More Praise for *And There Was Light*
by Jacques Lusseyran

"Most beautiful." — Oliver Sacks, author of *Musicophilia*

"Astonishing, life changing, and magical, *And There Was Light* is one of my favorite books of all time, and one I frequently give as a gift. A true story with the power to change what you think is possible."
 — Marc Lesser, author of *Less* and
Know Yourself, Forget Yourself

"Jacques Lusseyran's extraordinary memoir is a gift of light that brightens our darkest days. Blinded when he was eight, he learned to see with his inner senses, reading the world around him better than those who see only with their eyes, never losing his love of life, always expanding his capacity for friendship and his certainty that there is a saving power. That a blind teenager could become a moving spirit and key organizer in the French Resistance — knowing who to trust by the sound of a voice and the pressure of a hand — and could help to found one of France's leading newspapers, on clandestine presses, makes you want to stand up and cheer. His account of how he survived Buchenwald is one of the great narratives of human courage, giving us heart for the challenges in our own lives. This is essential reading, above all for its eloquent message that we only truly find joy, and light, within."
 — Robert Moss, author of *The Secret History of Dreaming* and
The Boy Who Died and Came Back

"Some years ago I asked the eminent historian of religion Huston Smith what he believed to be the greatest spiritual teaching of all. Without hesitation, he said, 'Follow the light, wherever it may lead.' If Jacques Lusseyran had been asked a similar question, I suspect his answer would have been startlingly similar, though as a blind leader of the French Resistance during the Nazi occupation, he would have insisted that the light does not come from without but comes from within. This incandescent memoir is graced with both, for light

radiates from every page, and glows within the heart of the reader who dares to brave the heart of darkness that Lusseyran illuminates."
— Phil Cousineau, author of *The Art of Pilgrimage* and editor of *The Hero's Journey: Joseph Campbell on His Life and Work*

"Hope is what pours over you on every page of Jacques Lusseyran's memoir. It's unavoidable. It's the DNA of the book."
— Jesse Kornbluth, www.headbutler.com

"Like Lusseyran's light, this inspiring book draws the reader into the experience beyond the ordinary, a world illuminated and quickened by a spirit of wholeness and humanness that is a joy to read and remember."
— *Noetic Sciences Review*

"*And There Was Light* is one of the most extraordinary books I have ever read. It is why books are published at all. Lusseyran's inner experience of blindness is a testament to the existence of a spiritual world, a guide for all of us."
— Mark Nepo, author of *Reduced to Joy* and *Seven Thousand Ways to Listen*

"*And There Was Light* is the little-known but thoroughly luminous autobiography of Jacques Lusseyran, a blind man who discovered the gift of inner sight after losing his vision in a childhood accident — and then put his gift to use in the struggle against Nazism. Lusseyran allows us to glimpse both heaven and hell on Earth through the eyes of a man who has lived through both. His description of what it is like to 'see' as a blind man is fascinating and inspiring; his account of Buchenwald, where he was condemned to the living hell of the 'Invalids' Barracks,' is one of the most anguishing fragments of Holocaust testimony that I have ever encountered."
— Jonathan Kirsch, *Los Angeles Times*

"A magical book, the kind that becomes a classic....How do you explain the incredible suspense of this book? You know he lives — he's gone on to write it down after all. So why is your breath caught in your throat and why can't you put this book down even the second or third time through it?"
— *Baltimore Sun*

AND
THERE
WAS
LIGHT

ALSO BY JACQUES LUSSEYRAN

Against the Pollution of the I:
Selected Writings of Jacques Lusseyran

AND
THERE
WAS
LIGHT

The Extraordinary Memoir
of a Blind Hero of the
French Resistance in World War II

JACQUES LUSSEYRAN

Translated from the French by Elizabeth R. Cameron

New World Library
Novato, California

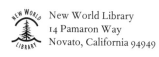
New World Library
14 Pamaron Way
Novato, California 94949

First published by Little, Brown and Company in 1963
Second edition published by Parabola Books in 1987
Third edition published by Morning Light Press in 2006

Text design by Tona Pearce Myers

Library of Congress Cataloging-in-Publication Data
Lusseyran, Jacques.
[Et la lumière fut. English]
And there was light : the extraordinary memoir of a blind hero of the French resistance in World War II / Jacques Lusseyran ; translated from the French by Elizabeth R. Cameron. — Fourth edition, First New World Library edition.
     pages   cm
Translation of: Et la lumière fut.
ISBN 978-1-60868-269-0 (pbk. : alk. paper) — ISBN 978-1-60868-270-6 (ebook)
1. World War, 1939–1945—Underground movements—France. 2. World War, 1939–1945—Prisoners and prisons, German. 3. Lusseyran, Jacques. 4. World War, 1939–1945—Personal narratives, French. 5. Prisoners of war—France—Biography. 6. Prisoners of war—Germany—Biography. 7. Guerrillas—France—Biography. 8. Blind—France—Biography. I. Cameron, Elizabeth R. (Elizabeth Ripley), 1907– translator. II. Title.
D802.F8L773 2014
940.53'44092—dc23
[B]   2013042898

First New World Library printing, March 2014
ISBN 978-1-60868-269-0
Printed in Canada on 100% postconsumer-waste recycled paper

New World Library is proud to be a Gold Certified Environmentally Responsible Publisher. Publisher certification awarded by Green Press Initiative. www.greenpressinitiative.org

10   9   8   7

For George and Virginia McMillan

Contents

WHEN YOU SAID TO ME: "Tell me the story of your life," I was not eager to begin. But when you added, "What I care most about is learning your reasons for loving life," then I became eager, for that was a real subject.

All the more since I have maintained this love of life through everything: through infirmity, the terrors of war, and even in Nazi prisons. Never did it fail me, not in misfortune nor in good times, which may seem much easier but is not.

Now, it is no longer a child who is going to tell this story and that is regrettable. It is a man. Worse yet, it is the university professor I have become. I will have to guard myself very carefully from trying to expound and demonstrate — those two illusions. I will have to return to the simplicity of a child and in addition reach back to France, leaving in thought this America where I live reassured and protected, to find again the Paris which held for me so many frightening experiences and so many happy ones.

CLEAR WATER OF CHILDHOOD

As I remember it, my story always starts out like a fairy tale, not an unusual one, but still a fairy tale. Once upon a time in Paris, between two world wars, there lived a happy little boy. I was that little boy, and today when I look back at him from the midpoint of life which I have reached, I marvel, a happy childhood is so rare. Besides, it is so little the fashion these days that one can hardly believe in it. All the same, if the water of my childhood runs clear, I am not about to muddy it up. That would be the worst kind of foolishness.

I was born in 1924, on September 19 at noon, in the heart of Paris in Montmartre, between the Place Blanche and the Moulin Rouge. I was born in a modest nineteenth-century house, in a room looking out over a courtyard.

My parents were ideal. My father, a graduate of a school for advanced physics and chemistry and a chemical engineer by profession, was both intelligent and kind. My mother, who had studied physics and biology herself, was completely devoted and understanding. Both of them were generous and attentive. But why say these things? As a small boy I was not aware of them. The small boy attributed no special qualities to his parents. He did not even think about them. There was no need, for his parents loved him and he loved them. It was a gift from heaven.

My parents were protection, confidence, warmth. When I think of my childhood I still feel the sense of warmth above me, behind and around me, that marvelous sense of living not yet on one's own, but leaning body and soul on others who accept the charge.

My parents carried me along and that, I am sure, is the reason why through all my childhood I never touched ground. I could go away and come back. Objects had no weight and I never became entangled in the web of things. I passed between dangers and fears as light passes through a mirror. That was the joy of my childhood, the magic armor which, once put on, protects for a lifetime.

My family belonged to "the petite bourgeoisie" in France in those days. We lived in small apartments but they always seemed to me large. The one I know best was on the Left Bank of the Seine, near the great garden of the Champ de Mars, between the Eiffel Tower, with its four paws spread apart, and the Ecole Militaire, a building which was only a name to me and whose shape I have quite forgotten.

My parents were heaven. I didn't say this to myself so precisely, and they never said it to me, but it was obvious. I knew very early, I am quite sure of it, that through them another Being concerned himself with me and even addressed himself to me. This Other I did not even call God. My parents spoke to me about God, but only later. I had no name for him. He was just there and it was better so. Behind my parents there was someone, and my father and mother were simply the people responsible for passing along the gift. My religion began like this, which I think explains why I have never known doubt. This confession may be something of a surprise, but I set store by it because it will make so many other things clear, my recklessness, for instance.

I was always running; the whole of my childhood was spent running. Only I was not running to catch hold of something. That is a notion for grownups and not the notion of a child. I was running to meet everything that was visible, and everything that I could not yet see. I traveled from assurance to assurance, as though I were running a race in relays.

I see myself on my fourth birthday as clearly as a picture hanging in the middle of the wall of my room. I was running along the sidewalk toward a triangle of light formed by the intersection of three streets, Rue Edmond Valentin, Rue Sédillot, and Rue Dupont-des-Loges where we lived. A triangle of sunlight opened out like a bit of seashore toward the Square Rapp. I was being projected toward this pool of light, drawn up by it, and waving my arms and legs, cried out to myself: "I am four years old and I am Jacques."

Call it the birth of personality if you like, but be sure that it was not accompanied by any feeling of panic. It was simply that the beam of universal happiness had fallen upon me like a bolt from the blue. I had my share of misery and grief as all children do. But truthfully I don't remember them. They vanished from my memory just like the presence of physical pain. As soon as it leaves the body, it leaves the spirit.

The violent, the ridiculous, the shady and the uncertain, all these I knew later on. But I cannot place any of them in the earliest years of my life. And that is what I meant just now when I spoke of the clear water of my childhood.

REVELATION OF LIGHT

FOR SEVEN YEARS I JUMPED, I ran, I covered the paths of the Champ de Mars. I scoured the sidewalks of the narrow Paris streets where the houses were crowded into the fragrant thoroughfares. For in France each house has its characteristic smell. Grownups hardly notice this, but children know it well, and can recognize the buildings by their odors. There is the smell of the creamery, the smell of the pastry shop, the confectioner's, the shoemaker's, the druggist's, and the smell of the shop belonging to the man who has such a beautiful name in France, "the merchant of colors." These buildings I knew by sniffing the air like a small dog.

I felt sure that nothing was unfriendly, that the branches I used to swing on would hold firm, and that the paths, no matter how winding, would take me to a place where I would not be afraid; that all paths, eventually, would lead me back to my family. You might say that I had no story, except the most important of all, the story of life.

Still, there was light, and light cast a spell over me. I saw it everywhere I went and watched it by the hour. None of the rooms in our three-room apartment has remained clear in my memory. But the balcony was different, because on the balcony there was light. Impetuous as I was, I used to lean patiently on the railing and watch the light flowing over the surface of the houses in front of me and through the tunnel of the street to right and left.

This light was not like the flow of water, but something more fleeting and numberless, for its source was everywhere. I liked seeing that the light came from nowhere in particular, but was an element just like air. We never ask ourselves where air comes from, for it is there and we are alive. With the sun it is the same thing.

There was no use my seeing the sun high up in the sky in its place in space at noon, since I was always searching for it elsewhere. I looked for it in the flickering of its beams, in the echo which, as a rule, we attribute only to sound, but which belongs to light in the same measure. Radiance multiplied, reflected itself from one window to the next, from a fragment of wall to cloud above. It entered into me, became part of me. I was eating sun.

This fascination did not stop when night fell. When I came in from outdoors in the evening, when supper was over, I found the fascination again in the dark. Darkness, for me, was still light, but in a new form and a new rhythm. It was light at a slower pace. In other words, nothing in the world, not even what I saw inside myself with closed eyelids, was outside this great miracle of light.

Whenever I ran across the Champ de Mars I was still chasing light. I was just about to jump into it, with my feet together, at the end of the path; to catch hold of it as you catch a butterfly over the pond; to lie down with it in the grass or on the sand. Nothing else in nature, not even the sounds to which I listened so attentively, was as precious to me as light.

When I was about four or five years old, I suddenly discovered that you can hold light in your hands. To do this you only need to take colored crayons or blocks and play with them. I began to spend hours doing all kinds of coloring, without much form I am sure, but I kept diving in, as you plunge into a fountain. My eyes are still filled with those colors.

They told me later that even at this early age I had poor sight. Myopia I think it was, a condition which positive people would think quite adequate to explain my obsession. But as a young child I was not aware that I did not see very well. I was not concerned about it, because I was happy to make friends with light as though it were the essence of the whole world.

Colors, shapes, even objects, the heaviest of them, all had the same vibration. And today, every time I assume the attitude of tender attention, I find the same vibration once again. In those days, when people asked me what was my favorite color, I always answered "Green." But I only learned later that green was the color of hope.

I AM CERTAIN THAT CHILDREN always know more than they are able to tell, and that makes the big difference between them and adults, who, at best, know only a fraction of what they say. The reason is simply that children know everything with their whole beings, while we know it only with our heads. When a child is threatened by sickness or trouble, he knows it right away, stops his games and takes refuge with his mother.

In just this way, when I was seven years old, I realized that fate had a blow in store for me. It happened in the Easter holidays in Juvardeil, a little village in the Anjou where my maternal grand-parents lived. We were about to go back to Paris and the buggy was already at the door to take us to the station. In those days, to travel from Juvardeil to the railroad station at Etriché-Chateauneuf, seven kilometers away, we used a horse and buggy. The grocer's truck was the first automobile I really knew in the village, and that was not until three or four years later.

That day in the country, as the buggy was waiting and jingling its bells, I had stayed behind in the garden, by the corner of the barn, alone and in tears. These are not the kind of tears they tell you about later, for I still feel them deeply whenever I think of them. I was crying because I was looking at the garden for the last time.

I had just learned the bad news. I couldn't say how, but there was absolutely no doubt. Sunlight on the paths, the two great box trees, the grape arbor, the rows of tomatoes, cucumbers and beans, all the familiar sights which had peopled my eyes, I was seeing for the last time. And I was aware of it. This was much more than childish sorrow and when my mother, after looking for me, finally found me and asked what the trouble was, I could only say: "I am never going to see the garden again." Three weeks later it came about.

On the third of May, I was at school as usual, the elementary school in the part of Paris where my parents lived on Rue Cler. At ten o'clock I jumped up with my classmates who were running for the door to the playground outside. In the scuffle, an older boy who was in a hurry came up from the back of the room and ran into me accidentally from behind. I hadn't seen him coming and taken off guard lost my balance and fell. As I fell, I struck one of the sharp corners of the teacher's desk.

I was wearing glasses because they had discovered I was near-sighted. The glasses were made of shatterproof glass, and it was just this precaution that was my undoing. The lenses did not break, but the blow was so violent that one arm of the spectacles went deep into the tissue of the right eye and tore it away.

I lost consciousness but came to immediately after being carried to the school playground. The first thing that occurred to me, I remember vividly, was, "My eyes, where are my eyes?" I could hear frightened people around me talking in panic about my eyes. But even without the voices and the pain I should have known where I had been hit.

They bandaged me up and took me home with fever raging through my body. There everything blacked out for more than twenty-four hours. I learned later that the distinguished specialist my family called at once had declared the right eye was lost and must be removed. As soon as they could they would do the necessary surgery. As for the left eye, there was little doubt that it too was gone since the blow had been so hard as to cause sympathetic ophthalmia. At any rate, the retina of the left eye had been badly torn.

The next morning they operated and with success.

I had become completely and permanently blind.

EVERY DAY SINCE THEN I have thanked heaven for making me blind while I was still a child not quite eight years old.

I bless my lot for practical reasons first of all. The habits of a boy of eight are not yet formed, either in body or in mind. His body is infinitely supple, capable of making just the movement the situation calls for and no other; ready to settle with life as it is, ready to say yes to it. And the greatest physical miracles can follow from this acceptance.

I am deeply moved when I think of all the people whom blindness strikes when they are fully grown, whether it is caused by accident or injury in war. Often they have a hard lot, certainly one harder than mine.

At all events, I have other reasons, not material, for thanking fortune. Grown-up people forget that children never complain against circumstances, unless of course grownups are so foolish as to suggest it to them. For an eight-year-old, what "is" is always best. He knows nothing of bitterness or anger. He may have a sense of injustice, but only if injustice comes from people. For him events are always signs from God.

These simple things I know, and I know that since the day I went blind I have never been unhappy. As for courage, which adults make so much of, children do not see it as we do. For a child courage is the most natural thing in the world, the thing to do, through life, at each moment. A child does not think about the future, and so is protected from a thousand follies and nearly every fear. He relies on the course of events, and that reliance brings him happiness with every step.

FROM NOW ON I shall find obstacles in my way, very serious ones, as I tell my story: first, obstacles of language, because in what I have to say about blindness, little known and almost always surprising, I shall run the risk of sounding either trite or extravagant; then, obstacles of memory. I went blind at the age of eight, and am still blind, and what I experienced then I still experience every day. Without wanting to, I am bound to confuse dates and even periods. But such barriers are more literary than real. Facts are facts, and I only need to rely on their eloquence.

I recovered with a speed that can only be explained by my extreme youth. Blinded on May 3, by the end of the month I was walking again, clinging to the hand of my father or mother, of course, but still walking and without any difficulty. In June, I began learning to read in Braille. In July, I was on a beach on the Atlantic, hanging by the trapeze, by the rings and sliding down the slides. I was part of a crowd of children who ran and shouted. I was building castles in the sand. But I shall come back to this later, for at the time other matters were more important.

It was a great surprise to me to find myself blind, and being blind was not at all as I imagined it. Nor was it as the people around me seemed to think it. They told me that to be blind meant not to see. Yet how was I to believe them when I saw? Not at once, I admit. Not in the days immediately after the operation. For at that time I still wanted to use my eyes. I followed their usual path. I looked in the direction where I was in the habit of seeing before the accident, and there was anguish, a lack, something like a void which filled me with what grownups call despair.

Finally, one day, and it was not long in coming, I realized that I was looking in the wrong way. It was as simple as that. I was making something very like the mistake people make who change their glasses without adjusting themselves. I was looking too far off, and too much on the surface of things.

This was much more than a simple discovery, it was a revelation. I can still see myself in the Champ de Mars, where my father had taken me for a walk a few days after the accident. Of course I knew the garden well, its ponds, its railings, its iron chairs. I even knew some of the trees in person, and naturally I wanted to see them again. But I couldn't. I threw myself forward into the substance which was space, but which I did not recognize because it no longer held anything familiar to me.

At this point some instinct — I was almost about to say a hand laid on me — made me change course. I began to look more closely, not at things but at a world closer to myself, looking from an inner place to one further within, instead of clinging to the movement of sight toward the world outside.

Immediately, the substance of the universe drew together,

redefined and peopled itself anew. I was aware of a radiance emanating from a place I knew nothing about, a place which might as well have been outside me as within. But radiance was there, or, to put it more precisely, light. It was a fact, for light was there.

I felt indescribable relief, and happiness so great it almost made me laugh. Confidence and gratitude came as if a prayer had been answered. I found light and joy at the same moment, and I can say without hesitation that from that time on light and joy have never been separated in my experience. I have had them or lost them together.

I saw light and went on seeing it though I was blind. I said so, but for many years I think I did not say it very loud. Until I was nearly fourteen I remember calling the experience, which kept renewing itself inside me, "my secret," and speaking of it only to my most intimate friends. I don't know whether they believed me but they listened to me for they were friends. And what I told them had a greater value than being merely true, it had the value of being beautiful, a dream, an enchantment, almost like magic.

The amazing thing was that this was not magic for me at all, but reality. I could no more have denied it than people with eyes can deny that they see. I was not light myself, I knew that, but I bathed in it as an element which blindness had suddenly brought much closer. I could feel light rising, spreading, resting on objects, giving them form, then leaving them.

Withdrawing or diminishing is what I mean, for the opposite of light was never present. Sighted people always talk about the night of blindness, and that seems to them quite natural. But there is no such night, for at every waking hour and even in my dreams I lived in a stream of light.

Without my eyes light was much more stable than it had been

with them. As I remember it, there were no longer the same differences between things lighted brightly, less brightly or not at all. I saw the whole world in light, existing through it and because of it.

Colors, all the colors of the rainbow, also survived. For me, the child who loved to draw and paint, colors made a celebration so unexpected that I spent hours playing with them, and all the more easily now they were more docile than they used to be.

Light threw its color on things and on people. My father and mother, the people I met or ran into in the street, all had their characteristic color which I had never seen before I went blind. Yet now this special attribute impressed itself on me as part of them as definitely as any impression created by a face. Still, the colors were only a game, while light was my whole reason for living. I let it rise in me like water in a well, and I rejoiced.

I did not understand what was happening to me, for it was so completely contrary to what I heard people say. I didn't understand it, but no matter, since I was living it. For many years I did not try to find out why these things were going on. I only tried to do so much later, and this is not the time to describe it.

A LIGHT SO CONTINUOUS and so intense was so far beyond my comprehension that sometimes I doubted it. Suppose it was not real, that I had only imagined it. Perhaps it would be enough to imagine the opposite, or just something different, to make it go away. So I thought of testing it out and even of resisting it.

At night in bed, when I was all by myself, I shut my eyes. I lowered my eyelids as I might have done when they covered my physical eyes. I told myself that behind these curtains I would no longer see light. But light was still there, and more serene than ever, looking like a lake at evening when the wind has dropped.

Then I gathered up all my energy and willpower and tried to stop the flow of light, as I might have tried to stop breathing.

What happened was a disturbance, something like a whirlpool. But the whirlpool was still flooded with light. At all events I couldn't keep this up very long, perhaps only for two or three seconds. When this was going on I felt a sort of anguish, as though I were doing something forbidden, something against life. It was exactly as if I needed light to live — needed it as much as air. There was no way out of it. I was the prisoner of light. I was condemned to see.

As I write these lines, I have just tried the experiment again, with the same result, except that with the years the original source of light has grown stronger.

At eight I came out of this experiment reassured, with the sense that I was being reborn. Since it was not I who was making the light, since it came to me from outside, it would never leave me. I was only a passageway, a vestibule for this brightness. The seeing eye was in me.

Still, there were times when the light faded, almost to the point of disappearing. It happened every time I was afraid.

If, instead of letting myself be carried along by confidence and throwing myself into things, I hesitated, calculated, thought about the wall, the half-open door, the key in the lock; if I said to myself that all these things were hostile and about to strike or scratch, then without exception I hit or wounded myself. The only easy way to move around the house, the garden or the beach was by not thinking about it at all, or thinking as little as possible. Then I moved between obstacles the way they say bats do. What the loss of my eyes had not accomplished was brought about by fear. It made me blind.

Anger and impatience had the same effect, throwing everything into confusion. The minute before I knew just where everything in the room was, but if I got angry, things got angrier than I. They went and hid in the most unlikely corners, mixed themselves up, turned turtle, muttered like crazy men and looked wild. As for me, I no longer knew where to put hand or foot. Everything hurt me. This mechanism worked so well that I became cautious.

When I was playing with my small companions, if I suddenly grew anxious to win, to be first at all costs, then all at once I could see nothing. Literally I went into fog or smoke.

I could no longer afford to be jealous or unfriendly, because, as soon as I was, a bandage came down over my eyes, and I was bound hand and foot and cast aside. All at once a black hole opened, and I was helpless inside it. But when I was happy and serene, approached people with confidence and thought well of them, I was rewarded with light. So is it surprising that I loved friendship and harmony when I was very young?

Armed with such a tool, why should I need a moral code? For me this tool took the place of red and green lights. I always knew where the road was open and where it was closed. I had only to look at the bright signal which taught me how to live.

It was the same with love, but let us see how. The summer after the accident my parents took me to the seashore. There I met a little girl my own age. I think she was called Nicole. She came into my world like a great red star, or perhaps more like a ripe cherry. The only thing I knew for sure was that she was bright and red.

I thought her lovely, and her beauty was so gentle that I could no longer go home at night and sleep away from her, because part of my light left me when I did. To get it all back I had to find her again. It was just as if she were bringing me light in her hands, her hair, her bare feet on the sand, and in the sound of her voice.

How natural that people who are red should have red shadows. When she came to sit down by me between two pools of saltwater under the warmth of the sun, I saw rosy reflections on the canvas of the awnings. The sea itself, the blue of the sea, took on a purple tone. I followed her by the red wake which trailed behind her wherever she went.

Now, if people should say that red is the color of passion, I should answer quite simply that I found that out when I was only eight years old.

HOW COULD I HAVE LIVED all that time without realizing that everything in the world has a voice and speaks? Not just the things that are supposed to speak, but the others, like the gate, the walls of the houses, the shade of trees, the sand and the silence.

Still, even before my accident, I loved sound, but now it seems clear that I didn't listen to it. After I went blind, I could never make a motion without starting an avalanche of noise. If I went into my room at night, the room where I used to hear nothing, the small plaster statue on the mantelpiece made a fraction of a turn. I heard its friction in the air, as light a sound as the sound of a waving hand. Whenever I took a step, the floor cried or sang — I could hear it making both these sounds — and its song was passed along from one board to the next, all the way to the window, to give me the measure of the room.

If I spoke out suddenly, the windowpanes, which seemed so solid in their putty frames, began to shake, very lightly of course but distinctly. This noise was on a higher pitch than the others, cooler, as if it were already in contact with the outside air. Every piece of furniture creaked, once, twice, ten times, and made a trail of sounds like gestures as minutes passed. The bed, the wardrobe, the chairs were stretching, yawning and catching their breath.

When a draft pushed against the door, it creaked out "draft." When a hand pushed it, it creaked in a human way. For me there was no mistaking the difference. I could hear the smallest recession in the wall from a distance, for it changed the whole room. Because this nook, that alcove were there, the wardrobe sang a hollower song.

It was as though the sounds of earlier days were only half real, too far away from me, and heard through a fog. Perhaps my eyes used to make the fog, but at all events my accident had thrown my head against the humming heart of things, and the heart never stopped beating.

You always think of sounds beginning and ending abruptly. But now I realized that nothing could be more false. Now my ears heard the sounds almost before they were there, touching me with the tips of their fingers and directing me toward them. Often I seemed to hear people speak before they began talking.

Sounds had the same individuality as light. They were neither inside nor outside, they were passing through me. They gave me my bearings in space and put me in touch with things. It was not like signals that they functioned, but like replies.

I remember well when I first arrived at the beach two months after the accident. It was evening, and there was nothing there but the sea and its voice, precise beyond the power to imagine it. It formed a mass which was so heavy and so limpid that I could have leaned against it like a wall. It spoke to me in several layers all at once. The waves were arranged in steps, and together they made one music, though what they said was different in each voice. There was rasping in the bass and bubbling in the top register. I didn't need to be told about the things that eyes could see.

At one end there was the wall of the sea and the wind rustling over the sand. At the other there was the retaining wall, as full of echoes as a talking mirror. What the waves said they said twice over.

People often say that blindness sharpens hearing, but I don't think this is so. My ears were hearing no better, but I was making better use of them. Sight is a miraculous instrument offering us all the riches of physical life. But we get nothing in this world without paying for it, and in return for all the benefits that sight brings we are forced to give up others whose existence we don't even suspect. These were the gifts I received in such abundance.

I needed to hear and hear again. I multiplied sounds to my heart's content. I rang bells. I touched walls with my fingers, explored the resonance of doors, furniture and the trunks of trees. I sang in empty rooms, I threw pebbles far off on the beach just to hear them whistle through the air and then fall. I even made my small companions repeat words to give me plenty of time to walk around them.

But most surprising of all was the discovery that sounds never came from one point in space, and never retreated into themselves. There was the sound, its echo, and another sound into which the first sound melted and to which it had given birth, altogether an endless procession of sounds.

Sometimes the resonance, the hum of voices all around me, grew so intense that I got dizzy and put my hands over my ears, as I might have done by closing my eyes to protect myself against too much light. That is why I couldn't stand racket, useless noises or music that went on and on. A sound we don't listen to is a blow to body and spirit, because sound is not something happening outside us, but a real presence passing through us and lingering unless we have heard it fully.

I was well protected from these miseries by parents who were musicians, and who talked around our family table instead of turning on the radio. But all the more reason for me to say how important it is to defend blind children against shouting, background music and all such hideous assaults. For a blind person, a violent and futile noise has the same effect as the beam of a searchlight too close to the eyes of someone who can see. It hurts. But when the world sounds clear and on pitch, it is more harmonious than poets have ever known it, or than they will ever be able to say.

Every Sunday morning, an old beggar used to play three tunes on his accordion in the courtyard of our apartment house. This poor sour music, punctuated at intervals by the metallic scraping of rails from the streetcars on the avenue nearby — these in the silence of a lazy morning created a thousand dimensions in space; not just the steep drop into the court and the parade of the streets on the ground, but as many paths from house to house and court to roof as I could hold with my attention. With sound I never came to an end, for this was another kind of infinity.

AT FIRST MY HANDS REFUSED TO OBEY. When they looked for a glass on the table, they missed it. They fumbled around the door knobs, mixed up black and white keys at the piano, fluttered in the air as they came near things. It was almost as if they had been uprooted, cut off from me, and for a time this made me afraid.

Fortunately, before long I realized that instead of becoming useless they were learning to be wise. They only needed time to accustom themselves to freedom. I had thought they were refusing to obey, but it was all because they were not getting orders, when the eyes were no longer there to command them.

But more than that it was a question of rhythm. Our eyes run over the surfaces of things. All they require are a few scattered points, since they can bridge the gap in a flash. They "half see" much more than they see, and they never weigh. They are satisfied with appearances, and for them the world glows and slides by, but lacks substance.

All I needed was to leave my hands to their own devices. I had nothing to teach them, and besides, since they began working independently, they seemed to foresee everything. Unlike eyes, they were in earnest, and from whatever direction they approached an object they covered it, tested its resistance, leaned against the mass of it and recorded every irregularity in its surface. They measured it for height and thickness, taking in as many dimensions as possible. But most of all, having learned that they had fingers, they used them in an entirely new way.

When I had eyes, my fingers used to be stiff, half dead at the ends of my hands, good only for picking up things. But now each one of them started out on its own. They explored things separately, changed levels and, independently of each other, made themselves heavy or light.

Movement of the fingers was terribly important, and had to be uninterrupted because objects do not stand at a given point, fixed there, confined in one form. They are alive, even the stones. What is more they vibrate and tremble. My fingers felt the pulsation distinctly, and if they failed to answer with a pulsation of their own, the fingers immediately became helpless and lost their sense of touch. But when they went toward things, in sympathetic vibration with them, they recognized them right away.

Yet there was something still more important than movement, and that was pressure. If I put my hand on the table without pressing it, I knew the table was there, but knew nothing about it. To find out, my fingers had to bear down, and the amazing thing is that the pressure was answered by the table at once. Being blind I thought I should have to go out to meet things, but I found that they came to meet me instead. I have never had to go more than halfway, and the universe became the accomplice of all my wishes.

If my fingers pressed the roundness of an apple, each one with a different weight, very soon I could not tell whether it was the apple or my fingers which were heavy. I didn't even know whether I was touching it or it was touching me. As I became part of the apple, the apple became part of me. And that was how I came to understand the existence of things.

As soon as my hands came to life they put me in a world where everything was an exchange of pressures. These pressures gathered together in shapes, and each one of the shapes had meaning. As a child I spent hours leaning against objects and letting them lean against me. Any blind person can tell you that this gesture, this exchange, gives him a satisfaction too deep for words.

Touching the tomatoes in the garden, and really touching them, touching the walls of the house, the materials of the curtains or a clod of earth is surely seeing them as fully as eyes can see. But it is more than seeing them, it is tuning in on them and allowing the current they hold to connect with one's own, like electricity. To put it differently, this means an end of living in front of things and a beginning of living with them. Never mind if the word sounds shocking, for this is love.

You cannot keep your hands from loving what they have really felt, moving continually, bearing down and finally detaching themselves, the last perhaps the most significant motion of all. Little by little, my hands discovered that objects were not rigidly bound within a mold. It was form they first came in contact with, form like a kernel. But around this kernel objects branched out in all directions.

I could not touch the pear tree in the garden just by following the trunk with my fingers, then the branches, then the leaves, one at a time. That was only a beginning, for in the air, between the leaves, the pear tree still continued, and I had to move my hands from branch to branch to feel the currents running between them.

At Juvardeil, in the holidays, when my small peasant friends saw me doing these magic dances around the trees and touching the invisible, they said I was like the medicine man, the man with an old secret who heals the sick by mesmerism, sometimes at a distance, and by methods not recognized by medical science. Of course, my young friends were wrong, but they had a good excuse, and today I know more than one professional psychologist who, for all his scientific knowledge, cannot account for these incongruous motions.

With smell it was the same as it was with touch — like touch an obvious part of the loving substance of the universe. I began to guess what animals must feel when they sniff the air. Like sound and shape, smell was more distinctive than I used to think it was. There were physical smells and moral ones, but of the latter, so important for living in society, I shall speak later on.

Before I was ten years old I knew with absolute certainty that everything in the world was a sign of something else, ready to take its place if it should fall by the way. And this continuing miracle of healing I heard expressed fully in the Lord's Prayer I repeated at night before going to sleep. I was not afraid. Some people would say I had faith, and how should I not have it in the presence of the marvel which kept renewing itself? Inside me every sound, every scent, and every shape was forever changing into light, and light itself changing into color to make a kaleidoscope of my blindness.

I HAD ENTERED A NEW WORLD, there was no doubt about it, but I was not its prisoner. All the things I experienced, however remarkable and however remote from the everyday adventures of a child my age, I did not experience in an inner void, a closed chamber belonging to me and no one else. They took place in Paris during the summer and fall of 1932, in the small apartment near the Champ de Mars, and on a beach on the Atlantic, between my father and mother and, toward the end of the year, a new little brother who had been born.

What I mean to say is that all these discoveries of sound, light, smell, and visible and invisible shapes established themselves serenely and solidly between the dining-room table and the window on the court, the bric-a-brac on the mantelpiece and the kitchen sink, right in the midst of the life of other people and without being put out of countenance by them. These perceptions were not phantoms which came bringing disorder and fear into my real life. They were realities and, to me, the simplest of them all.

But it is time to make it clear that, along with many marvelous things, great dangers lie in wait for a blind child. I am not speaking of physical dangers, which can well be circumvented, nor of any danger which blindness itself brings about. I am speaking of dangers which come from the inexperience of people who still have their eyes. If I have been so fortunate myself — and I insist that I have — it is because I have always been protected from perils of that sort.

You know I had good parents, not just parents who wished me well, but ones whose hearts and intelligence were open to spiritual things, for whom the world was not composed exclusively of objects that were useful, and useful always in the same fashion; for whom, above all, it was not necessarily a curse to be different from other people. Finally, mine were parents willing to admit that their way of looking at things, the usual way, was perhaps not the only possible one, and to like my way and encourage it.

That is why I tell parents whose children have gone blind to take comfort. Blindness is an obstacle, but only becomes a misery if folly is added. I tell them to be reassured and never to set themselves against what their small boy or girl is finding out. They should never say: "You can't know that because you can't see"; and as infrequently as possible, "Don't do that, it is dangerous." For a blind child there is a threat greater than all the wounds and bumps, the scratches and most of the blows, and that is the danger of isolation.

When I was fifteen I spent long afternoons with a blind boy my own age, one who went blind, I should add, in circumstances very like my own. Today I have few memories as painful. This boy terrified me. He was the living image of everything that might have happened to me if I had not been fortunate, more fortunate than he. For he was really blind. He had seen nothing since his accident. His faculties were normal; he could have seen as well as I. But they had kept him from doing so. To protect him, as they put it, they had cut him off from everything, and made fun of all his attempts to explain what he felt. In grief and revenge, he had thrown himself into a brutal solitude. Even his body lay prostrate in the depths of an armchair. To my horror I saw that he did not like me.

Tragedies like this are commoner than people think, and all the more terrible because they are avoidable in every case. To avoid them, I repeat that it is enough for sighted people not to imagine that their way of knowing the world is the only one.

At the age of eight everything favored my return to the world. They let me move around, they answered all the questions I asked, they were interested in all my discoveries, even the strangest. For example, how should I explain the way objects approached me when I was the one walking in their direction? Was I breathing them in or hearing them? Possibly, though that was often hard to prove. Did I see them? It seemed not. And yet, as I came closer, their mass was modified, often to the point of defining real contours, assuming a real shape in space, acquiring distinctive color, just as it happens where there is sight.

As I walked along a country road bordered by trees, I could point to each one of the trees by the road, even if they were not spaced at regular intervals. I knew whether the trees were straight and tall, carrying their branches as a body carries its head, or gathered into thickets and partly covering the ground around them.

This kind of exercise soon tired me out, I must admit, but it succeeded. And the fatigue did not come from the trees, from their number or shape, but from myself. To see them like this I had to hold myself in a state so far removed from old habits that I could not keep it up for very long. I had to let the trees come toward me, and not allow the slightest inclination to move toward them, the smallest wish to know them, to come between them and me. I could not afford to be curious or impatient or proud of my accomplishment.

After all, such a state is only what one commonly calls "attention," but I can testify that when carried to this point it is not easy. The same experiment tried with trees along the road I could practice on any objects which reached a height and breadth at least as great as my own: telegraph poles, hedges, the arches of a bridge, walls along the street, the doors and windows in these walls, the places where they were set back or sloped away.

As with the sense of touch, what came to me from objects was pressure, but pressure of a kind so new to me that at first I didn't think of calling it by that name. When I became really attentive and did not oppose my own pressure to my surroundings, then trees and rocks came to me and printed their shape upon me like fingers leaving their impression in wax.

This tendency of objects to project themselves beyond their physical limits produced sensations as definite as sight or hearing.

I only needed a few years to grow accustomed to them, to tame them somewhat. Like all blind people, whether they know it or not, these are the senses I use when I walk by myself either outdoors or through a house. Later I read that they call this sense "the sense of obstacles," and that some kinds of animals, bats, for instance, are highly endowed with it.

According to many traditions of the occult, man has a third eye, an inner eye, generally called "the eye of Siva," located in the middle of his forehead, an eye which he can bring to life in certain conditions by certain exercises. Finally, the researches undertaken by the French writer and member of the Academy, Jules Romains, have demonstrated the existence of visual perception outside the retina, situated in certain nervous centers of the skin, particularly in the hands, the forehead, the nape of the neck and the chest. I hear that more recently this kind of research has been carried on with success by physiologists, especially in the U.S.S.R.

But whatever the nature of the phenomenon, I experienced it from childhood, and its effects seem to me much more important than its cause. The indispensable condition for accurately pointing out trees along the road was to accept the trees and not try to put myself in their place.

All of us, whether we are blind or not, are terribly greedy. We want things only for ourselves. Even without realizing it, we want the universe to be like us and give us all the room in it. But a blind child learns very quickly that this cannot be. He has to learn it, for every time he forgets that he is not alone in the world he strikes against an object, hurts himself and is called to order. But each time he remembers he is rewarded, for everything comes his way.

[3]

THE CURE FOR BLINDNESS

THE RESPONSIBILITY MY PARENTS FACED was so heavy and so uncertain that they had to gamble on it. Should they keep me with them or put me in a special boarding school, the National Institute for Blind Children in Paris? This solution seemed the wisest by far, perhaps the only wise one, and they came very close to choosing it. But they ended by making the other choice, betting on the long shot, and for this I shall never stop being grateful to them.

But don't mistake me. I never had and still have no reason to think that schools for the blind are a bad thing. In any case there are some (and the Paris Institute is among them) where the teachers are intelligent and completely devoted. Many such schools in France, the United States, England and Germany have adopted the freest and frankest methods of up-to-date pedagogy, and have entirely abandoned both the stifling prejudice of the nineteenth century and the old policy of patronage.

I have met many former students of these schools, and I am

aware that many of them have grown into well-rounded men and women with nothing but gratitude for their experience as children. But unfortunately the problem is not so simple, or rather it is different. The only way to be completely cured of blindness, and I mean socially, is never to treat it as a difference, a reason for separation, an infirmity, but to consider it a temporary impediment, a peculiarity of course, but one which will be overcome today or at the latest tomorrow. The cure is to immerse oneself again and without delay in a life that is as real and difficult as the lives of others. And that is just what a special school, even the most generous and intelligent of them, does not allow. Even if the school has the ingenuity and the understanding not to block this course forever, at least it slows it up.

In making such a judgment, I run the risk of disturbing many people and many families. That is certainly not my intention, for I know there are parents of blind children whose circumstances, through poverty or work, make it impossible for them to keep their child at home. Most of all I am thinking of parents who have not been blessed with a thorough education, who find themselves painfully confused and completely disarmed when faced with this monster of strangeness, a blind person. I think of them above all for they are perhaps most numerous and in the most serious predicament.

In such cases the child should go away and be entrusted to experts, men and women who know what to do, and do it without any fear or sense of shame. There can be no greater misery for a blind child than the embarrassment of his parents, their sense of inferiority when they imagine or say that their child is not "normal." Anything is better than this kind of stupidity, and I repeat that the special school is not an evil, but at most a lesser benefit.

As far as I was concerned the problem was resolved within a

few days: I was to stay at home. Both intellectually and morally my parents were equipped to watch over me. On my behalf, at least for the first few years, they were ready to face all the difficulties I was unable to cope with because of my age and situation. They understood that the resources of blindness had to be explored to the limit, and that I must be thrown back into the world immediately.

First, as soon as the school year began, I had to go back to my sighted companions in the neighborhood public school, the school where my accident had happened in May. To do this, by October I had to learn to read and write in Braille. When they made it clear to me that this was a must, I plunged into the task with a kind of silent enthusiasm. At the end of six weeks I had turned the corner. The dots on the long wide sheet of paper, which had at first passed under my fingers like grains of sand, arranged themselves in columns, became fixed in groups, and one by one each of them took on meaning.

To teach me to read in Braille my mother had chosen the most appealing book she could find: *The Jungle Book*. Her method worked beautifully, because it was not Braille characters I was discovering, but the adventures of Mowgli, which I found fascinating. I am sure this way of doing things goes far to explain the speed with which I learned.

Besides, my parents had immediately ordered a portable Braille typewriter from Switzerland, to spare me the disillusioning and almost always futile labor of writing on a tablet. Later they taught me to use one, but I used it very rarely. I was embarrassed by this grooved steel slate to which one attaches a sheet of paper with a metal grid of its own. I disliked handling the thick punch, and the business of slowly and laboriously perforating the dots which made each letter inside the rectangles on the grill. This was the kind of groping which reminded me that I was blind, and my ideas always outran my movements.

But my typewriter was a toy. It had the smell of newness, and I liked its tapping sound and the six round keys which controlled six punches that made letters, words and sentences rise up like pictures in a film. With the typewriter it was like going out exploring. I was writing and, being mechanized, had the playful satisfaction of writing faster than my friends who could see.

By the first of October I was ready, but the school was not ready for me. Later on, the laws and institutions of society played me a number of bad tricks, and even at this time they were resisting me. Actually this was not surprising, for it was not long since blind people had been relegated to the fringes of society, pitied, reduced to playing the harmonium in small chapels, recaning chairs, even to becoming beggars.

In 1932 in France there were no laws which forbade public schools to admit blind children to their classes — no laws, but many entrenched prejudices. In other words, it took all my family's confidence, all their conviction that I could overcome every difficulty, added to the kindness and generosity of the good man who headed the school, to get me admitted. I was admitted on probation.

What disturbed people was their belief that a blind person must be in other people's way, that he must understand, read and write less quickly, see neither the sums nor the drawings on the blackboard, nor the maps on the walls. In short he would be like dirt in the machinery. They had reason to be uneasy, but it was up to me not to be that grain of dirt — up to me, my family and especially my mother.

What a mother can do for a blind child can be explained in a few words: give him birth a second time. That is what my mother did for me, and it was her courage, not mine, that was called out. My only job was to turn myself over to her, believe what she believed and use her eyes every time I missed my own.

She learned Braille with me, and watched over my homework for several years. In other words, she did all the work of a private and highly specialized tutor. But to competence she added love, and it is well known that that kind of love removes obstacles more effectively than all the sciences.

At the end of the first school year I was awarded the first prize in my class, a small honor, of course, but one which counted for her and for me as the modest sign of victory over material things. The rest was going to be easy.

You will excuse me for thinking my mother exceptional. But I don't believe it will weaken my tribute to her to say that there are a thousand other women with the capacity for the same gift and the same intelligence toward a blind child. To achieve it they only need to know that adjustment is possible for the child and, more than adjustment, keeping in step with the lives of other people. To gain confidence, they only need to hear people speak often of the riches of blindness.

And that is why I am willing to tell my story, by fortune a happy one. There is nothing I want more than not being an exception.

MY MEMORIES OF THAT FIRST YEAR of school are of a ship with myself on the forecastle. I must explain that since the accident imagination had become a passion with me. I was really living twice over: once in contact with the small objects and the small events of my everyday life, and then a second time in the world of fantasy. The second life was made of the same stuff, but bigger, brightly colored, turned into pictures and in harmony with the whole universe. There there was a stream of light and joy. I had found where it flowed and stayed close to it, walking beside its banks. Doors had opened inside me leading into a place of refuge, a cave, and everything that happened to me entered there, echoed and was reflected a thousand times over before it was extinguished.

As to my vision of the ship, it came to me quite simply from a table and chair. To do the same work as my classmates in school I needed more room. My typewriter was bigger than a pencil, and the Braille books I used took up nearly ten times as much space as ordinary books. The standard classroom desks were not big enough for me, so my parents had brought to school a large table of unfinished wood with ample pigeonholes. This table stood beside the platform where the teacher's desk was, and as a result it was slightly in front of the first row of pupils' desks. That is where I got the happy illusion of the ship. All year I heard the crew behind me working, giving the password, swearing, shuffling along the deck with their feet, and obeying the captain's orders as well as they could.

Our teacher that year was a slow-moving, gentle man who had an even temper except for rare outbursts of anger at the stupid ones. From these outbursts I felt secure, and set to work systematically to learn the foundations of arithmetic. It was impossible or very difficult with a Braille typewriter to arrange figures on the paper in the order they needed for addition, subtraction, multiplication and division. So they gave me a vulcanite slate with cube-shaped holes and a set of steel cubes. Braille characters were written in relief on the six faces of the cubes. Because the graphics of writing in Braille, made up of dots, are simpler than the writing of sighted people, no more than six faces were needed to make the ten basic figures. The six, rotated at a ninety-degree angle, became the four, and the four in its turn the zero, the zero eight and so back to the six. With the help of this device I learned to count as fast as the others, and they soon got used to the soft metallic click — like the sound of marbles — which they heard me making.

But within a few months I found I could dispense with the cubes and the holes. To make the mind work, only the mind is needed. I began to visualize all the processes in my head, except, of course, the ones which extended to an embarrassing number of data. Having a good memory, I became extremely adept at mental arithmetic, and that in turn helped develop my memory.

It is true that blindness considerably increases the ability to memorize, and it has to since the eyes are no longer there to reinsure and verify — an activity, by the way, to which they are too often limited and which consumes a large part of their energy. I remembered well, but above all I visualized. It was an enchantment to watch the appearance of all the names and figures on the screen inside me, and then to see the screen unfolding like an endless roll of film.

This screen was not like a blackboard, rectangular or square, which so quickly reaches the edge of its frame and has to give way to a useless piece of wall or a door which loses its meaning as soon as it is closed. My screen was always as big as I needed it to be. Because it was nowhere in space it was everywhere at the same time, and to manage it I only had to call out "Attention." The chalk on the inner screen did not turn to powder like other chalk. It was stronger and more supple, being made of the substance called "spirit." Let us not quibble over words. Call it matter or essence. In any case it is a reality closer to us than words can tell, a reality to be touched, manipulated and shaped. And when such treasures are unveiled how can a child fail to be consoled for the loss of his sight?

Of course I recognized that my sighted companions were quick and precise in many gestures over which I hesitated. But as soon as it was a question of intangibles, it was their turn to hesitate longer than I. They had to turn the switch to darken the outside world and light up the world of the mind. This was one move I almost never had to make.

Names, figures and objects in general did not appear on my screen without shape, nor just in black and white, but in all the colors of the rainbow. Still, I never remember consciously encouraging this phenomenon. Nothing entered my mind without being bathed in a certain amount of light. To be more precise, everything from living creatures to ideas appeared to be carved out of the primordial light. In a few months my personal world had turned into a painter's studio.

I was not the master of these apparitions. The number five was always black, the letter *L* light green, and kindly feeling a soft blue. There was nothing I could do about it, and when I tried to change the color of a sign, the sign at once clouded over and then disappeared. A strange power, imagination! It certainly functioned in me but also in spite of me.

That same year, geography was revealed to me through relief maps of the five continents and the principal countries — maps magnificently published at the end of the nineteenth century near Mulhouse, in what then was German Alsace.

Naturally, the broad outlines of the world became fixed at once on the inner screen, and I only needed to correct them and complete them as I learned. I got my bearings without trouble. A picture of the physical world, its courses and its barriers, settled in, and that is why, from childhood, my sighted companions preferred turning to me when we were walking around Paris and had lost our way. Then I referred to the inner screen and almost always found the solution. Today, when I am riding in a car, I am often first to tell the driver what route to take. I hardly need say that the feats of carrier pigeons far outdistance my own capacity, but still, what they do seems to me quite natural.

I know many blind people who are able to reopen within themselves avenues which have been closed to them in the world outside. Otherwise how can one account for the fact that they can travel alone around a city they don't know well, and more often without losing their way than people who see?

After all, isn't it true that the realities of the inner life seem like marvels only because we live so far away from them?

BEFORE LONG I SHALL BE WRITING about the friends who inhabited my childhood, telling how I lived with them and what miseries they spared me. But this is not yet the place for friendship. It is the place for the particular distress called "waiting." Whether deliberately or not, blindness is not well received in the world of people who see. It is so little known and often so dreaded. For that reason blindness always starts out with isolation. I have known solitude, known it with all its demons. But it is only fair to say that along with its evil spirits it has some that are good.

In the summer of 1933, a year after my accident, my parents took me to Juvardeil for the holidays as usual. Juvardeil was then and still is, despite the invasion of the automobile, one of those small French villages off the main road, as melancholy and meditative as the Angelus, hidden in the midst of hawthorn hedges and shrubs as high as walls, and all spread out along the river.

The river is the Sarthe, slow and deep and silent, in the middle of wide meadows which it covers with water at the flood season, bounded all along its course by a never-ending sheath of bristling poplars. The stream is like an old lady who has grown smiling and discreet with age, who tolerates life around her without taking part in it.

Juvardeil is a very old village, already mentioned in the ninth-century chronicles under the name of Gavardolium, which was undoubtedly the name of the inhabitants of that small province. Another etymology, suspect perhaps, but so poetic that I prefer it to all the others, attributes the name to the Latin words *juvare oculis*, joy of the eyes. Of all the places in the world, Juvardeil is still the one I love best.

At the age of nine I had a freedom there which Paris could not give me. Nothing in Juvardeil was unfriendly. The boat-builder's saw announced that I had left the river behind me. The blacksmith's hammer cut the straight line between the river and the church in half. The sound of lowing told me I had arrived at the gate of the great meadow where the cows gathered to watch the people passing by. I could go from my grandmother's house to my great-aunt's by myself, with a cane in my hand, without meeting anything more formidable than the snails.

That year the public school in the village, deserted during the holidays, was turned over to me. In other words, they left the doors open. The wide court, enclosed by walls as it is everywhere in France, and planted with linden trees, one of the classrooms and a storeroom belonged to me. When I think of it, I realize this store-room must have been just a room that was no longer used, possibly an old laundry, at the far end of the court, but sheltered even from the people who came in by the main door, and raised above the court by three or four steps at most. But in those days my idea of this room with a sloping ceiling was quite different. It was precious, secret, high up, and altogether fantastic.

You can imagine what a big empty room would mean to a blind child, with walls which were dilapidated but flat and with no beams to strike against, no hooks to catch on, and open all across one side to the rustling of the wind in the leaves. A slight overhang gave every sound the resonance of an arch. There was fresh straw and sawdust on the floor, and a pile of small logs in one corner, some of them round, some forked and some triangular — fabulous for all kinds of building games.

I spent endless hours in the storeroom that summer. I was almost always alone there, but this solitude was densely populated with all kinds of shapes and with the inventions of a personage I had never known before: myself. I was on an island, and one at a time I relived the adventures of Robinson Crusoe before he met Friday. I arranged the logs all across the room like a forest, like rocks, and I went off on voyages. Sometimes, wrapped in the rags of history they had given me at school, I made the logs into armies. And in that case, obviously, I was Napoleon.

There is no use asking whether I believed in my imaginary personage. I had no thought of believing or not believing. I was in the state that all children reach sooner or later when, thank heaven, there is no more past or future, no dream or reality, but only themselves riding on life at a gallop. But in my storeroom, solitude was added to divine imagination, a place where, for once, I had no one and nothing to contend with, since the room was quite empty except for the logs.

Inside my body I had thousands of gestures which had been shut up there through the year in Paris, all the ones I had had to make with careful calculation since I was blind, the thousand indiscretions and adventures my body was bursting with. It was so long since I had wanted to whirl around, to paddle with my arms, throw my feet in front of me, fall down, get up again, make an ugly face or a beatific smile, take dangerous objects in my hand and not hear people saying I should handle them carefully; and finally to experiment with space in all directions. I wanted to try it out in height and depth, in zigzags, to walk through it straight, or stagger through it like a drunk. And after a few minutes I really felt drunk.

I wish a storeroom like mine could be given to all blind children, whether in the attic or in the bowels of the house. But anyway it should be a free field from which all the sharp corners, the bumps, the tables, chairs, stools, washtubs, nails and wires have been removed, especially those terrible wires; a place swept clean of danger, as clean as emptiness, where all one's wishes can come true from one instant to the next.

With the logs I made plans for battles in the sawdust. I was doing it because of Napoleon and in his honor, and more for love of him than for love of battles, since I was not particularly aggressive. Besides, there was never any real battle except in words. The teacher I would one day become was already giving lectures.

How I made the storeroom resound with my voice! Instead of conquering my enemies, which was too quick and seemed too crude, I applied myself to convincing them. I explained in loud tones that they were wrong, or at least that I wanted them to be. And since games like this are better when they last, I managed it so that my enemies should not be persuaded by my first harangue.

What blindness had to do with my games in the storeroom is not easily explained. As a matter of fact, the games were quite ordinary, apart from the intoxication they made me feel, a feeling much more intense than pleasure. It was as if a rent had been torn in the fabric of my life, a rent through which I saw endless possibilities, all surprising and all crowding upon each other as I approached. I myself was intact, discovering it was enough to think of things to bring them into being, enough to want them to lift the ban against them. Only, being blind, I had to want them more intensely than other people.

Life did not fall on my face as cool as rain or into my hands as round as fruit, but was a wave rising inside me. I could hold it there and calm it down or allow it to burst out into the world outside. And what if my storeroom as a nine-year-old means nothing to other people? For me it foretold the things I should do later on, and spoke a language I understood because it was neither its own nor entirely mine. What it brought me was happiness.

Blindness works like dope, a fact we have to reckon with. I don't believe there is a blind man alive who has not felt the danger of intoxication. Like drugs, blindness heightens certain sensations, giving sudden and often disturbing sharpness to the senses of hearing and touch. But, most of all, like a drug, it develops inner as against outer experience, and sometimes to excess.

At such times the world unfolding before a blind person is perilous, because it is more consoling than words, and has the kind of beauty found only in the poems or pictures of artists with hallucinations — artists like Poe, Van Gogh and Rimbaud.

I have known this bewitched world, and have often withdrawn there and wrapped myself in its dreams. I have delighted in its luster, its maternal warmth, its license and its illusion of life. But, thank heaven, I did not remain there. For that is visceral life shut in upon itself, not truly the life of the spirit but its caricature. There is no real inner life for a man or a child unless his relation to real things inside and outside himself is a true one. Living entirely turned in on oneself is like trying to play on a violin with slackened strings.

Like almost all blind people I have had this temptation. But by good fortune the temptation was offset by another, that of contending with things, or rather loving them as they are, investigating the contours of objects and space, and mixing with people. The fact that there were men in the world was more vital to me than anything else.

Whatever puts a blind child in touch with physical reality is good, especially if it has to do with his movements and his muscles. I am not a good example of this because I never learned to swim, and that was a mistake. I never conquered my dislike for cold, for water and all the soft obstacles which abound on the edges of streams. But all the more reason for wanting blind people to know how to swim. And this should be increasingly easy now that the swimming pool is almost a part of the furnishings of the house. Fortunately, water was the only thing for which I felt this kind of distaste.

The first thing my parents put in my grandfather's garden at Juvardeil was a jungle gym, and I seem to have spent years hanging from the ropes, the rings, climbing the rope ladder, turning somersaults on the trapeze. This was my favorite spot in the holidays, the place where I threw my dreams overboard by the handful, and got rid of my vapors. When I pulled myself up by the arms on the parallel bars, I changed course and moved with all my weight towards air and sun.

The gym was much more than exercise. It was a marriage with space. Besides, I was never afraid of it. From the moment when I took a firm hold on a bar or a rope I recaptured the freedom which others get from their eyes. The trapeze swung as I pushed it, but in a limited range where I had only myself to reckon with. I felt more alive at some distance from the ground than level with it. I seemed to grow more knowing, and all sorts of shadows were swept away. I had keener senses of touch, hearing and sight. I saw the rounded top of the hundred-year-old box tree right under my toes every time the swing, going all out, made me touch it. I saw the sky open up beyond the garden walls and drop steeply down to the river.

I could see in all directions sitting, standing, curled up, hanging by my knees with my head down. It always ended with the marvelous sense of no longer being an animal standing up like a man, but a circular being.

From the jungle gym I ventured up into the trees, especially the apple trees, which were low with many branches. My grandfather owned and tended an orchard on the edge of the village. I would go there early in the morning with a book, climb up into one of the apple trees, sit down in the fork between two branches, and begin to read. But every ten minutes I would stop reading to explore higher up in the tree.

What about running? I couldn't do without it, yet running by myself was impossible. I had to find a teammate my own age, and this was easy. People are wrong in thinking that most children are not obliging, and don't like cluttering up their games with someone whom adults call an invalid. I assure you that for children there are no invalids. The bright boys hate the stupid ones, and the enterprising run from the cowards. It is as simple as that. Neither eyes nor legs have anything to do with it.

No boy in Juvardeil ever refused me his hand or arm, or gave it grudgingly. Sometimes they even bickered to see which one should have the right to hold me by the shoulder and run with me as fast as our legs could carry us, like good drivers who get the most out of their cars. I certainly covered much more ground in races than most children who see. I was guided back and forth through the rows of vegetables in the village gardens. Jumping from one lump of earth to the next, I crossed every newly plowed field, on forbidden ground. I climbed hundreds of hedges, scratched myself on the brambles, and landed in muddy ditches with water up to my thighs. I tried every rascal's trick.

Naturally, I was always harnessed to another boy, but the team ran so smoothly that for hours neither cart nor driver knew which was in the lead.

That is how I came to know the countryside around Juvardeil as well as any peasant child, and in September I took part in the ceremony which belongs to the end of summer — apple-picking. Or perhaps I should call it picking up, since it meant finding fallen apples in the thick grass and filling the great willow hampers with them. I was more at ease than ever, since I only had to crawl, hunt through all the holes with my hands and touch things nearby. In the process my fingers worked like searchlights. And in September the ground was ripe, heavy, rotting and had the pungence of a liqueur.

There were the apples and the hayricks. In the country in France hay is piled up in the meadow before it is taken into the barns, and that makes for the maddest and most fragrant days of the whole year. For those enormous blocks of hay which they call the *veilles* in Anjou stand up in the fields like volcanic islands or disheveled pyramids. The peasants don't like people to climb these cliffs, for it takes only ten determined urchins to pull the whole structure down in an hour. But the urchins, and I was not the least of them, have many other things to think about than the man who owns the hay.

Usually, a rope holds the rick together, making it into a solid block in the middle of the field. By taking hold of the rope you can climb to the top, and then an orgy of commotion begins — trampling, diving, shaking, with scratches and caresses, all in a whirlwind of aromatic dust. I don't think the game foreshadows anything in real life. If it does it can only be the first outburst of love.

THERE IS NOT A SINGLE ONE of my vivid memories which is not bound up with another human being. But why complain of that? In the nature of the case a blind man cannot carry anything through all by himself. The time always comes, in work or play, when he needs the hand, shoulder, eyes or voice of another person. Since there is no getting away from it, the question arises: Is the condition a happy or an unhappy one?

I hear blind people say this kind of dependence is their greatest affliction, turning them into poor relations or hangers-on. Some of them even look on this dependence as added punishment, quite unjust, and call it a curse. I think they are wrong in two ways. They are wrong for their own sakes because they torment themselves without cause. They are wrong as they face life, since they are the ones who make a misfortune of dependence.

But can these sad blind point to a single individual anywhere who has not been dependent, even with his eyes, not waiting for someone else, nor subservient to better or stronger men or ones far away; not bound in one way or another to every living creature? Whatever the bond, be it hate, love, desire, power, weakness or blindness — it is part of us, and love is the simplest way to cope with it.

I have always enjoyed having someone near me. Naturally, there are times when it is irritating, but on the whole I can thank my blindness for having forced me into bodily contact with my fellow men, and for making this an exchange of strength and joy more often than one of torment. The torment I have experienced has almost always been in solitude.

I cannot count my childhood friends. They still crowd around me, but I no longer know just who they are. They have left so much of themselves in me, and I so much of myself in them. Whom shall I see in this play of mirrors?

Of course, there are the dead. I belonged to a generation decimated a few years later in the Second World War. That is why so many of the people I am going to write about are no longer living.

But I don't believe we should mourn them. They would not have wanted that, having died because they loved life too much.

My first friend was at Juvardeil, and his name was Leopold. When I first knew him he was always a little too big for his age, not very steady on his long legs as he flew in big wobbly jumps over the stony roads, making a noise with his clogs. I was always afraid he was going to fall down. His father, a fine cabinetmaker, died when he was still very small. His mother ran the dry-goods store in the village. Leopold was a little deaf, or so everyone said because he made the teacher repeat his questions in class. Only I knew he was much less deaf than people thought, for the things that made sense or were beautiful he heard right off. He had a way of throwing his head back suddenly as if to say: "You don't need to talk so loud, I heard you perfectly."

He was a sort of peasant poet. People in the village snubbed him a little because he was hard of hearing, but mostly because they sensed that he was out of place. And he was out of place in the village, perhaps even in the world.

He and I became great pals because each of us had the same scenes going on in our heads. I could tell him about light, about sounds, the voice of trees and the weight of shadows. They didn't surprise him and, in return, he had a different story to tell me every day. It almost always had something to do with flowers. He said that flowers were made to save us. But to save us from what? As I said before, Leopold was a poet and a romantic.

In the country around Juvardeil we used to visit the haunted crossroads where there was a crucifix or a forked tree, or where ghosts had been seen once upon a time, according to folklore which was as old as the Sarthe itself. We didn't take the ghosts seriously, but we enjoyed their mystery. That last year the only thing Leopold liked was chrysanthemums. He planted them all over the place, and when they were not to be seen he imagined them and described them.

But more than that Leopold never had any coarse thoughts. He never boasted about tossing up the girls' skirts or watching them behind the hedges. When he spoke to them he was awkward and respectful, so of course they made fun of him. He didn't care because what he liked about girls were their warm hearts and their sweetness. Indeed, he was out of place in the village.

One winter day when he was sixteen (I was in Paris and only heard about it) Leopold died of a terrifying disease of the lungs. They told me he put up a tremendous fight. That seems likely, for he had really not had enough of life. He was my first friend — one of the dimmest and one of the dearest. But when one is blind it is amazing how many people of this sort one meets. Perhaps it is because they have the courage to reveal themselves to people who cannot see them.

In Juvardeil there was also promiscuity, especially out in the country on rainy days when people escaped to the barns from the garden and fields turned into ponds. Country boys have no modesty and no immodesty. With them one learns about life much faster than in the city, where civilized people play hide-and-seek.

Besides, to my knowledge no moral preachment has ever got the better of this kind of natural physical contact between boys and boys and girls. At least it leads to the realization that we are all one flesh and have the same foolish desires and the same limitations; that there are no differences between us except those which come from heart and spirit. In other words, we could all be thrown into the same basket and tossed like a salad without losing much of our dignity.

And, for that matter, what could a blind child learn about the world and other people unless like them he had the right to touch and meddle with them without being punished? If some sighted people are shocked by this notion, they should stop and think what their eyes do on the sly and often unconsciously, even when they are fully grown.

Beside the broken boards, the ladders, the firewood and the piles of hay in the barn there stood the "Little Republic." That was the name of a cart which everyone knew. It belonged to my great-grandfather in 1870 when the Third Republic was proclaimed. And since this particular ancestor, hardheaded as he was, had repudiated all the clerical and reactionary opinions of the rest of the family and shouted "Long live Gambetta, long live the Republic!" his two-wheeled cart was a symbol of the event, perpetuating the Revolution.

It stood there in the middle of the barn, so tempting with its shafts standing up in the air like arms. In principle we had no right to touch it, since it was being preserved for more serious work. But disorder has demands of its own, and we sneaked off with the Little Republic. Sometimes there were two of us, and sometimes ten, holding on to the shafts and pushing. When the Little Republic was empty, it sounded like a stream rushing over the pebbles. It danced up and down, fell into all the ruts and threatened to fall to pieces. Our fear of not bringing it home in one piece multiplied our pleasure ten times over.

But when the Little Republic was loaded it really gave tongue. Inside it we heaped up apples, wood shavings, weeds picked up along the way or piles of pebbles left on the roadside by the road mender. My playmates put me to the test. They were driving the cart while I, between them, followed along. But from time to time they took the wrong turn deliberately. They started the Little Republic on a shortcut or headed it straight for a wall. They said they did it to find out how much I could see. They hardly ever got anywhere, for the Little Republic, in front of me, told me right away that it was off its course, on the grass, having made a ridiculous turn, thrown out of line as it could be only by malicious design. Then I called out, protested, and stopped the cart. The boys were all glad, because they had seen that I was one of them.

I know the Little Republic was stalwart, but I don't know whether it survived. Anyway I still think of it often and with tenderness. Perhaps as a good republican, it knew the motto of the Republic. It certainly taught me Fraternity, also Liberty and Equality, and the fact that if I really wanted to I could go along with the others, for better or worse.

[4]

RUNNING MATES AND TEACHERS

I N PARIS, BLINDNESS WAS HARDER TO BEAR. The street was a labyrinth of noises. Each sound, repeated many times by the walls of the houses, the awnings of the stores, the grills over the sewers, the dense mass of the trucks, the scaffolding and the lampposts, created false images. I could no longer rely on my senses. People did not stay on the sidewalks. They cut their way through the crowds, with shoulders slumped forward and vacant eyes. Like all cities, Paris was a school for selfishness.

In the Champ de Mars, in the garden I knew as a little child, I heard mothers whispering to their sons: "Don't play with him. Can't you see he is blind?" I can't count the number of times I have heard sentences like these. They went through me like an electric shock.

I have no intention of putting stupidity and malice on trial. They were judged a long time ago. But I should like to say that those sulky, ill-tempered mothers, sickened by fear, ended by doing me a service. They may not have known how to defend their children, but at least they succeeded in defending me against them.

The parents of a blind child have little need to worry about the kind of people he chooses for friends. Thoughtless children, who are badly brought up, take good care not to get involved with a blind person. They prefer their mothers' skirts, and take no chances.

Until I was fifteen, when adult life began with its unavoidable exchanges, I was in a position to associate only with good children, weak ones or strong ones, but good children, prepared if not to give at least to lend what they had.

In the neighborhood school they had to find a guide for me, a boy willing to come for me at my table, take me downstairs as soon as the bell rang, and even stay with me during recess. A boy called Bacon volunteered his services. What a good fellow! An outcast for all that, for he was always at the bottom of his class. No matter how much he tried, and he did try hard and patiently, he could never find a single boy less bright than he was. As I remember it, the head of the school was scornful and made fun of him in the presence of the others. But as far as I was concerned the only effect of this injustice was to endear him.

The wretched Bacon had a mother who was a famous character in the Champ de Mars. All day long she drove her troop of small donkeys, and the children who came to the garden could ride on them for a few pennies. Because I was the friend and almost the only friend of her boy, the fat lady with the bass voice let me ride her donkeys for nothing.

In place of a quick mind Bacon had a heart of gold. He spent so little time thinking about himself that he thought of others instead, and knew more about them than the brightest students in the class. I told him stories which enthralled him, probably because the others never told him any. He loved me so much that I think he would have gone through hellfire for my sake. He was the first of a long series of friends whom heaven has thrown in my way, simple and crude if you will, but in whom my blindness aroused an irresistible feeling of tenderness. This alliance is as old as the earth. In the tales of nurses and in popular songs, there is always the never-ending brotherhood of idiots and blind people. And let there be no mistake, I say this without malice or contempt.

Still, many years went by before Bacon had a successor, for in the meantime I had gathered around me boys of quite a different kind. Children are much more ready to change their environment than adults. They haven't had time to be smug about the one they already know. To tell the truth, what embarrasses and depresses them is the fact that grownups, and their parents most of all, never change, believing this, criticizing that, calling the table table and money money, repeating the same phrases and always forgetting the heart of the matter: that the world is double, triple, countless and forever new.

My real friends always belonged to that special race of children, the seekers, the tireless ones, the ones they will call enthusiasts as young men. When people made friends with me, something rather astonishing happened to them. They were no longer satisfied with the kind of truth they were accustomed to. They had to take on some of my ways of looking at things, ways which were almost always new to them. It was not hours we spent comparing our worlds, among companions, but days. We took a real inventory, and I remember our surprise and our satisfaction every time we found out that there was a connection, a bridge between these two worlds. It was so easy for us to become identified with each other. At our age words made no trouble because they were used with such abandon, to be sure that everything got said.

My real friends did not appear until after I began going to the lycée. But there was not one of them, even in the first year, who was not drawn to me by the difference between us. That was even the case with Jean, and I shall soon be talking about him.

For the dreamers I had a bag full of dreams, so many we forgot time and even rain, and came home covered with mud. For the braggarts I saved up a lot of things to boast about. If you have an imagination it is there to be used, so we would fight duels for more than an hour, with tall stories for swords.

The gentle ones were sorry for me to begin with (they thought I must be unhappy since I couldn't see), but when they knew me better they no longer pitied me. By that time it was too late to go away, for already we were pals. For the tough ones, the ones determined to show their strength, I was the ideal protégé. I needed their protection but did not ask for it. They came around in a hurry.

I can still see one of them, Jean-Pierre, in my first year at the lycée. But mostly I remember his coarse wool sweater and his big shoulders which seemed to me superhuman. Jean-Pierre had taken it into his head to see that I made good. Before, between and after classes he led me around the school or, I might say, waved me like a flag. He made all the boys invite me to join their games, and the ones who refused never tried it again. He taught me to run right behind him holding on to his neck. He said that was the best way.

With Jean-Pierre ahead of me, there were no more dangers. If something unexpected came up, he took it all on himself. He almost thanked me for letting him hurt himself. Every day, he showed me off in the gym, the infirmary and the kitchen. And last of all we had to make our regular visit to the concierge, who was loud in support of Jean-Pierre.

To the people who think I am seeing my childhood through

rose-colored glasses, I say that is only because of their prejudice against childhood. Of course there are bad children, and I have been exposed to them. Sometimes I have lost a few feathers and come back wounded in my self-esteem. But more often than not there were the Jean-Pierres. I suppose that no real poet has ever had the mane of the real Pegasus in his hands. Still, at the age of ten, when I was holding on to the neck of Jean-Pierre, I was just such a poet. And I promise you I never doubted it.

IT IS OFTEN HARD to persuade individuals, but it is impossible to persuade organizations, and the best thing to do is to accept the fact. What hope is there that a school, a committee, an administration or department, a group entrenched in routine, will look with favor on exceptions? If you are blind you are bound to be an exception, because you are not just like other people, and because you belong to a minority, though fortunately a small one.

I had a chance to observe this again when I was ready to enter the lycée at the age of ten. I was admitted, but in the same way as two years earlier in the elementary school, on probation. They agreed to keep me if at the end of six months or a year I had demonstrated that I would not throw the train off the track. In October 1934, I was in my first year at the Lycée Montaigne, a building opposite the Luxembourg Gardens. Once I had passed beyond the administration and the door of the school, happily I had only individual men and not committees to deal with.

Of the many teachers I knew, first at Montaigne and then at Louis-le-Grand, not one ever opposed my being there, and many encouraged it beyond the dictates of conscience in their profession. If I mention the teacher of natural history who, exasperated by the clicking of my typewriter, held it under running water to get back at me, I should add that he had to be placed in an institution three months later because of mental illness. In seven years at the lycée I never really had any injustice to bear. It would be fairer to say that I was put in the ranks with all the rest, accepted, encouraged, even honored.

From this time on the story of my life is so like other people's that it often becomes confused with them. And since the studies of a young Parisian in the second quarter of the twentieth century hold no mysteries, for the first time I find I have to choose. My chosen subject is blindness, and what can be accomplished with it. All the other details I shall pass by.

I was bored at the lycée, bored almost all the time, and that was certainly not because of my companions or my teachers, but in spite of them. The boredom I am talking about was not the impatience of a child who wants to play instead of working (even though, naturally, I liked to play) nor the windiness of a mind which listens for five minutes, goes woolgathering, and then listens again. This process upsets conscientious children to the point of nausea, and throws those who are less tense into total mental sleep. I rarely fell asleep in class, at least no more often than my neighbors. I had a strong intellectual curiosity. Mathematics I did find dull, but Latin, Greek and German interested me, and literature, history, geography and the natural sciences made me feel as if I were visiting magic gardens. Lessons and homework, instead of tiring me, delighted me. I drank from the springs of knowledge as from a fountain. But all the same I was bored at school.

As soon as the classroom door closed, the smell of the room went to my head. It was not that my classmates were dirty, but each of them had a body, and forty bodies shut up in a small space were too many. It was like standing at the edge of a stagnant marsh. But why should it be so?

I HAVE ALREADY SAID that for blind people there is such a thing as moral odor, and I think that was the case at school. A group of human beings who stay in one room by compulsion — or because of social obligation which comes to the same thing — begins to smell. That is literally the case, and with children it happens even faster. Just think how much suppressed anger, humiliated independence, frustrated vagrancy and impotent curiosity can be accumulated by forty boys between the ages of ten and fourteen!

So that was the source of the unpleasant odor and the smoke which, for me, was like a physical presence in class. What I saw there was confusion, colors were faded and even dirty. The blackboard was black, the floor was black, the tables were black and so were the books. Even the teacher, in terms of light, was no more than gray. To be otherwise he had to be remarkable, not only for what he knew (learning in those days gave me little light) but remarkable as a person as well.

Boredom bound and gagged all my senses. Even sounds in class lost their volume and their depth and went lifeless. Every bit of my passion for living was needed to stand the test. At bottom I must have lacked discipline, not making up my mind to rebel, but still an incorrigible individualist. That was certainly part of my makeup, but then too there was blindness and its special world, to which school was doing violence. I had to wait years, at least until adolescence, to quiet the scandal which started inside my head at school. I doubt whether I have made peace with it even now.

I couldn't understand why the teachers never talked about the life going on inside them or inside us. They talked in great detail about the origin of mountains, the assassination of Julius Caesar, the properties of triangles, the way beetles reproduce and how often, and the combustion of carbon dioxide. Sometimes they even talked about men, but only as personages. There were the personages of ancient history, those of the Renaissance and of Molière's comedies, or a personage stranger than all the others, the one they called "individual" or "citizen," of whom I never had the slightest conception. There was never any talk of real people like the teacher or ourselves.

As for the subject of all subjects, the fact that the world is not just outside us but also within, this was entirely lacking. I understood that the teacher could not or did not wish to talk about what was going on inside him. That was his affair, and after all I was not anxious myself to talk about what went on in me. But the inner life was so much more than a personal thing. There were a thousand desires and goals my companions shared with me, and I knew it. To accumulate knowledge was good and beautiful, but the reason for men to acquire it would have been more meaningful, and no one spoke of that.

I could not help thinking that in the whole business someone was cheating somewhere. I felt I had to defend myself, and I did so by mobilizing all the images of my inner world, all the ones bound up with living creatures or living things. Sitting on my dark chair in front of my sickening table, under the gray downpour of learning, I set myself to weaving a kind of cocoon. Still, while I was a good boy I was sly, and managed it so that no one would guess I was hostile. This interior world of mine was so important to me that I was determined to protect it from shipwreck, and to rescue it I never stopped making concessions to the public, to books, to my parents and teachers. I owe my brilliance as a student to this rescue operation.

In order to be left in peace I undertook to learn everything they wanted me to, Latin, entomology, geometry and the history of the Chaldeans. I learned to type on an ordinary typewriter so I could hand my homework directly to the teachers like the others. Every day I carried my Braille typewriter to school, and put it on a felt cushion to deaden the sound, and then I took my notes. I listened, responded, listened, but was never in it heart and soul. As a boy I was cut in two. I was there and elsewhere, always going and coming between the important and the meaningless.

Now that the experience is behind me — the boredom thick as oil, the moral curvature which lasted for years — I can see that I owe them something, as the sign that some vital spirit in me refused to turn its back on childhood, and would never admit that truth was ready-made. There was no going back on it. I would never relinquish the sense of wonder I felt when I went blind. Even if there were not a book in the world to record it, I should still feel it.

WHATEVER THE DRAWBACKS, it was in school that I met my first allies: the poets and the gods. I found them in the dust of books and before me they opened avenues which were broad and bright. They seemed to be smiling on me and told me that all was not lost.

It is more than likely that humanistic studies will disappear before long. But in 1935 in a lycée in Paris they were still solidly entrenched. Our work was divided into two approximately equal parts: the world of today and the world of yesterday, the dreams of the ancients and the dreams of modern man. I can't believe that was a bad thing. At least we were not in danger of falling into the absurdity, so common nowadays, of confusing the era of Sputniks and Polaris rockets with the era of Genesis.

For hours on end we were compelled to consort with personages or, if you prefer, with supernatural beings, with Jupiter and

Venus, and with the mermaids and the elves; and then again with Jupiter, Prometheus, Vulcan, Apollo — a waste of time in terms of bookkeeping, a real bloodletting of learning and, for practical purposes, entirely foolish. Foolish it may have been, but who can prove it? As far as I am concerned I can assure you that it was a happy folly.

At all events, from 1934 to 1939 my task as a student was to gather in and make a harmonious household of people belonging to categories as different as Newton and Minerva, Franklin D. Roosevelt, Léon Blum, Adolf Hitler, Hercules and Neptune. The remarkable thing was that this odd mixture somehow resulted in a little more light.

I myself could see more clearly and knew more about myself, for inside me also the universe existed not just in two dimensions but in three. It revolved in the present but also in the past, revealing itself in the visible and the invisible, in things we can weigh and in others we cannot weigh; in things which bear a name which one can study in their elements or create, and not less in the process of change.

There was a vast agitation inside my head, a continuous fermentation, like a number of liquids poured into the same vessel and shaken up, but still lying one on top of another in neatly separated layers. It was Adolf Hitler who fell to the bottom and Apollo who rose to the top.

Everything I learned from Greek mythology, and through its long line of inheritance from Homer to Giraudoux by way of Racine, seemed clear. Yet this was the kind of evidence I had the hardest time explaining, especially when I had to write a theme. The Greek gods pleased me and were even important to me. Their way of behaving was almost always like a burlesque, and shocking. I remember that when I was twelve, the infidelities of Jupiter to Juno nearly made me hate him. I completely disapproved of him but still, behind those intimacies of the bedchamber and all the inane quarrels, the gods took on substance. And what they conveyed coincided almost exactly with what I was experiencing myself. Minerva, for instance, was wisdom, Venus beauty, Apollo light and Jupiter lightning, force, radiance, protection. For my part, I knew very well that these things existed, were not merely puppets or words, not just occasions of misunderstanding in the Latin.

The way adults said "this is beautiful," "that is reasonable" annoyed me, because I could see that, for them, "this" and "that" counted far more than "beautiful" or "reasonable." They were concerned only with things they needed right away, with things they used. I was not anxious to make use of things, anyway not yet. I just wanted to look at them.

I liked Apollo better than all the rest. I had definite reasons for my preference, because Apollo was the only one the books talked about for whom light was as important as it was for me. Besides, the particular responsibility of this great god was the part of light I knew to be essential — namely its source. He was less concerned with the way light strikes against objects all over the planet (this was good enough for the science of optics) than with its birth and rebirth, and the mystery which made it flow through everything inexhaustibly. Later on I understood that Apollo was not the only one nor even the best, that Jesus had considered light essential, and that it was one of the vital elements in the Christian mystique. But when I was eleven, Apollo was the one who spoke to me most clearly.

And then there were the poets, those unbelievable people so different from other men, who told anyone who would listen that a wish is more important than a fortune, and that a dream can weigh more than iron or steel. What nerve they had, those poets, but how right they were! Everything, they said, comes from inside us, passes through things outside and then goes back in. And that to them is the meaning of life, feeling, understanding, love.

Most of the time the poets were obscure — too much so for my taste — because of the wretched language they used, language which rose and fell endlessly, held you suspended to the point where, at the end of a few minutes, you could no longer hear them; a language which shimmered, bounded from one end of the universe to the other, called attention to something, then immediately replaced it by its opposite. Sometimes I suspected the poets of only adding fruitless complexities to their lives. But all the same they knew a great deal.

Speaking of complexity, three or four years later it was my turn to beat the record. When I was about fifteen I wrote poems as stormy and obscure as any you can imagine. I described gardens and fantastic grottoes. I made all the words in the dictionary knock their heads together, all the stars in the firmament run into each other, as I feel sure every man worth his salt must have done at some time in his life.

But the strange thing is that today, when I have become much more reasonable and more prudent, I often feel an unconquerable desire for the disorder of an earlier day as I have described it. Granted it was a mass of confusion, but at bottom luminous and containing more germs of life within the space of a single minute than there are in my happier days in the present.

At the lycée, when a friend, one of the "practical ones," asked one of us "visionaries" what a certain verse in Virgil or Victor Hugo meant, we had the answer ready-made. "It means what it means, and something more! Can't you see?" Most of the time he did not see, but he had something with which to console himself. He could always treat us as fools.

A VERY SHORT TIME after I went blind I forgot the faces of my mother and father and the faces of most of the people I loved.

From time to time I remembered a face, but it was always that of a person I did not care about. Why did memory work that way? It was almost as if affection were not compatible with it.

Could it be that affection, or love, puts us so close to people that we are no longer able to evoke their image? Perhaps we never see those we love, never completely, just because we love them. In the absence of their faces I had the voices of my parents ever present in my ears, and since the accident the shape of people and their appearance still concerned me, but in a different way. All at once I stopped caring whether people were dark or fair, with blue eyes or green. I felt that sighted people spent too much time observing these empty things. Every cliché of colloquial talk, "he inspires confidence," "he is well brought up," seemed to me superficial, the froth but not the drink itself.

For my part I had an idea of people, an image, but not the same as the one seen by the world at large. Often I saw them in a way diametrically opposed to that of others. The furtive boy I saw as shy, the one they called lazy as struggling all day long in imagination with an ardor which was the opposite of laziness. To tell the truth, my opinions of people had become so different that I often distrusted them. I ended by feeling that I was the one who was strange.

Frankly, hair, eyes, mouth, the necktie, the rings on fingers mattered very little to me. I no longer even thought about them. People no longer seemed to possess them. Sometimes in my mind men and women appeared without heads or fingers. Then again the lady in the armchair suddenly rose before me in her bracelet, turned into the bracelet itself. There were people whose teeth seemed to fill their whole faces, and others so harmonious they seemed to be made of music. But in reality none of these sights is made to be described. They are so mobile, so much alive that they defy words.

People were not at all as they were said to be, and never the same for more than two minutes at a stretch. Some were, of course, but that was a bad sign, a sign that they did not want to understand or be alive, that they were somehow caught in the glue of some indecent passion. That kind of thing I could see in them right away, because, not having their faces before my eyes, I caught them off guard. People are not accustomed to this, for they only dress up for those who are looking at them.

I heard my parents' voices against my ear or inside my heart, where you will, but very close. And all the other voices followed the same course. It is comparatively easy to protect ourselves from a face we dislike; sufficient to keep it at a distance, to leave it in the world outside. But only try the same thing with voices, you will never manage it!

The human voice forces its way into us. It is really inside ourselves that we hear it. To hear it properly we must allow it to vibrate in our heads and our chests, in our throats as if, for the moment, it really belonged to us. That is surely the reason why voices never deceive us.

I no longer saw faces, and knew in all probability I should go through life without seeing them. Sometimes I should have liked to touch them when they seemed to me beautiful. But society is careful to ban such gestures. As a rule it forbids any move which might bring human beings closer to each other. In doing so, society believes it is acting for the best, defending us against the assaults of immodesty and violence. Perhaps with good reason for men are often beasts. But how could a blind child recognize the danger? For him such bans were impossible to explain.

Nevertheless, I made the most of voices, in a domain which society has never intruded upon. It is strange that when laws men make are so ticklish in matters concerning the body, they never set limits to nakedness or contact by voice. Evidently they leave out of account the fact that the voice can go further than hands or eyes in licit or illicit touch.

Furthermore, a man who speaks does not realize that he is betraying himself. When people addressed me, a blind child, they were not on guard. They were persuaded that I heard the words they were saying, and understood what they meant. They never suspected that I could read their voices like a book. For example, the teacher of mathematics came into the classroom, clapped his hands and boldly began his lecture. He was lucid that day, as he usually was, perhaps more interesting than ever, a little too interesting. His voice, instead of falling into place at the end of the sentence, as it should have, going a tone or two down the scale, hung in the air, a bit sharp. It was as though the teacher wanted to hide something that day, put a good face on it before an unknown audience, prove that he was not giving in, that he would carry on to the end because he had to. Meanwhile, accustomed to the cadence of his sentences falling as regularly as the beat of a metronome, I listened attentively, and was distressed on his account. I wanted to help, but that seemed foolish for I had no reason for thinking him unhappy. All the same he was unhappy, bitterly unhappy. The terrible "intelligence" of gossip told us a week later that his wife had just left him.

I ended by reading so many things into voices without wanting to, without even thinking about it, that voices concerned me more than the words they spoke. Sometimes, for minutes at a time in class, I heard nothing, neither the teacher's questions nor the answers of my comrades. I was too much absorbed by the images that their voices were parading through my head. All the more since these images half the time contradicted, and flagrantly, the appearance of things. For instance, the student named Pacot had just been given 100 by the teacher of history. I was astonished, because Pacot's voice had informed me, beyond the shadow of a doubt, that he had understood nothing. He had recited the lesson, but only with his lips. His voice sounded like an empty rattle, with no substance in the sound.

What voices taught me they taught me almost at once. There were some physical factors which threw me off — boys who breathed badly, who should have been operated on for tonsils or adenoids, and whose voices remained blanketed in cloud. Some could never muster anything but a ridiculous falsetto which made you think at first they were cowards. Then there were the nervous ones, the timid, who only used their voices at the wrong moment, and made themselves as small as possible under the mumbling. But if I was deceived by them, it was never for long.

A beautiful voice (and beautiful means a great deal in this context, for it means that the man who has such a voice is beautiful himself) remains so through coughing and stammering. An ugly voice, on the contrary, can become soft, scented, humming, singing like the flute. But to no purpose. It stays ugly just the same.

How should I explain to other people that all my feelings toward them, feelings of sympathy or antipathy, came to me from their voices? I tried to tell a few people it was so, that they could do nothing about it and neither could I. But soon I had to stop because it was clear that the idea was frightening to them.

So there was a moral music. Our appetites, our humors, our secret vices, even our best-guarded thoughts were translated into the sounds of our voices, into tones, inflections or rhythms. Three or four notes too close to each other in a sentence announced anger, even if nothing made it visible to the eye. As for hypocrites, they were recognizable immediately. Their voices were tense, with small abrupt intervals between sounds, as though the speaker were determined never to let his voice go its own way.

Later people spoke to me of a new science, the science of voices or phonology, stimulated by developments in radio and methods of indirect persuasion used in advertising. Would such a science be possible? Surely. But desirable? I am afraid not, for if the time should ever come when greedy and unscrupulous men mastered the art of the human voice, knew how to decipher it and modulate it at will, all that is left of liberty would be lost. Such men would have their hand on the hidden tiller. They would be like a latter-day Orpheus, charming the beasts and making the stones come to life. But remember that Orpheus had the right to his secret only as long as he refrained from abusing it.

[5]

MY FRIEND JEAN

For some time since I have been talking to you, I have not been alone for Jean has joined us. You could not have known it, but he is there in everything I do and say. If I were not afraid of being needlessly obscure, for the nine years of my life which lie ahead I should never say "I" but "we."

In my first year at the lycée, in almost all my classes Jean sat at the table behind me. He chose this place himself. He didn't want to leave me, but he had not told me so. For my part, I always wanted to turn around and hear his voice closer by — it was a wise voice, brighter than all the others, and it made me happy.

We were not yet intimates, and didn't dare suggest it to each other. Toward the end of the school year, his mother came to ask mine if he could come home with me every evening, to read me the books I needed and work with me. To our delight it came about right away. But who could have guessed then that this growing friendship would end in tragedy? Neither he nor I, I assure you. We were children and knew only that we loved each other.

Jean was the son of an architect, a happy man and a good one who was to die of a heart attack four years later. His mother had been a painter. She was imaginative and gentle and unbelievably respectful of other people.

At the age of eleven Jean was more innocent than any of my companions. He knew nothing about life, and at the time didn't want me to teach him about it. With him it was partly modesty and partly the sense that things come about in their own time. He kept telling me that he could wait.

In everything he was slower than I was. Sometimes his movements were a little heavy; he either bore down or fondled. When he shook your hand, he shook it too hard and too long. It almost hurt. He had the voice of an angelic countertenor. Till he was fourteen, it made him very anxious, for he wondered whether he was ever going to speak like a man. Then in two weeks in the spring of 1938 his voice fell three octaves, and turned into a noble and protective bass.

To protect: the word expresses all the desires of which Jean was capable. Later on, when we had both learned about introspection, he told me how glad he was to be weak, since that would always keep him from abusing other people. But was he really weak? As far as the teachers were concerned, he was. Although he was very intelligent, the rhythm of his mind was slow and his speech grave. They accused him of being too phlegmatic. His face always wore a slightly surprised expression which stupid people mistook for irony.

Jean entered life by all doors at the same time: through studies, imagination, affection and a sort of communion which can only be compared to the spiritual intimacy of marriage — such marriage as one rarely sees. He was serious, he was grave. Other words are really needed to express it, words like *nobility* and *majesty*, if only you could strip them of their stiffness and solemnity. He was more serious than I, less open to all the follies of instinct, and in these things, toward me, he acted as a brake.

We were both hard-working boys, for books had caught us in their trap. The best present I ever gave Jean (or so he said) was a copy of *Pelleas and Melisande* by Maeterlinck. We worked and we dreamed. For our two bodies we had only one head.

His body grew much faster than mine, so that every year his hand had to drop farther to my shoulder. He held me by the shoulder only, and heaven is my witness that he held me tight! At sixteen, he was eight inches taller than I, a great strapping fellow, but thin and more and more serious.

We had been together at the lycée from the beginning. That was the first of the seven years when we were never separated for more than forty-eight hours. And after the seven came two more, two stormy years. But it is too soon to talk about that. For nine years there was not an idea or an emotion which we did not share. And yet we were as different as could be.

We listened to the same teachers, read the same books, had the same friends, made the same trips, awaited the same pleasures at the same hour, walked at the same pace, and, believe me, as he grew taller, that was hard for me. We were crazy together, sad at the same moment. When one of us didn't know something it was because the other also was unaware of it. We were one to the point where we could communicate by telepathy. Yet for all that, we were still two, joyfully and freely two, so much so that each of us lived twice every day.

What bound us together was not just friendship, it was a

religion. The apartment house where I lived was halfway between the lycée and Jean's house. Twice a day Jean made the trip on foot, picked me up and dropped me off on his way. I waited for him downstairs in the vestibule of the building. I loved waiting for him. When he was a little late, I could feel the ends of my fingers tingle, my throat tighten, not with uneasiness — but with joy. All of a sudden he was there in front of me, straight as a die, dependable as your word of honor. For a second or two he never said anything. Neither did I. We needed silence to find each other once more.

When we were sixteen we solemnly decided that we would never exchange any of those trite phrases, none of those horrible expressions like "How are you?" "Pretty well. And yourself?" which make the noise of friendship and then collapse like bubbles a minute later. We had sworn to tell each other the truth, nothing but the truth, and if we couldn't, to be silent. Just imagine two boys, one tall, the other of medium height, striding along paths in one of the forests in the Ile-de-France (Rambouillet, St-Germain, Chantilly), smiling at each other now and then but not talking for hours on end. There you have Jean and me, at fifteen, one day when we were not sure of ourselves, not sure we should not hurt each other if we spoke.

How demanding we were in those days! Both of us were so certain that being honorable and respectful gives greater delight than all the pleasures in the world. Jean was born knowing it and had taught it to me. And I was not a bad pupil.

We also knew how to chatter. In September 1940, one Sunday, I remember fourteen hours of talk, without interruption and with no witness. But when we talked on that way it was to search out and find each other. This was not just making sentences, it was exploring. Hours before our heads had stopped recording words and we had been speaking through intentions and movements of the spirit, communicating through lives open as a book.

Jean picked me up every day to go to the lycée, whether it was raining, blowing or snowing. When we were together I don't remember feeling that we were hot or cold, at least not enough for us to notice it. Physically I was never ill, but Jean sometimes was. For reasons which medicine never explained, he had terrible and frequent headaches. Then he got dizzy and had to lie down all day. Or, if he ventured out, his hands shook and his voice sounded smothered. I always knew he was unwell before he told me so, but I never talked to him about it. He had made me promise not to. As soon as the attack was over, his voice sang again. The first thing he did was to ask me to tell him what had happened in the world while he was out of it.

In the end, people became so accustomed to seeing us together that they could hardly distinguish between us. Sometimes Jean said to me and I said to him that that was a pity and we should someday have to separate. But for us this idea was like thinking about death, and we rejected it immediately.

Jean loved my being blind, because he thought that if I weren't our friendship would never have been so complete. Besides, we were constantly lending each other our eyes. One day it was he who saw, the next it was I. Of that too we made an adventure.

So as you see, Jean is here with us. So far I have not been able to show him very clearly and I am not sure I can do better. But I shall carry him along with me up to the time when he and I were both nineteen. In the end you will surely know him well.

HAVE I TOLD YOU — I probably haven't yet — that Jean and I made a pact from the start, declaring that both of us had the right to make friends as we liked, independently? This was not done to conserve our liberty (since for us liberty only seemed to begin with sharing all we had), but to protect the freedom of others. Anyone could confide in Jean and not in me, or vice versa. Sometimes people are so queer.

The measure was a wise one as it turned out. Till 1938 most of my friends would not have tolerated Jean. They would have mistaken his innocence for silliness, and made life miserable for him. I knew there was no doubt about this, and kept these people at a distance. Now and then I felt ashamed of it, but it takes time for shame to affect our actions.

I was still at the mercy of my passion for violent games. I still needed to run, either on the Champ de Mars or at Juvardeil. After school every afternoon I had to run around the Luxembourg hugging the fences — it came to about two and a half breathless miles. I had to cut across the grass in spite of the signs which said not to, or rather because of them. Running and shouting we spread panic among the baby carriages and the young mothers, who seemed very old to us in those days and deserving of such treatment. We made the dust fly up in clouds, sniffing the acetylene of the merry-go-round, tearing through the crowds, alarming the people passing by, raiding a record shop on the Boul Mich to hear the latest songs of Maurice Chevalier and Tino Rossi — all these experiments we regarded as the height of boldness. And for these exploits you can understand that Jean was not the man I needed.

I needed boys ready for anything, ready if need be even to fake innocence to their families or in school.

In all this, I was far away from Jean, in a no-man's-land, an uneasy terrain suspended between childhood and adolescence. Like all the rest of my companions, I was full of clownish ignorance and precocious knowledge.

I began to suspect that man has a body, and that it is sometimes a nuisance. He wants to enjoy it, but is not always allowed to. In the world of pleasure one comes upon innumerable rites, most of which are hidden. My pals in the Luxembourg were not like the ones at Juvardeil. When they looked at girls it was always on the sly. They thought about them but never touched them and in the long run this was a bad thing. In this respect they seemed to be living under the eye of some nameless police. Picture magazines, the movies and the radio turned their heads, and their heads turned in a vacuum.

That's why we made those frequent visits to the part of the Luxembourg where lovers were in the habit of meeting at night. We wanted to surprise them in the midst of the mystery, but we were disappointed every time, for there was no mystery. Here and there we saw an arm around a waist, a kiss that lasted a little longer than was sensible. But it was just like the movies and no more. We came home unsatisfied, and discussed feverishly the bits of life that we had picked up.

I wasn't happy away from Jean, especially away from that purity of his. But how was I to resist, especially when all these boys, who were trying so hard to forget their childhood, needed me? They told me so. Several of them had the idea that, being blind, I must be an expert in matters of feelings (that's what they called the movements of their bodies, and it would be ungracious to reproach them, since most adults do exactly the same thing). Besides, a blind person was a witness beyond their dreams! Since he could not see the girls, it was necessary to explain them to him. Then too, there was no danger of his contradicting what he was told.

I took part in all these games, though not content with them, until the time when Jean set me free. When he was there the good side of me blossomed. Soon, I couldn't even understand how only a few hours earlier I could have been interested in things that held so little of the ideal, so little hope. The boys in the Luxembourg became ugly to me, no longer children but not yet men. Already there was something unhealthy in them. I don't know what it was, but Jean, for his part, kept his pride.

He also talked to me about girls, but in the same manner as he would have talked about the stars: they were made to stay far away and to shine with a small flickering light for a long time. They never touched ground, and must neither be knocked against nor taken hold of, since they were the essence of gentleness. One should not even think about them all the way, since they were as important as the future.

This kind of talk did me good. It held so much promise, and I knew that Jean, in himself alone, was more right than all the others put together.

I knew this because even if all my escapades at the Luxembourg never carried me to the point of speaking to a girl, still I did meet some at home, the sisters of my companions or childhood friends. Jean, who in his innocence could foresee everything, kept telling me I should take advantage of their being there, for soon this would no longer be possible. He was quite right, for these were the last hours of that wonderful ease.

I felt comfortable with girls. They were better listeners than boys. If only they didn't pretend! But at the time the suspicion never occurred to me. Whenever I told a story, invented a make-believe scenario, or changed a book to fit my dreams (and when the girls were there I was inexhaustible) they were always willing to follow. Unlike boys, they never quibbled over ridiculous points of accuracy. They felt so much at home in the imagination that with them I could dream twice as hard. They always gave back an echo, and the more unreal my inventions, the happier the girls. They managed to dramatize the impossible.

From time to time I was obliged to remind myself that they were girls hiding something essential from me, and that made me uneasy. But as a rule I didn't think about it. I lived with them outside the real world, and benefited from this liberty.

Then the day came — and it was difficult — when they stopped coming to see me. They had turned into *jeunes filles*, and Jean and I had a long way to go to recapture them.

Between the ages of thirteen and sixteen, both the bad boys and the pretty girls had left us. It was the time for holidays shared between the two of us; for those interminable and often pointless confidences; for the world you discover with its ever new life, a world reminding you that you are not yet fully alive; the time for thoughts which are born but have no time to grow before others take their place; the time for the pure joy of living which, for want of a better word, we called love.

WE HAD BEEN CLIMBING in shale and brush along the side of a hill above the Seine Valley. All of a sudden, having just noticed that the landscape had made a final dip on my right, I said to Jean: "Just look! This time we're on top. You'll see the whole bend of the river, unless the sun gets in your eyes!"

Jean was startled, opened his eyes wide and cried: "You're right."

This little scene was often repeated between us, in a thousand forms. And if it surprises you, that is only because you forget how hard it is for people who have something — eyes, luck or happiness — to realize it and make use of it. When we came in from our walks, Jean would say to his family, "It's fantastic how many things he made me see today!"

I should add, but perhaps you have already guessed it, that Jean spent hours dreaming. He was continually diving down into his inner world. He believed me when I told him that this world, if not richer than the other, was certainly as rich, and almost completely unexplored. I had pointed out to him ways to approach it, for I knew the route well. And now he came very close to going further along it than I.

Still, though he had learned to go down into himself, he was clumsy when it came to climbing up again. The ascent is always the most difficult part of this journey. I had been making the return trip regularly for five or six years, and for me it was routine.

I explained to Jean that it was a preconceived idea which made the process hard for him — an idea, by the way, which almost everyone shares — that there are two worlds, one without, the other within. I kept having to explain all over again, because Jean wanted to believe me but couldn't. The preconceived idea always stood in the way.

We talked about this at least once a week in the frame of mind of people going to Mass on Sunday. After all, it was a religious subject. The reality — the oneness of the world — left me in the lurch, incapable of explaining it, because it seemed obvious. I could only repeat: "There is only one world. Things outside only exist if you go to meet them with everything you carry in yourself. As to the things inside, you will never see them well unless you allow those outside to enter in."

To pass from the inner light to the light of the sun was not the work of the senses. A click sufficed, a slight change in point of view, like turning one's head a hundredth part of the circle. It was enough in the end to believe. The rest came by itself.

To convince Jean (which mattered terribly to me) I assembled all my arguments. If he wanted to be completely happy, there must be only one world, for this was the indispensable condition.

This joy was well known to me. It was the Grace of my state of being. When I read in the gospels that the Word was made Flesh, I told myself that this was indeed true. At the same time I was aware that I had done nothing to deserve it. It had simply been given to me, and I prayed God that Jean, too, should receive it.

If there is a difference between a boy of fifteen years and a man of forty, I am afraid, alas, that it is to the advantage of the former. The boy does everything by attention. The man no longer does anything except by habit. Jean knew how to pay attention, to the point where nothing could distract him, neither nightfall, nor my endless chattering, not even hunger. Fifteen years old! The age when you dare to say anything, when you always find someone to listen. I, too, knew how to listen to Jean. When one of us was try-ing to draw an idea out of his head, or a whole scene which stub-bornly refused to take shape, the other found that entirely natural. He waited and already understood.

Try telling a grown-up person that you don't see things as he does! Beware! You will annoy him and probably even shock him. And if you embark on the description of your differences, you have a fifty-fifty chance of making an enemy. But Jean and I were able to bear everything coming from each other. We were on the watch for even the smallest novelty.

For a whole hour he would tell me about the effect that Schubert's music had on him, and how different was the effect of Beethoven's. For my part, I would unroll for him the film of history. I simply don't know how it all came to me. But every time someone mentioned an event (whether it was in the reign of Tiberius or in the First World War), the event immediately projected itself in its place on the screen, which was a kind of inner canvas. This canvas could open out or fold up — like the altarpieces artists painted in the Middle Ages — and could do this as often as I wanted. If I needed the century of Augustus, I fixed it on the canvas and left hidden the Roman Republic on the left, and the rest of the emperors and their decline on the right.

I could widen or narrow my field of vision at will. Periods when not much happened — like the sixth and seventh centuries between the prophecy of Mohammed and the crowning of Charlemagne — I saw in shades of gray. Crowded periods, like the ones which began with the American and French Revolutions, I could cut up into as many pictures as they needed. In this way, I hardly need to say it, the study of history became a game for me. And what a vivid game!

In these pictures, large or small, it was not figures or lines of print I saw, but the great people and places of history, in all the detail which I had learned about them: Joan of Arc at Reims, Joan of Arc at the stake, the plague in Marseilles, Gutenberg and his first Bible, Santa Sofia sacked by the Turks, Christopher Columbus on his caravel.

Jean had the right to all these details, a hundred times over, and never tired of them. Comparing my world with his, he found that his held fewer pictures and not nearly as many colors. This made him almost angry: "When it comes to that," he used to say, "which one of us two is blind?" That is why when I asked him to see, he was willing and really looked. Then, immediately, I made use of his eyes. And when my turn came to say, "I have seen the forest, I see the sun setting," he believed me.

Still, it was necessary to keep these secrets to ourselves, for they were not really commonplace enough to be spread abroad. And, when Jean was gone, I had to wait years before I got back the courage to confide in anyone. It is not always easy to be different.

[6]

THE VISUAL BLIND

T HE FIRST CONCERT HALL I ever entered, when I was eight
years old, meant more to me in itself alone in the space of a
minute than all the fabled kingdoms. The first musician I heard
there, right in front of me only a few steps from my seat in the
orchestra, was another child, Yehudi Menuhin.

Every Saturday from October to May for six years, my father
came to get me when school was out, called a taxi and took me to
one of the concerts given by one of the large symphony orchestras
in Paris. Paul Paray, Felix Weingartner, Charles Munch, Arturo
Toscanini, Bruno Walter became so familiar to me that I knew,
without anyone having to tell me, who was on the podium that
day. The orchestra followed Munch's pace or Toscanini's, and who
could mistake them?

Going into the hall was the first step in a love story. The tuning
of the instruments was my engagement. After that I threw myself
into the music just as one tumbles into happiness.

The world of violins and flutes, of horns and cellos, of fugues, scherzos and gavottes, obeyed laws which were so beautiful and so clear that all music seemed to speak of God. My body was not listening, it was praying. My spirit no longer had bounds, and if tears came to my eyes, I did not feel them running down because they were outside me. I wept with gratitude every time the orchestra began to sing. A world of sounds for a blind man, what sudden grace! No more need to get one's bearings. No more need to wait. The inner world made concrete.

I loved Mozart so much, I loved Beethoven so much that in the end they made me what I am. They molded my emotions and guided my thoughts. Is there anything in me which I did not, one day, receive from them? I doubt it.

Today, music for me hangs from a golden nail called Bach. But it is not my tastes which have changed but my relationships. As a child I lived with Mozart, Beethoven, Schumann, Berlioz, Wagner and Dvořák, because they were the ones I met every week. Before becoming the word of a man, even if the man is Mozart, all music is music. A kind of geometry, but one of inner space. Sentences, but freed from meaning. Without any doubt, of all the things man has made, music is the least human. When I heard it I was all there, with my troubles and my joys, yet it was not myself exactly. It was better than I, bigger and more sure.

For a blind person music is nourishment, as beauty is for those who see. He needs to receive it, to have it administered at intervals like food. Otherwise a void is created inside him and causes him pain.

My father was in the habit of walking home from the concert, making me a present of some of the most beautiful hours of my childhood. How can people call music a pleasure? Pleasure satisfied impoverishes and saddens, but music builds as it is heard.

Holding my father by the arm, I was filled with sounds and guided by them. My father whistled, hummed a melody. He talked to me about the concert. He talked to me about all the things that life, someday, would offer me. He no longer needed to explain them. Intelligence, courage, frankness, the conditions of happiness and love, all these were in Handel, in Schubert, fully stated, as readable as the sun high in the sky at noon. If only fathers would share with their sons, as mine did, something beyond themselves, life would be better for it!

However — though who would believe it — I was not a musician, not really. I learned to play the cello. For eight years I practiced scales and did exercises. I played some simple pieces respectably. Once I belonged to a trio and managed not to destroy it altogether. But music was not my language. I excelled in listening to it, but I would never be able to speak it. Music was made for blind people, but some blind people are not made for music. I was among them; I was one of the visual blind.

I did not become a musician, and the reason was a strange one. I had no sooner made a sound on the A string, on D or G or C, than I no longer heard it. I looked at it. Tones, chords, melodies, rhythms, each was immediately transformed into pictures, curves, lines, shapes, landscapes, and most of all colors. Whenever I made the A string sound by itself with the bow, such a burst of light appeared before my eyes and lasted so long that often I had to stop playing.

At concerts, for me, the orchestra was like a painter. It flooded me with all the colors of the rainbow. If the violin came in by itself, I was suddenly filled with gold and fire, and with red so bright that I could not remember having seen it on any object. When it was the oboe's turn, a clear green ran all through me, so cool that I seemed to feel the breath of night. I visited the land of music. I rested my eyes on every one of its scenes. I loved it till it caught my breath. But I saw music too much to be able to speak its language. My own language was the language of shapes.

Strange chemistry, the chemistry which changed a symphony into moral purpose, an adagio into a poem, a concerto into a walk, attaching words to pictures and pictures to words, daubing the world with colors, and finally making the human voice into the most beautiful of all instruments!

With Jean, who was more of a musician than I, I had long arguments on this subject. All of them ended with an exciting discovery, and it was always the same one: that there is nothing in the world which cannot be replaced with something else; that sounds and colors are being exchanged endlessly, like the air we breathe and the life it gives us; that nothing is ever isolated or lost; that everything comes from God and returns to God along all the roadways of the world; and that the most beautiful music is still only a path. Yet there are enchanted paths, and those which bear the names of Vivaldi, Beethoven and Ravel went further, I knew, than any roads on earth.

In 1937, at the age of thirteen, I went on a journey that holds a peculiarly unique place in my life. My parents and I traveled to Dornach, a Swiss village not far from Basel. There, at the top of a hill, rose a singular building: the Goetheanum. Rudolf Steiner had had it built [before his death in 1925], in order to have a place for the working and meeting together of all those who followed his teachings. He himself had spoken there. And he *spoke*; he did not prophesy. In a wonderfully simple, completely sober method of speaking, he showed that spiritual worlds do exist. Deliberately and without pathos he affirmed with quiet force that it is the spiritual worlds that determine our physical one. He explained what these spiritual worlds consist of, why we generally know nothing of them, and the reasons for our ignorance and its significance. But now the time had come, he said, openly to reveal these secrets, even though they had been withheld up to now by a small number of initiates.

By birth Rudolf Steiner was an Austrian and in the German language he held hundreds and hundreds of lectures in which he seemed never to invent but rather to describe spontaneously what was before his eyes at the very moment. Dornach, in its wreath of surrounding hills, still cherished the marks of his earthly path, profound yet not austere, respectful yet not idolizing.

My father had for many years been active and influential in the French section of the Anthroposophical Society. He devoted all his free time to a regular lecturing schedule. To me, too, he spoke a great deal about Steiner and his work. Gradually I began to understand more and more, and a quiet and unforced veneration filled my mind and thought. The teachings of this astonishing man — at least, those that impressed me at the time — struck me with a feeling unknown until then: namely, a feeling of certainty, a feeling that the teachings were self-evident. The cycle of successive reincarnations, in particular, gave to my consciousness complete tranquility. I can still experience it today. For in accord with this new insight, any indignation about earthly injustice and unmerited suffering is wiped away. The misfortune that meets us can only be measured by our own responsibility; our anxiety and despair are now revealed as a result of our ignorance. We must pay for our past mistakes and answer for our present faults, but we shall be able to atone for them in a future life.

Only our outward, visible history seems absurd and arbitrary. Our inner destiny knows only equilibrium and compensation. To some extent we are masters of our own personal fate, no longer

— as so many religions would teach — condemned to exist, to be born, to die, but guilty only when given over entirely to matter and forgetful of our essential Self. And thus eternity is no longer so inexplicably projected into the future but rather encompasses our life on all sides, this life of ours which is both trivial and at the same moment so significant.

I used to listen to these teachings, one after the other, but without ever summoning in myself the will to accept them. I was not fostering a belief. I was merely willing to see what was shown to me. Life itself would decide my choice.

I spent two weeks in Dornach and paid careful attention to everything. One event, however, absorbed my interest more than anything else. I was allowed to attend a eurythmy performance. On an ordinary theater stage in the Goetheanum men and women were dancing, or rather, they seemed to dance. For eurythmy was not stylized choreography, but an art, a new art, just as complete and original an art as poetry or music. Steiner had created its foundations and established its first laws. One can say that eurythmy would reconcile word and motion, would let a movement of the body correspond to each spoken sound, would make the sense of poetry or prose visual, pictorial. There was, accordingly, a eurythmic alphabet based on the inner spiritual meaning of the sounds of speech, and a freely applied grammar to hold them together. Sometimes the eurythmists developed their art in connection with music, sometimes with a recited poem.

On that evening poems by Goethe and also several by Steiner himself were recited. They touched me deeply, for without quite understanding them (they were spoken in German) I could guess their meaning without any effort. The speakers brought the words to life in the same way that one makes a gesture with the hand or the arm or with the whole body.

The German language seemed immediately to me of an extraordinary, musical beauty; most of all, it seemed imbued with a miraculous and unique flexibility. It never sounded finite, never closed or dead. It brought sounds into uninterrupted motion, rich invention. It let them rise or sink in an uninterrupted flow, always following certain curves that were impossible to predict. Though often rough and sometimes heavy or, at least, ponderous, it struck the air with solemn drumbeats. But it never was satisfied with itself; it seemed always to be in search of and following its moving forms.

Its grace beguiled me. Yes, I say: its grace — certainly not that brilliant and proportioned grace of the French language, but more ardent, more willed. I heard how the vowels or the warm diphthongs — ü ["au" as in "how"], ä ["ai" as in "light"], ö ["eu" as in "oil"] — following a slow, very determined rhythm, soften the piano-like tones of the st, pf, cht; how at other times they put their feet on the ground and emphasize their strength in the endings -g or -t: *Wirkung, aufgebaut.* German became for me the language of a musician-architect, to whom the speech sounds have given building-stones and the impulse of will patiently to erect his speech edifice.

Through all this I was filled with an enthusiasm which was to last for almost ten years without diminishing — and which today can still seize me at every new opportunity: I simply had a passion for the German language. Soon there followed a passion for Germany as well, and for everything it conceals of menace and of treasure. I found myself confronted with a mystery.

FROM 1937 TO 1944 A WHOLE PART OF MY LIFE was unfulfilled. Every day for eight years I would hear the call of Germany. I felt myself irresistibly drawn to the east. It seemed to me as if every day were the eve of a possible departure. Germany gave me the joy of life, it brought all my possibilities and capabilities on to a higher level.*

When I was fourteen I was a small edition of the Tower of Babel. Latin words, German words, French and Greek words led a riotous life inside my head. Every night I went to sleep with my ears ringing. That's what happens when you are too conscientious as a student, with too much memory, when you have a bent for literature, when you read more than is good for you, and when words have grown as real to you as people.

Luckily I had found a way of protecting myself. I had discovered, contrary to what all the books taught, that the less seriously you took words, the more sense they made. The proper way to look at them was from a distance, in the mass. The more numerous they were, the more chance they had of taking on significance.

I used to stop reading all of a sudden, lift my head above the waves of language and keep my ears open. I caught words on the fly, and it wasn't hard for there were always words floating around me in the room. I trained my headlights on each one of them for a second, and then quickly replaced them with others. The associations, the marriages that resulted often seemed to me admirable. But I didn't take note of them for this would have spoiled my pleasure.

My greatest pleasure was in hearing words sound, in watching them make all those comical attempts to convince me that they had meaning. Besides, they were not abstract figures moving around in

---

* The preceding eleven paragraphs were not included in the original American publication of *And There Was Light*. They were translated from the original French edition separately and published, with the author's permission, in the *Journal of Anthroposophy*, no. 8, 1968.

the world of the mind. Each of them had a voice, a voice that fluttered, but one my ear could hear distinctly.

On Thursdays, I felt like a truant when I went off to the Comédie Française. But can you imagine a more serious form of diversion? I was going to hear *Polyeucte* and *Britannicus, Tartuffe, Athalie, Zaïre*!

For once, Jean was not with me, since he always had some schoolwork to finish. I turned to more frivolous boys, less conscientious, all of whom, more or less recently, had fallen in love with an actress. I catered to their passion by making it their responsibility to accompany me. From the top gallery they looked down on the object of their desire, caught by the cruelty of a Trojan prince or absorbed in taking poison. I was intoxicated by this weekly dose of classical alexandrines.

Since the seats farthest from the stage were the only ones we could afford — especially if we wanted to allow ourselves the luxury of an eskimo pie between the acts — we usually had trouble hearing the lines. Only the tragic cries rose to the place where we were. The blank spots we had to fill in with our imagination, but that kept us forever awake and entranced.

Wandering through the marble busts of all the French playwrights since the Renaissance, along the solemn galleries of the theater, we made all kinds of assumptions about episodes in the play we had not heard. And without exception, they went to our heads. For hours after the show was over, my brain swayed right and left to the rhythm of the alexandrines, as they say the sea does through the attraction of the moon.

Up there in "the gods" I heard poorly because of distance and also because the theater fans — they were as thick as flies those days — could not refrain from reciting Marivaux's prose or the verse of Racine along with the actors in loud and passionate tones.

And finally, I heard badly because my blindness kept me from seeing what was happening. But at the same time my powers of invention flourished.

A nudge from my companions was enough to make me understand that the traitor, the executioner or the lover had come onstage. Fragments of sentences whispered in my ear set the scene, described the action: "She is falling down....He is dying....There is an armchair on the right....He is lifting his hat...." That was all I asked, I didn't need anything more.

In the intermission, my buddies, who had seen the hat or the dagger, asked me, in the most serious way, for my opinion of the production. It was a habit with them. I gave my opinion and corrected their judgment. They never for a moment thought me ridiculous.

It was true that I had seen the play. I had chosen the position of the columns for every vestibule in the Roman palace. I had seen to the makeup of Agrippina and Nero with the greatest care. I had changed the lighting from one act to the next. Why shouldn't I say so?

From time to time, I came upon an unbeliever, but his doubts did not embarrass me for very long. "After all," I said to him, "when you read a novel, you don't see the characters. You don't see the places. Yet you do see them, or else it is a bad novel." Already my friend's resistance softened.

What I liked in the theater was that, like music, it opened doors to life which I had not seen. In real life I had never met the Misanthrope, or Phèdre, but I realized that these people were not unreal, no more and no less than my parents or my teachers. The astonishing thing in seeing Phèdre or the Misanthrope was their transparency. These characters hid nothing.

For me, everything happened at the theater as it did with

voices. Appearances melted as fast as snow under the sun. After all, for some time I had been in the habit of recognizing the cruelty in the languid voice of a society woman, the silliness in the rhetoric of a professor stuffed with learning, and a hundred similar kinds of ugliness. Theatrical people must be like me, endowed with a double ear.

Naturally, some incomprehensible things remained. Adultery, lust for power, premeditated murder, infidelity and incest, which abounded in the plays at the Comédie Française, left me befuddled. Whenever, miraculously, my companion and I had enough money left over to pay for a glass of beer after the show, these great problems took on an air of conspiracy around the table at the bistro. At the time we thought the world was an uneasy affair, doubtless still more extraordinary than all of Racine and all of Shakespeare. We were so anxious to see for ourselves that we went home on the run.

In those days the Comédie Française was somewhat contemptuous of Shakespeare. It is amazing that the love of Shakespeare has always been subject to eclipse in France, as if Frenchmen, from time to time, were unhappy to meet such a great man away from home. Still, one evening on the radio, I came upon a production of *Hamlet*. I remember clearly that I understood nothing but was fascinated.

This play was as convincing as Racine, with mist added, fog everywhere, between the lines, between the scenes, characters of whom you never knew exactly where they were or what they should be called. Were they mad or rational, ambitious or good? The ambiguity of the English seemed to me more true than all the definitions of the French.

In Shakespeare I had at last discovered a spirit as complex as life itself. I began to read the whole of it in translation. Dramatizing Shakespeare in my head was a joy. And how much help he gave!

He poured out upon you all the shade and all the sun, the songs of birds and the groans of ghosts. He never said anything that was abstract. With him you no longer had to imagine Romeo and Juliet. You touched them and even thought you yourself were Romeo.

No more need for the small or even the broad bounds of the intelligence. The suitable and the unsuitable, the probable and the improbable mingled, as they should and as they do in real life. Shakespeare was greater than the others, because he had what I had looked for vainly everywhere in the French theater: the divine excess. Puck, Mercutio, Prospero, Henry VIII, Lady Macbeth, King Lear and Ophelia tripped over each other in my head. They ended by obsessing me. There was only one thing left for me to do to get free of them: to put myself to work.

In two years I composed ten Shakespearean tragedies. Granted not one of them reached the stage of being written down. I was not at all concerned with the written text. I was not composing, I was creating! Between a Latin translation and a problem in geometry, I took refuge in fantasy and in the theater. Walls spotted with blood and haunted castles moved in procession.

It must be said that the French side of my nature was not long in coming back at a gallop. At the end of the Shakespearean drama, my heroes, who thought dying in bunches was premature, not to say primitive, turned to reasoning. They made very long speeches to each other, and these in the end appeased them. They calculated with passion, but what they calculated was compromise, reconciliation.

In short, to bring back the dead — through an exchange arranged for in good time — to prevent Hector's body being dragged in shame around the walls of Troy, seemed to me a noble poetic function. And I decided that this function would be mine.

TO GO TO THE LYCÉE, Jean and I had a choice between two different routes. We could take the Rue d'Assas and cross the

Luxembourg on the diagonal till we came to the Boulevard St-Michel, or we could go directly to the gardens of the Observatoire, and cut straight across the Luxembourg. The same distance in each case, the same encounters, but two climates and one so different from the other.

If we took the Rue d'Assas, silence fell upon us. We could not speak. Words hung suspended in our heads, till they gave us a feeling of impatience or grief. On the other hand, going by the Observatoire, we had so much to say that we had to restrain each other. I should never have been able to communicate my impressions to other people, for they would have laughed in my face. But with Jean, I didn't even need to describe them. He was living them at the same time as I.

To us, no two places in the world were ever alike. No sidewalk was unimportant, no wall blind, no crossroad nameless, no tree replaceable by another, nothing without its own individuality. Ours the observation, ours the familiarity, and we clung to it as if it were treasure.

At last, one summer our parents planned a vacation for us together. The two of us were going to spend a month in the mountains. The place was the Haut Vivarais, in the foothills of the Massif Central to the east, at the exact point where it plunges down on two levels, rounded off but as clearly defined as steps, toward the valley of the Rhône. It was a land of pastures scented with lemon balm and marjoram, low bushes blue with bilberries, pine forests humming with flies and bees, valleys sloping steeply with grass- and moss-covered sides where the rocks seldom broke through the soil.

I had discovered the mountains a few years earlier, but then Jean was not there. The joy they brought me I had kept secret. This time I could describe them in detail and sing about them aloud. For Jean was not the one to think it silly! We set out in the morning and came back at night, working hard on the way. Our legs could not carry us any farther, and yet we still longed to stay up there in the air.

In order to guide me better, Jean had invented a code. The pressure of his hand on my right shoulder meant: "Slope on the right. Shift the weight of your body to the left," and vice versa. Pressure in the middle of my back said: "No danger in a straight line in front of you. We can walk faster." Pressure on my back but on the left side was a warning: "Slow up! Right turn ahead." And when the weight of his hand became heavier, it was because the turn ahead was a hairpin bend.

For every obstacle there was a sign: a stone to climb over, a brook to jump across, branches to avoid by lowering your head. Jean declared that in less than an hour he had perfected the method, that for me it was as if I had found my eyes, that for him it was so simple that he hardly had to think about it.

As a matter of fact, his system of radar worked so well that going down a narrow path, along the edge of a precipice and on rolling stones, created a tension hardly greater than walking along the Champs-Elysées for an aperitif. Physical problems could always be solved. That was the lesson of radar. "In any case," said Jean, "I have to look where I am going, and telling you about it is only a matter of mechanics."

To get our bearings, we used the plan of the sundial. When Jean wanted to tell me about the rosy mists which bathed the peak of Mont Chaix around six o'clock in the evening, or show me where they came from or where they were going, he only needed to say: "A minute ago, they stood at three o'clock. But while I am speaking they are moving toward two." To understand, it was enough to state, once and for all, that noon would be right in front of my face from where we stood. Since in the physical world everything is point of view or convention, there was only one thing to do to master it: invent an equal number of conventions and points of view for ourselves, and put them to use.

When we were climbing hills or going down through the valleys, everything took care of itself. I no longer asked anything of Jean except, from time to time, to point out a landmark: the tree with the split trunk, the rock with the horns, the roof on the house you could not see, the stile the goat had just crossed. I did the rest.

Jean was absentminded as you may remember, but never about things that were pressing. Then he felt his responsibility, and never made a mistake. But as for looking at the landscape continuously, it was too much for him. For me it was good, and that was my job on the team.

Even at the cost of interrupting the conversation, it was up to me to point out every change in the view to Jean. If, at the turn in the road, the forest grew thicker, giving us the chance to catch the light along a darker channel; if the meadow sloped straight down to the stream, then climbed up again on the other side at the same angle, suggesting black and blue reflections at the base, I was supposed to describe it.

I reported the stages along the way. I pointed out the villages: "Satillieu is down there, behind that hill. When the trees are not so high you will see Saint Victor." Altogether this made some pretty strange dialogue. The one who saw was in the lead. The blind one described. The seeing one spoke of things nearby, the blind one of those far away. And neither made mistakes.

The mountains for me were the blessed place of perception at a distance. Was it the buzzing of insects which encircled the forest for me? Was it the bouncing and silent echo of stones which defined the peak in front of me? Was it the acrid smell, suddenly rising from heavy plant vapors, which told me about the rock glistening with cool water? These were questions I no longer asked myself.

Everything talked, that was sure. There was no tree with exactly the same thickness as the tree near it, etched or twisted in the same fashion. The perfume of wild mint had two ways of diffusing itself as it grew on a rich meadow or a pebbly field. The light crowned the rises in the land or filled the depressions, following their contours faithfully. To know them one had only to follow the light.

Landscapes composed, changed for me from one second to the next and, when the air was cool, when the wind did not cap my head, did so in a manner so precise that I seemed to be seeing them through a magnifying glass. What a surprise, then, when I pointed out to Jean, without an error, two chains of peaks in series. We stopped at this point, but found nothing to say about it. It was like that — whether or not people believe it, and whether or not they read it in books. On the mountain paths and everywhere else, Jean and I ran into a hard fact — the fact that limits do not exist. If there are any, they are never the ones they taught us.

People around us seemed satisfied when they said that a lame man walks with a limp, that a blind man does not see, that a child is not old enough to understand, that life ends with death. For the two of us, in our summer of green fields, twilight and dawn continually revolving, none of these statements stood its ground.

We had friendship on our side. We had ignorance and bliss, and we looked at everything through these channels. They taught us all we knew. The blind man himself saw, and the sighted one close behind him knew it. Life was good, very good.

[7]

THE TROUBLED EARTH

O N MARCH 12, 1938, I turned the buttons of the radio to
make the small tour of Europe I made every night. What
was that noise I heard all of a sudden on Radio Vienna?

Waves of shouting hammered against the loudspeaker, a mass
of humanity in delirium. *"Deutschland über Alles,"* the *"Horst Wes-
sel Lied,"* music and voices aimed at you point-blank like loaded
pistols. *"Anschluss! Heil Hitler. Anschluss."* Germany has just fallen
on Austria. Austria is no more. German, this language I love, has
been disfigured to the point where I no longer recognize the words.
My thirteen-year-old imagination wants to stand up to the shock,
but it is too great, coming all at once. History hurls itself on me,
wearing the face of the murderers.

They had spoken to me of suffering, and made much of it. Along
with love, it was the only subject in the books. Besides, love and
suffering in books almost always came together. I wonder why! In
my own life there was no suffering. Immediately after my accident,

I had felt a lot of pain. But it did not last long, and then it was an accident. Everyone knows there are things which are inevitable.

One morning at the lycée during recess, I was present when the boy with the shrill voice threw himself on one of my companions, claws out to scratch his eyes. Luckily the other boy dodged and ran away crying. I was horrified. But everyone in the end concluded that the aggressor was crazy. That at least was an explanation.

One evening about midnight — it was February 6, 1934 — my father came home from the neighborhood of the Etoile and told us, with tension in his voice which was unfamiliar to me, that demonstrators on the Champs-Elysées were tearing up the metal railings around the flower beds, and throwing them in the faces of the police; that a bus was burning on the Place de la Concorde. I did not really understand. It sounded like a tragedy or a novel. It resembled the history books — only a little hotter. It didn't seem real.

I had never seen a person die. Of course all men died, but only when God called them back to Himself. It was not a thing to be angry about. On the contrary.

In March 1938, I knew enough German to follow the news broadcasts on the Nazi radio. But I was determined to learn the language thoroughly — to be sure, to feel what these men wanted of us. Europe was rocking toward the east, toward Berlin, Hamburg, Nuremberg and Munich, and I was going to rock with it. I could not overcome the feeling. Where this would end I had no idea but I was making my preparations. For the next five years I studied German for two hours every day.

Between Anschluss and the Capitulation of Munich I made so much progress that I could read Heine's *Book of Songs*, Schiller's *William Tell* and the autobiography of Goethe. Each one of these books baffled me. I could see no connection between them, their harmonious and humane language, their thoughts so exalted one could not always follow them to the end, and the armored divisions, the SA and SS, those assemblies of hate in the Sportspalast in Berlin, on the fairgrounds in Nuremberg; Jews insulted and arrested — they said even tortured — all these people fleeing from Germany, because a free man could no longer live there. War and death.

War! There really were men who loved it. Already I knew that for sure. As for death, there were men who were killing for pleasure. So history was all true, all the slaveries, all the punishments, all the battles, all the massacres. And it was about to start all over again in our time. It was only a matter of weeks or months. In the summer of 1938, if there were still politicians in Europe who doubted it, they should have consulted the thirteen-year-old schoolboy, for there was no hesitation left in him.

Every night on the radio I hung on the statements by Daladier, Chamberlain and Ribbentrop. In September in the weeks before Munich, there was not an interview or a speech that I missed. If I happened on the BBC, my ignorance of English caused me real regret. I waited patiently for two hours until the BBC gave out the same news in French or in German.

I was not afraid, not yet. Of that at least I am sure. I passed through a series of interesting states of mind: curiosity about trouble, need to understand, fascination with mystery, the poetry of the future and the unexpected — the unexpected most of all.

Because of my father we had German friends. Having made several trips to Germany in his profession as an engineer, my father had established connections. But, above all, devoting his leisure time to philosophical and spiritual studies, he had made real

friendships in Germany with some remarkable men: one a professor of mathematics, another a former minister in Bavaria. And
now these peaceable men, who seemed to me to resemble Heine,
Goethe, and Beethoven, were in flight. I learned they were all
threatened with imprisonment, perhaps with death.

At the beginning of August 1938, my father made plans which
threw me into the midst of adventure. He took me with him to
spend three days in Stuttgart. On the slopes of the Uhlandshöhe,
above the city, we visited the director of a German school who was
a friend of my father's. I was struck by the man's calm, his mod-
eration and his sadness. He told us that all Germans who wanted
peace, or preferred it to war, were already suffering or preparing
for suffering ahead. He spoke little and in a low voice. Still, he
made it clear that everything we could imagine was less horrible
than the reality. For it was not only Germany, but France, England,
the whole world, which was on the point of bursting into flame. For
his part, he would have to leave his country before the end of the
year. He knew it but could not decide to act on it.

When we got back to Paris, naturally I played the prophet to
my companions. Almost without exception they failed to understand. In their families they heard nothing out of the ordinary.
There had always been incidents, and always would be. Three
years before there had been colonial war in Ethiopia and threats
of blockade from the Western powers, but nothing came of it. At
this very moment there was civil war in Spain. It had all been in the
newspapers.

But one of the rules of bourgeois comfort — comfort in the
family — was that newspapers were read but not believed. The
press lied, now more, now less, but continually. It was best to think
about it as little as possible. From my point of view, this refusal to

face reality was the stupidest thing I had met in my thirteen years. For my companions and their parents, I was ashamed. If I had only known how, I would have made them understand.

Most grown-ups seemed to be either imbeciles or cowards. They never stopped telling us children that we must prepare for life, in other words for the kind of life they were leading, because it was the only good and right one, of that they were certain. No, thank you. To live in the fumes of poison gas on the roads in Abyssinia, at Guernica, on the Ebro front, in Vienna, at Nuremberg, in Munich, the Sudetenland and then Prague. What a prospect!

I was no longer a child. My body told me so. But all the things I had held dear when I was small I loved still. What attracted me and terrified me on the German radio was the fact that it was in the process of destroying my childhood.

Outer darkness. Here it was. A place worse than any melodrama, where men must shout at the top of their voices to be heard, where they talk honor when they want to dishonor, and fatherland when they want to pillage.

In such a school I should have learned to hate the Boches. But no more, thanks be to God. My family dissuaded me. Books and symphonies told me it must not be so. I went on calling them Germans, and with respect.

Some of my companions declared themselves patriots. Not I. I had no desire to be like them, for they were all braggarts, and not one made the slightest effort to understand what was going on. Besides, inside their anti-German families, it was amazing how indulgent they were toward Hitler and his crimes.

Without admitting it to myself, I had already imagined the Nazis everywhere. From now on the world was like a giant kettle heated by rancor and violence. I was still dreaming at the end of

1938, but for the first time the dream did not come of itself. You had to watch over it, to keep the gate of the Kingdom open behind you. The great unity had been cut in two, with love on one side and hate on the other; fear one way and joy another.

There was no doubt everything was going to be hard, a little harder from day to day. But after all, even if life was not good, it still looked as though it was going to be exciting.

THE YOUNG GIRL JEAN MET ON SUNDAY for the second time was called Françoise. Why should he have concealed her name after their first meeting?

The girl was of no consequence to me since I had never met her. Besides, I should probably never see her. She was the daughter of some rather distant friends of Jean's family. Still, everything had been going at cross purposes for me since she came into the picture.

Jean had a strange way of talking about her. He said she had the eyes of an angel, hazel brown. He said again and again that she had a slim waist and shoes you couldn't take your eyes off. He kept coming back to her figure, her shoes, the fabric of her dress, and to a mole he said was just at the hairline on the back of her neck. When he mentioned these things he spoke in a whisper which got on my nerves. I wanted to tell him he was ridiculous, but I didn't dare for fear of interrupting him so he would not give me any more details. I wondered whether Françoise would interest me. Was that possible? I was not as happy as I had been. No doubt about it, I had worries.

That Monday morning, the day after his second meeting with the girl, because he could no longer contain himself, Jean had told me her name was Françoise. On his way to my house, he had run into her by chance on the platform of the bus. It was so crowded he had had to stand pressed up against her for five minutes. She was smaller than he, and to answer him, to look at him, she had to lift her eyes. So he had a good look at her eyes, and at once they became the center of his world.

I listened to Jean and was miserable, truly miserable. There was a lump in my throat, and Jean did not seem to be aware of it. He talked on all by himself. In a way that was lucky for, if he had asked me a question, I couldn't have opened my mouth. But why? There was nothing novel about a girl named Françoise with hazel eyes.

My anguish lasted for days, growing bigger and more and more formless. By this time Françoise had nothing to do with it. She might as well have been called Monique or Jeanne, or have blond instead of dark hair like Jean's Françoise. I should have suffered just the same.

The only thing to do was to tell Jean about it without waiting any longer. I would find no other doctor, for Jean still loved me and would do something to help. Only this time, instead of declaring myself frankly as usual, I saw myself making endless preparations. I was calculating the attack. I was afraid of myself.

Frankly, I was frightened, and that was my trouble. As soon as the idea occurred to me, I launched into confession boldly. I took Jean for a three-hour walk near the Porte d'Italie, because I knew that this neighborhood would be deserted until the factories let out.

First I begged his pardon for all the wrong I had not yet done him (but which, in all probability, I was already doing). I made it clear to him that Françoise was only a pretext. Because of her I had remembered that I was blind. Or rather I had realized for the first time that this was so. I would never be able to see the girls' hair, their eyes or their figures. As for their dresses and their shoes, I knew very well they were important but what could I do about it?

It frightened me to know that I should always be kept away from these marvels. And girls as a rule were so intent on your looking at them that perhaps for them I might never exist.

While I was talking, I had already begun to say to myself that I was wrong, that there were girls of a different kind. But Jean was terribly embarrassed when I had finished speaking. I had never seen him in such a state. He couldn't express himself, and was fiddling with my shoulder as though he wished he could make his hand talk in his place.

The incident had no sequence. In the first place Jean did not see Françoise again, or hardly ever. In the second place he treated me with a kindness which broke my heart more than once. No doubt about it, the danger must be real if pity was the treatment I deserved.

Without realizing it, I had just faced one of the toughest obstacles a blind person ever has to meet, and from here on I had to go from one fall to another for two years, until I regained my common sense.

I used to stand at the window in my room listening to the noises in the court below. I touched, I heard, but I no longer perceived as I had. A veil had come down. I was blind.

Then I closed the window and shut myself up. I told myself stories of boundaries that could never be crossed. I ridiculed my childhood dreams. My heart was full and my hands were empty, without arms in a world where everything is made to be seen, where there is no place to go unless one goes there by oneself. I felt myself reduced to doing the thing in which I excelled, but which interested me least: shining in studies. My throat tightened with envy when they told me about the boys who were going out on their bicycles with girls. I would stay at home. That was inevitable.

Fortunately jealousy and foolishness never took hold of more than half of me, even during those two years. And even then it was the smaller half. Above all, there was Jean, who with every argument, with overwhelming patience, tried to prove that he had no special advantages: "If you only knew how few things we really see! Girls do not let us see anything."

Then too, there was the voice speaking inside me. Whenever I had the strength not to silence it, I heard it clearly, calling me a fool. The voice said I had fallen into a trap, had forgotten the true world: the world within, which is the source of all the others. I must remember that this world, instead of disappearing, would grow with the years, but only on one condition: that I believe in it unshakably.

The voice added that what you have seen one day as a child you will never stop seeing. According to the voice, great things lay ahead of me. The easy girls, the ones who think of nothing but themselves, would drop me. But there would be others, the ones who were genuine. And they would be more worth having. They would expect me not to doubt them. They would not want me to give up what I loved, for they would love it too. Above all, they would forbid me to compare my position with that of the average man. This much I understood, that to make comparisons is to suffer, and without reason since, in any case, no two things are ever comparable.

All the same, I listened to the good voices in vain. I would have given so much to recapture the peace that was mine when I was twelve. Since I had been fifteen the universe had taken on a kind of dense coarseness. People worked, talked on the radio or made love to girls, as if each one of them were all alone in the world.

No way now to share, except possibly with Jean. But even with him would it last forever? The question tortured him as it did me, to the point where we made solemn vows to reassure each other in the summer of 1939. Each of us swore to tell the other the whole truth, every time, whatever it might be, and swore that no girl would ever come between us.

The pledge was no sooner made than we found out to our amazement that we had never yet told each other the whole truth. There were countless secret places in our consciences where we had never looked. We were so badly made, so timid, so selfish, fickle, jealous, prudish and forgetful. We had to admit we were not deep. To put it simply each of us had a double or triple base, a mechanism to deceive himself and deceive other people.

Still, we had taken the pledge, and we were going to keep watch loyally. No more mysteries or prudishness between us. We would spare each other nothing. We would go the limit with words, and if words hurt, then we would console each other.

Life being what it was, with all those ministers and fathers of families preparing to make war, with all those girls who laughed for no good reason, and kept giving looks you could never understand, surely it would take two of us to man the attack.

[8]

MY COUNTRY, MY WAR

T HE BUS DRIVER, after stopping in front of me to make sure, said with the kind banter that is typical of the south: "So, young fellow! You can't see. Well, for the first time you're in luck. It could last a hundred years this war, without your being in it."

Then he turned around briskly, sat down behind the wheel, and drumming with his fingers on the dashboard, began to sing a military tune. But why should the man say I was happy not to go to war?

That was at Tournon on the Rhône on September 2, 1939, a few hours after the orders for general mobilization had been posted on every wall in France. For a few days Jean and I had been staying with my godmother in the little town where the streets smelled of peaches and onions. The World War had started the night before.

All the men were going away to war, the bus driver as well. He was twenty-five years old, and had a wife and a small daughter. He told us the whole story of his life. This was the last trip he was making in his bus. Next day he would be a soldier. From time to time he grumbled or sighed, but mostly he did not seem sad. He was waiting for the customers who would be taking the bus to Lamastre. But today — he said so in a loud voice — there were no customers, and that made him laugh. "No one will come," he said, and then repeated himself as if to get the full flavor of his conclusion.

Five o'clock struck. As it turned out, Jean and I were the only travelers. Then our driver started up, singing. He burned up a strip of the big highway along the Rhône at sixty miles an hour; then, hardly slowing down, took the first curves along the mountain road. He turned left, he turned right, and kept blowing his horn like a madman. Had he been drinking to get up his courage? Not even that. He was as fresh as paint. Only he was going off to war and was already dreaming about it.

Ever since the night before, when the radio announced that Nazi tanks had gone deep into Poland, people were not the same any more. I could see it clearly.

Some of the women wept, some of them held back their tears. On the square in front of the town hall the old men were reminiscing about 1914 to 1918. It was not exactly heartening. Obviously, Frenchmen had no idea in the world why they should have to fight now. The Danzig Corridor, the treaties with Poland meant nothing to them.

By the time our driver had climbed down from his seat, Jean and I were as stirred up as he was. And who knows, perhaps for the same reasons. Besides, everyone was excited.

Was it with pain or pleasure? It would have been hard to tell. But everywhere there was a sense of adventure. People were not taking the bus. They were not going to bed at the usual hour. The express trains blew their whistles twice and stopped at the small stations. The radio played military music till the middle of the night. People no longer wrote each other letters. They telegraphed instead. There were rumors that Göring's planes had already bombed Paris; others said it was London. Everyone was arguing and trying to find out whether there would be poison gas, germ shells, or trenches as in the last war. But one thing no one talked about was victory. This time no one was on his way to Berlin.

The reality of war made its way into my consciousness drop by drop, like the effects of hard liquor. Once the first intoxication was absorbed, a single question grew till it blotted out all the others: "Is the war our business?"

We had not yet come to a decision, either Jean or I. But that was not because we didn't know the answer. On the contrary, it was because we knew it too well, and it seemed to us unreasonable, frankly childish. Since we were still only fifteen, we were still protected, and the rest was only smoke.

Still, the smoke kept getting thicker and thicker, from one day to the next. It gathered in front of us, in the path of our future, like a cloud. None of the shapes in the cloud stood out clearly, but in the end, we could read the signs: "It will be your war, for both of you." And even if we were shocked into discomfort, or worried till it hurt, there was no way out of it.

Jean finally told me that in his case, leaving all fantasy aside, the premonition was not necessarily silly. The war might last two years, and if it did he would enlist. Why not? Or four, like the last war, when even the youngest classes were mobilized. But in my case it was ridiculous. There could be no foreboding. I was completely out of it.

Wise reasoning, but it solved nothing for either Jean or me. I saw that at once with a joy I cannot describe. He didn't believe what he was saying. He had the same visions of the future as I.

Foolish or not, they were as insistent as prophecy. They drew us on by their weight. As far as we were concerned they were more like an appeal than a threat, a kind of dizziness, a magnetic force. In the end I said to Jean, "I am going to make war. I don't know how, but I shall make it."

September passed, so empty. There was hardly any fighting at the front. Poland was conquered already, but who had delivered the final blow? Nobody knew. Suddenly on September 17, Russian troops had invaded her from the east. In Europe nothing was left but enemies.

A great change (or a change which seemed great to us) happened in our lives. My father, mobilized as an officer in the Engineer Corps in a powder factory, was called to Toulouse. My mother, my brother and I were going to join him. Jean was going too, for, not wanting to leave me, he convinced his mother that she should settle in Toulouse. For the first time we were not going to live in Paris. I remarked to Jean that something impossible was coming about.

For a while, our premonitions were masked by the life of another city, the South of France, new voices, a different sun. Still, forebodings kept pouncing on us all over again at the most unlikely moments. But was war something we cared about — that we could like?

To hear people talk they all hated it, but that didn't keep us from noticing that since the first of September melancholy faces were much less common than they used to be. What was written on these faces was perhaps not gaiety, but interest. At least no one was at the accustomed place at the same hour. At night the men didn't come home to the same woman and the same children right next to the same neighbors.

There was a sense of freedom everywhere. People were more

willing to say what they thought. Even time had grown precious. You counted it, said it was going too fast or too slow, in short you were concerned about it, and it was exciting.

The dead were not troubling us, not yet. There were a good many of them at the end of the year, on Finland's icy lakes: thousands of heroes fighting for a freedom which was unattainable and therefore more beautiful, if that were possible, than our own. But who, in France, cared about Finland? Students of geography like us, who conscientiously followed all the advances and retreats on the big map. No one else, or hardly anyone.

The war seemed unreal. Some already whispered that it would never happen, that it was a huge political production. I didn't agree. War would come, in full force. To know it, I only needed to listen to the German radio every night. There it was, the dark prophecy — I could no longer doubt it that winter in 1940. It was there, my war.

The cloud, the monster, was in the Nazi meetings. The voice of these crowds had gone too far, cutting itself off from the world of man. It would have to be silenced, or I must do something about it. I was upset, caught between passionate anger and the sense of the absurd. A blind boy, fifteen years old, facing Hitler and his people. That was something to laugh about. Still, it was all I could do to keep from spreading the news.

HAVING TASTED HAPPINESS to the point of intoxication at Toulouse, I can give you this piece of advice: if you are happy when you are a boy or girl of fifteen, don't tell anyone. Or, if you do, choose your confidant, and take one your own age.

If you really can't contain yourself, show the grown-ups that you are happy, but don't hope for great things. Almost all adults have a short memory, and they always think happiness begins only at eighteen or even at twenty-one. Whatever you do, don't ever give them your reasons for being happy. The most liberal and loving family would be disturbed right away, and think you were out of your mind. By keeping your secret you will lose nothing, for the secret only makes happiness grow.

This policy really worked for Jean and me. All year long we concealed ourselves. The more unlikely our hiding places the better they were. Some of our joys were so intense that we couldn't confide them to each other in any ordinary place like the street. Yet in Toulouse the streets were narrow, winding, badly paved or not really paved at all. The gutters wound down the middle of the road. The smell of cats, of moldy stones, soapy water, food fried in olive oil, garlic and honey assaulted you at every step. Yet even those poetic streets did not serve our purposes. We needed some ugly spot, to give more tang to our happiness. The waiting room of the railroad station was the place we chose.

Or else we fled to the country for all-day walks, without any destination on principle. To know ahead of time where we were going would have been a mistake. We had the good sense to know that. The important thing was to lose ourselves, in the dry deserted hills south of the city, in the fertile valley of the Ariège, among the ruined houses of deserted villages, on land lying fallow around those little hamlets with high-sounding names, Sayss-en-Gayss, Courtousour, La Crois-Falgarde. No matter where, but somehow losing ourselves! Never thinking of finding the way, nothing in our heads but happiness, walking zigzag or straight ahead till we were tired out — this too another kind of happiness.

Every day we became friends again as though it were the first time, and this too was essential. Friendship was a fragile state of mind or body, one that vanished as soon as you made a habit of it. To renew it every day was an obligation and hard work. Sometimes we had to set friendship free, making it garrulous and lenient; emptying out all our dreams, without choosing among them and without scruple. Sometimes our censorship held no pity. Jean literally did not have the right to say one foolish thing, nor did I. We examined everything, the articles of agreement one by one: loyalty, faithfulness, tolerance and sharing. Of all the clauses the thorniest was the one about sharing. We did not succeed in stipulating how far it should go. Theoretical at first, this became a practical matter in March. Then there was a crisis.

Since he had come to Toulouse Jean had lived in a small apartment in a house with dark stairways on a narrow street. But this somber house was lighted by the presence of a young girl. Out of "virtue," Jean said, he had tried at first not to see her. But as time went on his efforts failed completely.

Aliette, for that was the girl's name, was really unavoidable. She was eighteen years old. She was beautiful without giving it a thought. She didn't touch the ground, she flew. She didn't walk down stairs, she glided down them like a flower tossed into the wind. She sang from morning to night, so much you wondered how she could manage to learn her lessons. And you were not learning yours, because you were always trying to hear through the partition, because your one idea was to be with her, to drink her song from her eyes and her lips, and then sneak home without being seen. Or if she wasn't singing, that was surely because she was sad or perhaps sick, and you wanted to run and help her. Consoling Aliette would be such a marvelous thing!

She said nothing and did nothing the way the rest of the world did it. Jean told me that with a conviction that I was beginning to share. He asked himself what was the difference. She used ordinary words, but as soon as they were out of her month they took on a thousand different meanings. You no longer had time to listen to them. The sun began to play on them as it does on the wings of a butterfly, and your vision became blurred.

To make everything more complicated, for a week or two Jean had been certain she was interested in him. The proof was she talked to him, even let him talk to her. On the landing they had exchanged tips on problems in mathematics. She said mathematics meant nothing to her. Finally, she invited him to play the piano at her house, and while she was bending over to turn the pages, Aliette's hair had brushed against his cheek.

In a word Jean was in love. But love, you understand, is a very feeble word for it. The fact was my poor Jean was no longer living, he was bursting with life. And this is where my story, inevitably, gets confused. For I too was not just living, I too was in love.

The discovery was terrifying. Everything became unsettled all at once: friendship, its rights and its limits, the future, our studies, the serenity of our lives, and last of all our love itself. To whom did it belong, this love? To Jean or to me?

If there was nothing between Aliette and Jean but a partition, that, after all, was only luck. And thanks to another piece of luck, I had been the first to meet Aliette and the first to talk to her. From the point of view of history, I had definite rights.

I can joke a little today when I tell you this story, but we were certainly not joking at the time. We made longer excursions into the hills than ever before, and from beginning to end these walks were a single storm. We weren't fighting, you mustn't think that. We weren't angry, we were meditating. The intensity and the size of the problem were so great that almost always at the end of the hour we forgot the problem itself. The rest of the time the two of us were alone with our double girl. We kept on looking at the double image we carried around with us, and after this nothing in the world seemed to us divided.

I must say, to Jean's glory and mine and Aliette's, that no one of the three of us ever went about spoiling the image. On the contrary it grew so gentle and so pure that no one bothered to compare it with its model. Still, the model was there, alive, more and more vibrant, more and more familiar. From now on we were meeting Aliette every day, but always together, never separately.

We met her on the squares in the town, at the corner of the little streets in the reddish shade of the brick houses. We waited for her after school. We had conversations under the damp arcades. When I went to her house, she and Jean took me back to mine, we went out again to hers, they went back with me, and all the time the summer night spread around us and cradled us.

I am not very sure what we said all those hours. We counted the stars, I remember that. Each one of us held Aliette by the arm, not with too much pressure, for she was sacred. We let her voice make the rounds of our hearts and our thoughts. We may have made her talk for the joy of it. I think we ended by forgetting her, our Aliette, while she was frisking around between us, laughing and light-hearted, because she was more beautiful than anything, because nothing meant anything anymore. To the devil with reality!

Was this a girl dreamed about, or lived? Lived, for sure, sometimes to the point of tears, so great was the pleasure she gave. But lived at the one moment in life when things don't need to have happened to be alive.

In the distance, to the north, throwing a weird light on our happiness, the war went on. It ended in catastrophe. In five weeks in May and June, France was conquered. The armies of Hitler were rushing southward, heavy with calamity. They alone had the power to separate us.

ALIETTE, WHEN SHE LEFT US the night before, told us it would be better for us not to see each other again, at least not all three together and not so often. We didn't know why she said so and she didn't explain. But suddenly, ten minutes later, the radio announced that German troops had entered Paris and that Paris had yielded without resisting. Paris a prisoner! Aliette going away! Which should we think about first?

At last in the morning at the main entrance to the lycée, this notice appeared, written by hand in large clumsy letters (they certainly had not had time to have it printed): *Because of what has happened, the written tests for the first and second bachots are postponed till a later date. From today on classes are suspended throughout the Toulouse school district until further notice.*

Events! Aliette! And again events! Our heads were about to burst. Jean agreed with me. We must not continue to think of ourselves. Within a week perhaps our country would no longer exist. At such a time the interest of the community is so much more important than the concerns of the individual.

That is easily said! But emotions were beating in on us from every side at the same moment. Each wave was more violent than the last. We didn't know where to head in.

As for France, we were agreed that the war was lost. Our English allies were in flight, climbing into the boats at Dunkerque. You couldn't blame them. French armies were fleeing too, to the south of the Loire according to the reports.

In the last two weeks, three hundred thousand refugees had poured into Toulouse: women, old people, children, even men.

They came from Holland, Belgium, Luxembourg, from northern and eastern France, from Paris, Normandy and Orléans. They had no idea where they were going. They were heading south, that was all. Toulouse was a big city, so they stopped there.

They crowded into tents in the athletic fields along the Garonne. Two thousand of them, most of them women and babies, spent the night in the chapel of our lycée. Private houses in the city were taking in all they could hold. Often they were putting up five, even ten, in the same room.

The city authorities were uneasy. Such a concentration of people was an ideal target for attack from the air. It was rumored that Toulouse was about to be bombed.

In the middle of the city, it was easy to believe yourself in Paris one day in the Revolution. The crowd was all concentrated in a single mass, immense and purposeless. The fact was that people did not seem either threatening or frightened. They gave the impression of understanding nothing.

Cars covered with mud, their fenders pierced by machine gun fire, were standing driverless at any angle against the curb. But where was the army and where were the generals? Where was the government? They said it had fled to Bordeaux.

Terrifying rumors were going the rounds, confirmed by the papers and on the radio. Planes were machine-gunning civilians who were in flight along the roads. On the roads in the north the planes were German, in the south they were Italian. A man passing by said, "There is no time left for crying. This time, it is the end." What was he saying, this man? We were outraged. A nation does not die like that. Not France...

But by this time, we were in a side street which was less disturbed, and the memory of the night before came back to us. Aliette didn't want to see us anymore!

Could we possibly have offended her? Was she mistaken about our intentions? All of a sudden I said to Jean: "I know. It's because she is in love with one of us. It can't be anything else but that."

The idea was unbelievably simple. We had loved Aliette for months without even asking ourselves whether she loved us, or even whether she was thinking about loving us, or which one of the two of us she would choose. Because she would have to choose. That too we had completely forgotten. We had lost sight of the fact, deplorable but inescapable, that love is a personal matter. We had been ridiculous, that's all. And how angry she must be. Jean pulled himself together and said, "Don't let's think about her, shall we?" But how could we manage to avoid thinking of everything at the same time when it was all so serious?

At night we slept well (you sleep whatever happens when you are fifteen), but we had hardly opened our eyes before the double tragedy hit us full in the face: our love and our country.

You must realize how well informed we were in spite of our youth. Everything that happened meant something to us. We knew about the parties, the governments, political systems and alliances. We were well able to tell the difference between armistice and defeat.

On June 17 at noon, when Marshal Pétain spoke to the French people and said that the army could no longer keep on fighting, that it was necessary to surrender, that all further resistance would be wrong and that he, the oldest and most famous soldier in France, the victor of Verdun, had agreed to sign an armistice with Hitler and the German generals, thus offering to France "the gift of his own person" — we were there listening and did not believe him. The idea that he could be a traitor never occurred to us. But we were sure that he was wrong. The cause of France was not just the cause of her armies in the field.

On the evening of June 18, when a young general, almost unknown and bearing a name sounding like that of a legendary hero, Charles de Gaulle, made his first appeal from London for Frenchmen to resist, to keep the war going in all the overseas territories where France was still in a position of command — in North Africa, West Africa, Equatorial Africa, and Indochina — and also in metropolitan France, called on Frenchmen to resist with all the moral and physical arms they had left, we were there too. But this time we believed, and our answer was yes.

Not a shadow of doubt remained. We were about to become the soldiers of Free France. But when? And how? What arms would Jean have? And — the more difficult question — what arms were there for me? I can say only one thing. We knew nothing, and yet we already knew everything. We were embarking upon the serious things of life just as a well-hammered nail bites into wood and takes hold.

It was not bravado. It was not even patriotism. For us, France was a rather vague idea, and somehow belied by events. The things in our heads and our hearts we called freedom: the freedom to choose our beliefs, our way of life and let others choose theirs, the freedom to refuse to do harm. But why should freedom need to be explained?

Aliette too was free. She was calling us again. She had the right to see us or not to see us. She even had the right to tell one of us to go away. If only we had been able to ask her which of the two of us she loved! We almost decided to do it. But, in this affair, what was to become of friendship?

Jean retreated before my anguish. I drew back before his. If we spoke, one of us would have to withdraw. Whatever the outcome, it was certain to cause suffering. It was at this point that Jean said something entirely confused in its expression but absolutely clear to me.

I was blind and for once, he said, that had its effects. My chances of talking to Aliette, of being alone with her were not on a par with his. My chances in the material world, I mean. But that was not quite fair, for Jean still felt he had a moral obligation to support me. He promised to do nothing to win Aliette that I, for my part, would not be able to do too. He would go on talking to her (if she still wanted him to), but at times and places where I too could have gone without anyone's help. He would tell her everything he wanted to, with one exception: he wouldn't tell her he was in love. I wouldn't do that either. Like Jean I was going to give my word. Jean kept repeating, "Don't say thank you. It's a fair exchange."

Jean thought that after a defeat like ours, there must be terrible years ahead. Terrible for us, that was sure. Hard choices would have to be made, and dangers met. No one could say that death might not be part of it.

"You have more imagination than I have," he said. "I love life but you love it more. I shall need your strength. With you there I shall never be at a loss." We were very romantic, weren't we? Yes and no. For we kept our promises to the bitter end: the promise about the war and the one about love. We seemed to be laughing at ourselves just a bit. Our enthusiasm was so great that it could stand a little humor.

Aliette was all changed since the armistice. Had she guessed our decision — secret though it was — to love her without letting her know? You might say that she had suddenly begun to respect us. Women in wartime need men so badly. She was getting ready for the *bachot* too, just as we were, and since we didn't know when the examination would be, we had agreed to work very hard to hold on to our patience.

Working very hard was a thing Aliette didn't care for very much. She admitted she could not do it alone. She asked us, as a service, to make her work. Knights in the days of chivalry were never more exalted by their lady's demands.

We took Aliette out into the woods and sat her down at the foot of a tree in a clearing and made her go over her courses as well as we could.

Jean was the specialist in science. To lure Aliette he was trying to draw from algebra, solid geometry and electricity everything that these subjects, so unsympathetic to girls, can of fantasy or beauty.

My job, I admit, was simpler. The advantage I had almost embarrassed me. I was supposed to teach German, history, and literature, that divine subject, in which everything was somehow related to love.

I hardly dare to admit that Aliette failed her exams three weeks later, and that Jean and I passed. For us it was a personal defeat. Fortunately, Aliette, drying a few tears as she read the list that was posted, looked prettier than ever. And she knew very well that we were men, and that men were supposed to be first in this kind of competition. That was only natural.

So the *bachot* was behind us as I knew very well. The morning we took the French composition I was so happy about a kiss Aliette had given me, like a little sister, on the cheek, to bring me luck (she had given one just like it to Jean) that when I came out I had no idea what I had written. For this composition I got the best mark I had ever gotten for one in my six years of lycée attendance.

When July came, a silence like mourning had fallen over France. The Germans had forced us to cut our country in two, north and south. They took over the Northern Zone themselves. And there was no one around us who had the courage to think what that meant.

As for the Southern Zone, they were already calling it "the free zone." But that seemed to us a mockery. On July 10, a French government had been set up at Vichy under Marshal Pétain. It was a government, but not the government of France.

Military defeat had opened a breach into which all the enemies of the Third Republic and of France could rush. Within a few days words had changed their meaning. People no longer talked about liberty but about honor, for honor was more reassuring. No more talk of parliament or institutions! Now it was the fatherland. No more talk about the French people or its wishes. Now it was the family. The family was smaller and more manageable.

My father, who was sincerely devoted to democratic principles, said that France was going through one of those onslaughts of the spirit of reaction which have been so common in her history but which seemed this time to be more formidable than ever before.

At the end of August trains were set up in convoys to repatriate all the refugees and all those who needed to go back to their homes in the north. My parents had no choice. We were headed for Paris. Jean's family decided on the same course. Our hours of love were numbered.

[9]

THE FACELESS DISASTER

A GIGANTIC CONVENT with its parlors deserted, that was Paris at the end of September 1940. The year before you never heard the church bells except on Sunday morning when traffic was moving slowly. Now you heard nothing but the bells.

In our apartment on the Boulevard Port-Royal, at the far edge of the Latin Quarter, all day long I heard the bells of Val-de-Grâce, St-Jacques-du-Haut-Pas and, whenever the wind was in the west, those of Notre-Dame-des-Champs. If it was from the north, there were the bells of St-Etienne-du-Mont, farther away on the square in front of the Panthéon. The bells reached my room in all their force, for to reach it they had only to cross those vast soundless stretches.

Paris under the Occupation looked to me as if she were praying. She seemed to be calling on someone, but hers was a voiceless cry. Still, I had better wake up. These were nothing but dreams. Since I had returned I had really seen nothing. We had come into the Austerlitz Station in the evening on our way back from Toulouse. My heart had stayed behind with Aliette. We had not been able to find a taxi. There were no more taxis, and we had had to carry our suitcases and walk the two miles to our house. Along the whole length of the Boulevards de l'Hôpital, St-Marcel and Port-Royal, we never met a single car. The few pedestrians we saw were walking in the middle of the street, moving straight forward and very fast. Paris seemed much bigger and much quieter than I remembered it. Except for that I was not aware of anything unusual.

But where was the disaster? No one seemed to know. There were hardly any cars left and no buses, only trucks. Rich people or poor, they all had to take the Métro. The price of cigarettes was a bit higher. So were the prices of bread and meat, but not much. All this was really nothing, it was surely not calamity. And the Germans, where were they? They kept out of sight, hiding in barracks or in hotels. To keep from seeing them, all you had to do was stay away from the Place de la Concorde, the Champs-Elysées and the Etoile. There you could smell them, smell their cigarettes, sweeter than ours because of the blend of Oriental tobacco they liked.

In other parts of Paris you hardly ever saw them. If you did, they were riding in cars and making the tires scream at the corners of the deserted streets. If they happened to get out, you heard their shoes scraping, their step stiff, always stiff, and loud. They had the grave and satisfied look of people who knew where they are going. But did they really know?

From day to day we were waiting for them to land in England. But the date kept on being postponed. I was watching for the agony in the street but not finding it. It may be that the calamities of history, when they are as real as the one we were living, don't proclaim themselves all at once. No doubt it takes time. The next day

I would surely hear cries, learn that people were suffering. Paris as prisoner would pound on the door to be released. But the next day came and was filled with the same silence as the night before.

The silence caught you by the throat, made sadness press into your thoughts. The houses had grown too tall, the streets too wide. People were separated from each other by spaces that were too big. Even the air which flowed down the empty streets was furtive and kept its secrets.

No one knew what to think about. One thought about oneself. Perhaps everybody was thinking only of himself and of nothing else. I used to say to Jean: "This is a queer war. We are never going to see our enemy, and it won't be easy to have courage."

But courage to do what? There was not a single direction marked for us to follow. There was nothing to do but stay at home, think of Aliette, each from his own corner, think of her for hours on end with every ounce of our strength, and get only a battered picture in return, a little face as sad as our own, almost without eyes and without voice, a photograph that hadn't turned out. Here was grief that grated on your nerves, made you jump up, wanting to fight, longing all at once for the one thing that was not there — Aliette, Aliette so far off, Aliette who had gone away — but no, it was I who had left her — Aliette whom I longed to take in my arms and hold tight.

How strange! In Toulouse that was not what I had wanted. I would not have wanted to touch Aliette. For, at my touch, she would only have vanished into thin air. But ever since her body had been separated from mine, it existed as a body. What I was embracing was only shadow.

We no longer had our beloved and we had not met our enemy. We were heavy and empty at the same time, and our fever rose. Besides, we should never again know what was happening to

Aliette. Letters exchanged between the two zones were forbidden. The occupying authorities allowed only the cards called "interzones" — a piece of pasteboard with forms printed on them to be filled out. "I am..." ran the formula, and you wrote "well," "very well," or "fairly well." "I received your card from..." and you looked at another card just like it to find the date on which the people you loved had written these meaningless phrases the last time.

The French are resourceful, they always find a way of making rules serve their own ends. We managed to slip in words loaded with meaning, loaded with meaning at least for us, for what could the others understand from their side of the wall? People were not talking much anymore about the war, for they were not learning anything. The only newspapers that were appearing were German or had sold out to the German side. Radio Paris too was German and it was forbidden to listen to the BBC. Of that there was no doubt, for it was the only precise order that had been issued by the German military government up to this time.

Naturally, hundreds of thousands of people were listening in all the same. This is how it went: "London calling, Frenchmen speaking to Frenchmen." Here were General de Gaulle, Jean Oberlé, Pierre Bourdan, Jean Marin, Maurice Schumann. They were the ones giving the news. Confidence rang out in their voices. But after hearing them we never spoke of it. We were afraid of our neighbors. A country in disaster is swarming with traitors.

We should never again know what people were thinking. There would be no way of asking them, and in any case they would not have replied. There it was — the real anguish of Paris — five million human beings on guard, ready to defend themselves or to hide, determined not to talk whatever happened, to do good and evil alike. We should no longer be able to tell cowardice from courage, for everywhere there would be silence.

The lycées were reopening. We began our philosophy classes on the first of October at Louis-le-Grand. We were preparing for our second *bachot*. On the first day we had a new history professor. He walked rapidly and seemed to know exactly what he wanted. All of us stood up. With a small gesture of annoyance he told us to sit down. "Gentlemen," he said, "I ask you to listen to me, not to obey me. This land will surely perish if everyone obeys." He was young, wore thick glasses and was short. He never stayed still, but kept moving around between the benches. He put his hand on one boy's head, or on the shoulder of another. He questioned us by word of mouth and face to face, about our age and our plans, the June defeat and the reasons for it, about the correct behavior of the army of occupation, about de Gaulle, Hitler and Pétain. He asked us if we knew what Russia was, and America and Japan, or if we knew what parts of the world have coal, steel, oil or manganese.

He talked fast. I had to pay the closest attention to understand him. In an hour he said more than I had ever heard before in two weeks. Paris was still occupied, but the occupation had a new meaning, and so had the future. His voice was flexible, warm, like the voice of a creature full of life. Each word held a gesture. Ideas were germinating in my head at such speed that I no longer had time to stop them so I could really see what they were. Never mind. I would recapture them at night when I was alone. But what was he actually saying, this teacher of ours? That our class held at least one traitor and that he knew it? A boy ready to inform the occupation authorities about things that might be said in school? Impossible. I must have heard wrong. But no, there was no mistake, and the teacher repeated it. Along my spine ran a hot wave. I felt as though I were coming to life. So, after all, there was an evil to reject. And there would be something good to be done.

BEING BLIND SEEMED TO GIVE ME nothing but advantages. For instance, after two or three weeks of hard adjustment, I could see Aliette again. Jean, for his part, couldn't see her yet and said to me, "I never manage to close my eyes tight enough to see her."

I was spared that particular pain, there was no doubt about that. I was not only closer to the inner world than Jean, but for nearly eight years I had identified myself completely with this world within. I had had no choice. The investment had surely been good, and here I was drawing the interest.

Only the visible Aliette had been taken away from me, her outside shell. I was rebuilding her presence inside myself, and without even thinking about it. I had no idea how the operation was performed, but I had noticed that the less I worked at it the more successful I was. Memories and emotions are fragile things. You should never bear down on them, or draw on them by main force. You should barely touch them with the tips of your fingers, the tips of your dreams.

The best way to bring love back to life, and happiness with it, was to catch hold of a reminder of love, catch it lightly as it passed by — no matter whether it was the hem of Aliette's dress or the sound of her laughter — and then let memory do the rest. For it was memory and not I as a person who was happy and in love. My will did not count and was nothing but an obstacle in the way. I tried to hold it captive, but from time to time it got away from me, wanting to see Aliette and see her more clearly. But the will has a horror of half-measures, and as soon as it took over, I had to start again from the beginning.

But when I held my will in leash, not letting it move, my

beloved girl filled the whole room with her presence. Aliette was no longer on my right or my left, as she had been in Toulouse, divided from me now more, now less by holding my arm or letting it go. She was above me, behind and within. I no longer had to pay any attention to silly limitations of distance or space.

She still had a face and it was her prettiest, and she still had a voice. But now the face and the voice embraced and accepted me. When they had been with me in the real world, the divided world, I had not always been sure of joy in the same measure.

My parents had turned the back of their apartment over to me — two small rooms next to each other, opening on a courtyard and completely isolated from the rest of the house down a long corridor with a bend. This was my own domain where I had free rein. I changed the furniture around and planned order and disorder to suit my whims.

I was not always alone there. People came to see me, and I was the one who received them. After dinner, when I had said good night to the rest of the family, I had a place of retreat. The two little rooms became a shrine.

I sat up late at night. I had thrown myself furiously into the study of philosophy. I wanted to understand it all, and felt it was urgent. I don't know exactly why, but it seemed to me that such a chance would not come again, that I was going to be snatched away to more worldly responsibilities.

All the ideas of men who had dedicated themselves to thought found their way into my head for the first time, from Pythagoras to Bergson, from Plato to Freud. I examined them as closely as I could. Truly, the human spirit — or whatever there was of it in me — was not a good glass to look through, for it did not hold steady. This lapse in attention often worried me, but not overly, since the philosophers themselves did not always appear to have seen clearly.

As a rule they had chosen a direction which the best of them had been able to follow through an entire volume, in some cases for a lifetime. This was true of Plato and Spinoza. But the choice in itself and their obstinacy in pursuing it were limiting, and prevented them from looking about them. I saw their thinking as to the surface of a sphere, but only at one point, thus losing touch with the reality of the universe which could be nothing less than the sphere as a whole. In this way, the more deductive and systematic a philosopher was, the greater his defeats as I saw them. Poets and most artists said and did many foolish things, but at least they reached out in all directions, multiplying risks and opportunities at the same time. There was something good in their turmoil.

I tormented myself that autumn of 1940. I thought a lot, or at any rate gave exercise to my thoughts. I tried all the avenues, one after another, the realist and the idealist, the materialist and the spiritualist, the empirical and the rational. All the way from Heraclitus to William James, no one of them seemed to me without function, but none satisfied me completely.

As for psychology — they were making us study its foundations and its doctrines for nine hours a week — I had a grudge against it. For me, it was way off the track. Either psychology was analyzing the properties of mind and spirit without taking into account that their very existence was open to question; or else, in a trice, it turned its back on mind and spirit alike. Outward manifestations were the only concern.

Manifestations and reflexes! But these were nothing but effects. How could they be taken for the sum total of human life? Perhaps they were signs, but their interpretation could not help being insecure since it was made by individuals who did not know themselves any better than those they were judging.

When I came upon the myth of objectivity in certain modern thinkers, it made me angry. So there was only one world for these people, the same for everyone. And all the other worlds were to be counted as illusions left over from the past. Or why not call them by their name — hallucinations? I had learned to my cost how wrong they were.

From my own experience I knew very well that it was enough to take from a man a memory here, an association there, to deprive him of hearing or sight, for the world to undergo immediate transformation, and for another world, entirely different but entirely coherent, to be born. Another world? Not really. The same world rather, but seen from another angle, and counted in entirely new measures. When this happened, all the hierarchies they called objective were turned upside down, scattered to the four winds, not even like theories but like whims.

The psychologists more than all the rest — there were a few exceptions, Bergson among them — seemed to me not to come within miles of the heart of the matter, the inner life. They took it as their subject but did not talk about it. They were as embarrassed in its presence as a hen finding out that she has hatched a duckling. Of course, I was more uneasy than they were when it came to talking about it, but not when it came to living it. I was only sixteen years old, and I felt it was up to them to tell me. Yet they told me nothing.

The philosophers put my brain to work, and my brain followed them willingly. The discipline they imposed on it strengthened its muscles. My brain used its powers better, and found its way faster from day to day, but it never reached port. I heard questions everywhere, but answers never.

Our philosophy teacher was very weak that year. The poor man had aged badly. Fortunately, there were the books, and we discussed them among ourselves with a passion which was new to me.

EXASPERATING VAPORS SEEMED TO BE RISING from occupied Paris, lying there as silent as the tomb. All the words that people held in because they were frightened were turning to defiance. Almost all the boys my age were worried. Those who weren't were fools, and we dropped them. Our uneasiness was more intense than the uneasiness of people fully grown. It did not consist in asking ourselves who would win the war and when, whether there would be food rationing — indeed there would, it was already beginning — whether the more dangerous enemy was Nazism or Bolshevism. For our part, we wanted to learn how to live, and that was a much more serious matter. And we wanted to learn fast, because we felt that the next day it would surely be too late. There were signs of death on land and in the air, from the Spanish border to the frontiers of Russia. Not just signs but battles to the death.

The feeling grumbled inside us, pressing to come out in the open. Unless we were up to making a better life than the life of our elders, the orgy of stupidity and killing would go on till the end of the world. Let people be silent if they were able to go on living without speaking out. We were incapable of it. As for that fear of theirs, it was indecent, and made us feel sick. We had no forbearance toward the philosophers, our teachers or our families. It was better so, since we needed our strength to prepare ourselves.

Students were very serious that winter in Paris. Some of them even had the tragic look. And why not? On November 11, 1940, there had been a demonstration on the Champs-Elysées, in memory of the 1918 victory, which refused to be snuffed out. That was the first demonstration, the first and only time that the Parisians had said no to Germany. The students had done it, and next morning at dawn some twenty of them had been shot.

Most people were still laughing and having a good time. The balance of life is not destroyed at once in one season. But each morning we woke up having lived weeks, though we didn't know how, since the day before.

In a happy land children never stop being children. But those who live in a land of suffering are men even before they want to be, before their bodies allow it. They still have the mouth of the ten-year-old ready to pull a long face, the brightness of tears in their eyes, ink on their fingers, the slang of schoolboys, and little girls they have not touched bothering their heads. Yet they are already men, with a zeal for understanding and doing which must be assuaged without delay. They have a thousand times as many questions as there are answers the world over.

I was like that, and so were my companions. We were gulping down our studies for want of more solid food. But, at any rate, we were not taken in by words, by science or philosophy, by newspapers, complacency or fear. We were afraid of not living, no doubt about that, of not having the right or the time for it, and afraid of people telling us we must do it this way but not that. As if they knew! We were in a hurry and we were determined. In spite of everything we were going to give life a try.

Leaving my house there were two of us as there always had been. But by the time we got to the lycée we were eight or ten or twelve. It never failed. My companions converged on us from all the streets along the route. Some of them even went a long way out of their way to join us. The concierge at the lycée, who was much amused at the sight, used to stick his head out of the window at the gate and call out: "Well, well. So it's the Lusseyran parade."

In a way it was my parade, for under the broad guiding hand of Jean I was always in the middle. Sometimes the presence of the others became almost a nuisance. From now on, to recapture our old intimacy, Jean and I had to retreat to my apartment, to the two little rooms, my monkish cell in the Boulevard Port-Royal.

Outside there was always the crowd. "You attract them," was Jean's way of putting it. "They need you." I, who thought it was I who needed them. After all, perhaps it was a little of both. The mysteries of attraction have never been solved. But Jean went on, "Don't you realize you are the one they are always looking at? Even when it is difficult, when they have to look over the shoulder of the boy next to them? They think you don't see them. Maybe that's why they do it."

Our procession went down the Rue St-Jacques and then climbed up again, side by side but with no confusion. Sometimes I wondered where all this order came from. Everyone talked in his turn. There was a time for joking and a time to be serious. All the boys were so levelheaded, and when they were excited they were so secretive about it that it was as if they were lining up in battle formation. Whatever happened there was always one subject that was taboo — school. By unanimous vote the one who talked about that had to leave the procession. Serious questions had priority, and how serious we were! Even when we were talking about girls.

I walked in the middle and was happy, without knowing exactly why — happy to be with men who, like me, were not willing to shut their eyes to life. I completely forgot we were going to the lycée. Once I was in school I forgot I was in class. I was already walking in the midst of the future. Yet I had no idea what the future would bring.

François, one of the boys in the parade, was born in France, but his family was Polish and poor. His father had emigrated twenty years before, and had become a metal worker in one of the factories in the north of France.

François was full of ardor. In itself that would not have been enough to single him out among us, for the temperature of our group was high. But his ardor was different, as we used to say, "in the Slavic manner." Emotions flashed from his tall thin body — perhaps a shade too thin — like a battery discharging. They caused him to make motions he could not control; to fold his arms across his chest, put his hands on your shoulders while he was talking, always on a level with your face and in a voice that was inspired and rounder and warmer than other people's; made him stop suddenly in the middle of the street two steps ahead of the others and greedily hold us there crying, "Life is beautiful," or something very like it. François was celebrating his private Mass.

Did I say he had a passion? The fact is he had all the passions, but the greatest of them all was his passion for France. He loved his country, and seemed to know it better than we did. Sometimes he called it France in the usual way. Sometimes he called it Poland. For him it came to the same thing, and for my part I thought he was right.

In the presence of our teachers we had to pretend and we hated it. We had to look reasonable — how shall I put it — detached. Our fire had to be turned down low, except with the man who was so different from the others, our history teacher. He wanted us to be exactly as we really were, funny if we couldn't help it, furious if we were angry. This remarkable character was as much alive after six months as he was on the first day. His learning made us gasp. He made numbers and facts pour down on us like hail. Every now and then he rubbed his hands in a lively and happy way, and laughed a small friendly laugh. We were beginning to know him well, and saw that that meant an idea had occurred to him.

The syllabus for history stopped at 1918, with the kind of nearsighted caution people thought suitable for courses in school. But for him that was no obstacle, for he would go ahead without any syllabus. He went on past all the barriers, even after the hour for the end of school. If he knew we were not scheduled for other courses he kept us an hour, even two hours longer. Smiling, he announced: "I am not keeping you. Those who want to leave may do so. It's all right with me." Naturally, we all stayed, consumed by that unbelievable whirlwind of facts, information, new angles on all the countries and all the periods; and by his pleas for clarity, common sense, energy and alertness. All of us, that is, except two. We had noticed them, for they went out right on the hour. It was not long before we found out that they had enrolled in a youth movement for collaboration with Germany.

As soon as they had closed the door behind them, the teacher said, "Now we are among friends, let us go on." He followed the history of Germany beyond the defeat of 1918, through the Weimar Republic, Stresemann, the venerable Hindenburg, inflation, strikes, misery and the failure of the Social Democrats, all the way down to Hitler's *Putsch* and the birth of the Nazi monster, which was weighing down upon us now with all its strength.

He told us about the Reichstag fire and the people who were really responsible for it, about the creation, in 1933, of a place unique in history for the scientific organization of cruelty: Dachau, a concentration camp, six miles from Munich in Bavaria.

From his worn briefcase be pulled out incredible documents, whole pages translated from *Mein Kampf*, the statements of Alfred Rosenberg, Joseph Goebbels, Julius Streicher — all the teeming nightmares of National Socialist Germany. He made it clear to us that this was race murder and how they went about it — not in theory but here and now and in actual practice, and not so far away from us, in Poland and in Czechoslovakia. Though François was not Jewish, I could hear him grumble in protest.

Our teacher had no fear, and what a deliverance that was! Whatever choice he had made in this war of ours, he knew the reason for it. And he would not take leave of us until he had told us the whole story. At last, one day, he met us head on. He asked us what France was, what it was good for, what part it was playing in the world. We had to answer, for his questions were not just rhetorical.

As might be expected, François spoke more eloquently than the rest of us. He said that France had just been beaten, but that that meant nothing, only that there was a general infection in the body of Europe. This infection must be cured, or else the world, the whole world, would be poisoned from the same source. And besides, said François — he was almost on his feet because he couldn't keep his seat — France was not just a country, it was a way of life. While this was going on, our teacher was rubbing his hands with more conviction than ever.

To him it seemed clear that François was right. France had to be loved, but with intelligence, and that was the hard part. We must recognize that the French Empire was wounded, perhaps dead, and times were changing fast with the balance of power turning on its own axis. There was no denying that Germany, for all its Gestapo and its Wehrmacht, was not the whole of the problem but only a part of it.

He wanted us to look beyond frontiers because, as he said, frontiers were only the bones of an old corset which was about to burst. His sentences were interrupted by the familiar laughter we had come to love so much. "Young gentlemen," he said, "this is not a war of nations. There will be no more wars of that sort. Get that into your heads! The world is one. That may be uncomfortable, but it is a fact. And every nationalist is behind the times, just an old stick-in-the-mud."

Fascinated, we followed him across the frontiers, eastward toward Russia and westward toward America. As he saw it, only those two countries counted now, the U.S.S.R. and the U.S.A. The power of Germany was of the moment, nothing but a gigantic frenzy. It could not last.

The Russians and the Americans might not be any better than other people, but they were certainly more alive, and in the end life was always what mattered. The U.S.S.R. and the U.S. were not at war yet, but they would be. That was not just a hope but the inevitable sequence of events.

Then for six weeks he devoted himself to explaining the birth of Bolshevism, the rule of Lenin, the rule of Stalin and the Moscow purges. For our benefit he analyzed the constitution of the U.S.S.R., relying upon the Russian texts which he had had translated. He made it plain that for a good three years Russian heavy industry, concentrated in the region south of Moscow and around the cities of the Ukraine like Kharkov and Dnepropetrovsk or in the Donbas, had been systematically changed over to new cities to the east in the northern Urals, Magnitogorsk, Chelyabinsk, and even farther off in Siberia in the Kuznetsk Basin. Even more recently food industries as important as pastas and canning had moved in the same direction.

Wasn't it clear what this meant? Didn't it throw a new light on the Nazi–Soviet Pact of August 23, 1939? Could the U.S.S.R. really be the friend of Hitler? If the Bolsheviks were sincere this was impossible, for in that case they were fighting for the freedom of man. If they were not sincere it was still impossible, for in that case they were secretly harboring the dream of world domination, and could not tolerate the domination of the Nazis for any length of time.

The U.S.S.R. weighed heavily in the balance. We had no right to let ourselves be put to sleep by the illusions the Western powers had entertained on that score since 1917. Russia was a nation at once very old and very young. Its strength lay in the humility and guilelessness of its people, and the impatience for well-being which had piled up over centuries under despotic rule.

The U.S.S.R. was an unknown quantity but America was no less so. "As for them," our teacher used to say when he was talking about America, "if they are only as skillful as they are generous, we shall all be saved!"

The portion of the future which lay on the other side of the Atlantic was greater than Europe liked to admit. There was a vast continent there, filled with resources, teeming with people, growing in almost geometrical progression. America represented the greatest triumph of the spirit of adventure that man had ever managed to achieve. Excitement and egotism were part of it, as they are with all young nations, but America also had one of the most solid reserves of tolerance and confidence to be found anywhere in the world.

Americans loved to invent, to build, in other words they loved action, and if they could only keep this taste intact for a long enough time, they would become Europe's first hope, perhaps her only hope, ghastly as it might be to admit it.

We had a course of lectures on the 1929 crash, the depression, Franklin Delano Roosevelt's first term and his second. We were told about the New Deal, the rapid recovery of America from depression, the TVA, the plans for reforestation and the development of electric power in the Rockies. For the first time in our lives,

New York, Philadelphia, Pittsburgh, Cleveland, Detroit, Chicago, San Francisco, Los Angeles, even Minneapolis and Duluth, Toledo, Rochester, the Mississippi and the Missouri, the Appalachians and Lake Huron became something more than just names — remarkable places where every year millions of people thought of hundreds of new ways to harness life.

I listened and I understood. The frontiers of France, my frontiers, were breaking apart on all sides. The wand of a schoolteacher, or better his charm and his ability, were turning a sixteen-year-old French schoolboy into a citizen of the West.

In March 1941, I was called to the blackboard, or rather to the rostrum, as my history teacher put me to the test. Within a month I had had to read some twenty books, some about Russia and others about the United States. Now I had to summarize them for my classmates and make the synthesis, as we rather pompously called it. Since it was really the first time I had had to talk in public, I was overwhelmed by fears and weighted down by notes. The anguish stayed with me, but the notes disappeared.

I had sat down in the teacher's seat to begin my statement. My hands moved back and forth over the top of the desk but in vain. The notes were no longer there, and I felt dizzy. Then I heard the familiar rubbing of hands and the small affectionate laugh. "I am the one who took your notes," the teacher said. "When someone takes off on a trip, he puts his luggage in the baggage car."

In the emergency I felt even dizzier. Then something cleared in my head. I remembered the inner screen and discovered that I could read my notes on it with ease. They were even more legible than on paper. How could I have gone on for several months forgetting the existence of this marvelous tool? What a fool I had made of myself!

Besides, all the time I was talking my voice was growing more assured. It sounded almost natural. As for the silence of my classmates, it was a good sign meaning they wished me no harm, and that some would even have liked to help me out. I was sure of it for I felt them leaning toward me, François and Jean in particular.

At the end of an hour — they told me it lasted an hour though I couldn't believe my ears — I heard myself drawing to a close and the teacher applauding. He never applauded, especially not his own students. What could I possibly have said?

I found out only a few seconds later from the others. It seemed I had said something astonishing, specifically that the war had only just begun, that we should only know where it was leading us after the USSR and the USA were in it, and that this double intervention would certainly not be long in coming. Dear God! How could I have said such things? I had not prepared them, what is more I didn't even know them — literally had no idea of them! But I had to reconcile myself to the fact that my mind was outrunning my knowledge. In itself this modest discovery gave me something to dream about, and I did dream.

10

THE PLUNGE INTO COURAGE

W EISSBERG WAS THE NAME of the thin little man with the short beard and white hair. He was always polite and always welcoming. As an old schoolmate of Jean's father, he had a deep affection for Jean, and asked nothing more of him than a brief visit once a month. Being a bachelor he said he loved Jean like the son he had never had himself. His life had been devoted to patient research in biology. He had made some real discoveries in pharmacology, but was too modest and too absentminded to make capital of his own inventions. He had always been poor.

When Jean came back from those visits to Weissberg, he blossomed. The old man had made him see and love so many things that were new to him.

One evening at the beginning of April Jean had gone off toward the Avenue de Clichy for his regular visit. But the concierge stopped him as he was passing and told him that the old gentleman who lived on the fifth floor was no longer there. Two days before, at five o'clock in the morning, the German police had come for him. "Three of them were looking for him," said the concierge, "all of them very polite, especially the tallest one, who spoke French." But as they were taking the poor man away, the tall one, obviously an officer, had turned around and said to her: "Don't be upset. It is only a Jew."

Some days after this, Radio Paris, which was German, announced that French terrorists had cut the telephone lines used by the German army near the coast of Brittany. As a result ten French hostages had just been shot.

Then one day, as I was coming out of the lycée at noon, a young man I didn't know took hold of my arm as I was going by. He drew me into the corner of the entrance hall and said to me in an anxious voice, "The Gestapo arrested Gérard this morning. I think he is at the Santé." The Santé! It was the first time the name of that Paris prison had sounded so close and so personal in my ears. The young man went on: "I am Gérard's oldest brother. I am in danger myself. Our father joined the Free French Forces in London last June, as you know. They must be holding Gérard as a hostage. I thought I should tell you, since you were his best friend."

Three days later, I fell ill. I am not sure whether it was because of Weissberg, Gérard and the hostages. The illness itself was common enough. A bad case of measles declared itself in a few hours and broke out in a rash after four or five days. When it left me, it set a torrent of energy free. I hesitate to say so, but that is really what I think. There is no doubt that I believed it at the time. In the first hours of fever it became obvious that my system was purging itself of a poison and spewing out foreign bodies. But the poison was moral as much as it was physical, of that I am sure.

When the fever was at its height I had the shivers. But, strange as it may seem, my head was still clear and I watched the battle going on. Emotions were driving my body and my mind every which way. I threw myself forward with fury, as though I were driving off the enemy. Soon the notion that I was sick no longer mattered to me. This was no microbe or virus making its way in. It was resolve.

It took me over from head to foot like a conquered land. I could not resist it, for it had taken the wheel. It was driving me to definite destinations which I had not thought about before it came.

This resolve gave me orders, telling me first of all that I must say nothing to my family, at least not right away. I must have a meeting with two of my comrades, with François and Georges by themselves. Even Jean would not be there. Later I should have to get in touch with about ten more. The list was already made up.

My new resolution didn't tell me what to say to them. And that didn't matter, for when the time came, I should know well enough. My only haste was to get my body well again, to risk it in the great adventure.

What a fortunate case of measles that was! In me it had catalyzed a pack of fears and desires, intentions and irritations which had held me closed in a tight fist for weeks, and which I should never have been able to break open myself. On the first day of convalescence I said to myself aloud in my room: "The Occupation is my sickness."

That was in April in our first Nazi spring. Youth, the Occupation, convalescence whirled around in my blood. My temples throbbed when I saw everyone saying nothing and doing nothing while my country lay motionless. Recently a new name had been going the rounds, a name which described all such people: *les attentistes*, the waiting ones.

What were they waiting for? For the terror to clamp down?

For it to consume our joy of living, working on us like an enormous microbe? — this would soon be accomplished, for not much of the joy was left. Waiting for all the Weissbergs to be arrested or missing? For France to be made up of only two kinds of men, the hostages and those on whose behalf they kill the hostages? That I did not want.

Of course, once again "want" was an empty word. Nothing could convince me that all the people who were waiting were doing it because they liked it. They were doing it in spite of themselves. And besides, were they all really waiting? How could you tell? In those days there was no communication.

In conversation, when words like Nazis, Gestapo, torture or shooting came up, then all of a sudden something was turned off in the person you were talking to. I had grown so sensitive to this phenomenon that I thought I could almost hear a characteristic sound. In such cases one never knew whether people were closing their eyes, their fists or their mouths. All that was left of them was a bundle of rejection. This was especially true of the adults, but recently the sickness had spread even to my contemporaries.

There it was, I had grasped it, the subject I must discuss with François and Georges. I would talk to them about the reasons why everyone was holding his tongue. I could prove to them that all the reasons were poor. I would make them speak, or I would speak in their place.

I had words in my head and words in my throat. But nothing was to be gained by making them into a novel or into verse. This was not a time for speeches. I had words enough to fill my arms and hands.

If I didn't know yet precisely what the Occupation was, that was because it was too important and, after all, almost invisible. The Nazis had perfected a new way of inserting themselves into the body of Europe. They held themselves in rigid order, at attention quite correctly, at least in France. They stole from us, looted us, taking home 85 percent of the agricultural and industrial production of our country. But they didn't talk about it, or hardly ever. They never made threats. They were satisfied with signing requisitions.

Behind the army — everyone knew it, and those who were not sure were afraid of it, which had an even greater effect — behind the army there was something hidden. This was not a war like other wars. It was not violence which lay behind this war but something worse, an obsession: make Europe Nazi, kill everything un-German, or grind it under the German heel.

And this obsession was not just mad. No one saw the foaming at the mouth. There was a directing body, and that was the secret. All the plans had been set down in advance. They were under cover, in desk drawers in offices from Narvik to St-Jean-de-Luz, and lately as far off as the island of Crete. In Paris the drawers were in the Rue des Saussaies, the Rue Lauriston, and in all the apartment houses the Gestapo had occupied.

By now I felt I understood the Germans. There would be no massacres, for one could count on the Nazis to be more adroit. Or, if there were any, they would happen one at a time, man by man and disappearance by disappearance. One day, perhaps after several years had gone by, it would become clear that not a single Gérard was left in our France, not one free man, not one Weissberg.

Once the measles were cured, my determination to speak out became a second malady. This one too gave me the shivers and pricked my tongue. The pain I felt was certainly real.

Then I said to Jean: "Why don't we learn to dance?" I suspect the relation between the rhumba, the fox-trot and my new fever for liberty will probably escape even the attentive reader. Nevertheless there was a very simple bond between them. I was not yet ready, not entirely. The seething of my mind, transmitted to my body, gave me a strength which I would be at a loss to call by name. Cosmic might be the word for it. There was in me such a train of forces preparing themselves for deeds that all roads had to be cleared at once to allow them to pass.

I learned all the basic dance steps in two weeks, as fast as parched people quench their thirst in midsummer. I covered the whole range from waltz to swing and became a real fan of swing, not for aesthetic reasons as you may guess, but because swing was really a dance to drive out demons. When you had whirled a pack of girls at arm's length for five or six hours, with all their perfume coming back to you by the handful, you were dead beat. But still you had driven off the devils. And they are made to be shaken, these devils, whether they are political or individual.

Besides, the distinction people made between the problems which concerned them personally and those that concerned them only generally, as they put it, seemed to François, to Georges, to Jean and to me absolutely repulsive. The life of the country was our own affair, there was no question whatever about that! It was a fact, and one which burst forth in the first talks I had with each of them at the end of April.

AT THE BEGINNING OF MAY I had adopted the ascetic way of life which befits a soldier of the ideal. Every day, including Sunday, I got up at half-past four before it was light. The first thing I did was to kneel down and pray: "My God, give me the strength to keep my promises. Since I made them in a good cause, they are yours to keep as well as mine. Now that twenty young men — tomorrow there may be a hundred — are waiting for my orders, tell me what orders to give them. By myself I know how to do almost nothing, but if you will it I am capable of almost everything. Most of all give me prudence. Your enthusiasm I no longer need, for I am filled with it."

Then I washed quickly in cold water, and looked out of the window of my room to listen to Paris. I was taking Paris more seriously than I ever had before, yet without getting my blood up, without feeling myself accountable for the whole city. But three days before, in this city lying half stupefied and frozen by the curfew every night from midnight to five o'clock, I had become one of the responsible ones. There was nothing anyone could do about that, not even I myself.

It was the others, my comrades, who wanted it so. And only the week before, when I had my first confidential talk with François and two hours later with Georges, I was still wondering whether the storm of sentences pouring from my lips would mean anything to them. François had nearly cried for joy at the first words. He had embraced me, a thing we never did among ourselves, and stammered: "We all expected this from you." I had to bite my tongue to keep from saying, "From me? But why from me?"

The rest of the hour had to be spent throwing water on the fire. I had barely said to François that we no longer had the right to stand the Occupation when he burst out with a whole column of plans. Not crazy ones; on the contrary, they were drawn up like reports on tactical maneuvers. Clearly he had been thinking of nothing else since the summer before. But these plans were so rash they would have put all our lives in jeopardy in an hour.

I was forced to admit it, I had thought of everything but the danger. And here was François throwing danger straight at me, like a clenched fist full in the face: my danger and his and at the same time the danger of all those to whom I was about to speak. I needed time to accustom myself to the harsh fact that from now on

I should not be speaking a word which was not also an act. I was in urgent need of God, and I promised myself to pray every day.

Georges's reaction turned out to be quite different from François's. Georges was a little man, full of boldness but also reserved. Besides, his lack of intellectual gifts had held him back in his studies. By now he was twenty, and by contrast with François he understood only practical things. He had been badgering me to give him my plans in detail. But what I had was only a purpose, and that was not the same thing as having plans.

I recognized in these circumstances that I must improvise an organization on the spot. Already Georges was asking, "What kind of people do you want to get in touch with? How many? When will you need money and how much? Where are you going to put the headquarters of your movement? What sort of discipline are you thinking of using to keep the activities of the members under control? When are you going to tell London about your existence?"

Your existence! Your movement! They were all moving faster than I was. But if I was surprised to see the pace they were setting, I was even more surprised to see my own. By a feat of acrobatics which I didn't believe I was capable of, and which I had certainly never learned anywhere, I was not only following François and Georges but going ahead of them. By very little, but very definitely: by a sentence, by a head.

For instance, I heard myself saying to Georges that we would not know how extensive the movement was until after a two months' trial period; that until this period was over, we must not treat the comrades we had been in touch with as full-grown men but as Boy Scouts. It seemed inevitable that among the first twenty some ten would drop out, and that this kind of dropout could only be permitted in the earliest stages before the organization was really established. After that there would be martial law because we would be in the underground.

Georges had certainly heard what he wanted to hear because at the end he had said, "I swear to you..." Then he hesitated before taking the plunge: "I swear to you by the head of my mother that I am with you."

The next day I called on three other schoolmates to come to my room. I had met two more going back and forth to the lycée. Now I was feeling uneasiness verging on doubt as I realized that I was not saying the same thing to all of them. Some I was encouraging. Others I was calming down. Without figuring it out exactly, but for reasons which seemed compelling, it was only to Georges and François that I told the whole story. To Jean I told only half of it.

At the end of four or five days, about ten boys were gathered around and pressing me to act. To me this meant embarrassment very like panic, making me feel a painful stiffening of the muscles in the back of my neck. What action was I capable of, blind as I was? Yet it was for me all of them were waiting.

I sought no one's advice and did not have time for it. I had already sent out invitations for a preliminary meeting in the apartment of Jean's family on the following Tuesday. The ten comrades we were in contact with would be there at five o'clock on the dot.

And they were there, not ten of them but fifty-two. When I heard the wave of voices climbing the narrow stairs of the apartment house, I had the foolish idea that someone had denounced us.

But ten minutes later, when the fifty-two boys were sitting on their heels in the middle of the big room with the stained-glass windows, with all eyes turned in my direction, when suddenly they fell silent as I had never heard men fall silent, and when one of them, I think it was Georges, said to me, "The chips are down. It's up to you to speak," then an unaccustomed radiance filled my head, and my heart stopped beating out of rhythm. All at once I began to understand everything I had been seeking and not finding for the past weeks.

The consciences of my companions seemed to lie wide open before me, and all I needed was to read them. As to my own conscience, it no longer troubled me. I had dedicated it to a cause which must have the power of truth since it was teaching me to speak all those words I had never uttered before.

To the fifty-two I said that there was no turning back from their commitment. They would not be able to close the door they had opened that night. What we were making, they and I together, was called a Resistance Movement. The fact that the oldest of us was not yet twenty-one, and that I was not quite seventeen, though it did not make all our operations simple, made some of them possible. So long as people thought of us as kids, they would not suspect us, at least not right away. In the six months ahead, we must make the most of this prejudice and this piece of luck.

For the first six months, for a year if need be, our resistance would be passive while we were preparing the way. First we would proceed to set up the cells of the Movement, one at a time. There would be no appeal from this rule. The meeting of the fifty-two had been madness, not deliberate of course, and perhaps necessary, but it would be the last. From now on the members of the Movement must never meet more than three at a time, except in serious emergencies.

In the preparatory stages, all childish dreams must be thrown away without pity, all those dreams of cloak-and-dagger, those dreams of conspiracy and guerrilla war. Until new orders were issued, there would be no arms in the Movement, not even a single hunter's gun. And there would be no talk of arms.

Besides, in ordinary conversation, nothing that meant anything must be discussed. Starting that very evening we must lead a life divided right down the middle, on one side the life of innocent young people, open with their families, their teachers, the class-mates they didn't know well and with their girls; on the other side the other life. Those who had time for affairs could still have them, but they would talk to their girls about love and bedroom slippers and nothing more. Families were the most dangerous; since by def-inition they meant well, they might get in our way or gossip.

IT WAS LESS THAN A WEEK since I had said all these things. Already the wheels were turning, and I was at the head of a Resis-tance Movement. In the courtyard in front of me, when the early sun cast its first musical rays, the delectable aroma of salt and sugar mixed together came up from the bakery next door. It smelled as sweet as it always had, before the days of the Resistance. It made you want pleasure, not serious deeds. Among all the dangers that beset me, there would always be that one to reckon with, the one that comes from the enjoyment of everyday things.

I had stripped myself of the right to dream. At any rate, now my dreams could take only one path, and I should never know what lay at the end of the road until it was upon me.

Under pressure from Georges and François, and then from two others, Raymond and Claude, we had already had to form a Central Committee for the Movement. Central Committee! It sounded like a farce, almost as if we had been playing at tin sol-diers. All the same that wasn't true. The need was real and we were working at it.

What I could not devise was devised by the other four. You see there could be no question of getting expert advice, not from politicians, officers, newspapermen, or even from our parents. And when fifty boys have to be persuaded to do something, or worse, be prevented from doing it, tactics are a must.

The first Central Committee had met the evening before near

the Porte d'Orléans on the south side of Paris, in one of those poor apartment houses which are like beehives, and where there is constant coming and going on the stairs. Still, we arrived and departed each according to an itinerary decided on in advance, and different from that of all the others. Only Georges and I were paired. I would have to be the exception to the rule.

The Central Committee, by unanimous vote, with a single abstention, mine, had come to a decision. For the first three months, I would be in sole charge of recruiting. The Committee thought this risk was mine by right, as the moral initiator of the whole affair, and because I was blind.

That was my job, my specialty. They claimed I had "the sense of human beings." In my first encounters I had made no mistakes. Besides, I would hear more acutely and pay better attention. People would not easily deceive me. I should not forget names or places, addresses or telephone numbers. Every week I would report on the outlook without resorting to scraps of paper or lists. Everything written down, even in code, was a risk that none of us had the right to run.

I had abstained from voting but also from refusing what they offered me. Nothing in the world could help me more to live than this confidence on the part of my friends, and this danger itself, which for some weeks might be even greater than theirs. Later on, if it was necessary to spy, to carry arms, to flee or to fight, I would turn the task over to someone else. I would stay in the rear, necessarily. But before my eyes condemned me not to make war, as they might one day, I should have my eyes to thank for the chance to make it first, in the front lines.

IN LESS THAN A YEAR nearly six hundred boys took the road to the Boulevard Port-Royal. They came to see the blind man. It will be easier to understand the times and the burden of their secret if I explain that in most cases these people did not know my name, and didn't even ask what it was.

One of the fifty-two from the original group would watch a classmate for several days, sometimes for several weeks. Eventually, if they believed he could be trusted, they sent him on to me. The rules were strict. I was never to receive individuals whose coming had not been announced. And I was not to receive them unless they arrived within five minutes of the appointed hour. If their coming did not meet these conditions, and if I was unable to send them away — a difficulty which was very likely to arise — I would ask them in, but, pretending there had been a misunderstanding, would talk of nothing that mattered. The members of the original group knew I wasn't joking. They knew it all the better because they were not playing games themselves. "Go to the blind man," they would say to the neophyte. "When he has seen you, I shall have something to tell you."

Then they explained that I lived on the Boulevard Port-Royal, opposite the Baudeloque Maternity Hospital, and that the door of my house was between a drugstore and a sweatshop; that they must take the main stairway in the building to the fourth floor, and give two short rings and one long on the bell. I would open the door myself and take them to my quarters. After that they were to let things take their course, and answer any questions I might ask.

In the first weeks only the very young ones came, boys between seventeen and nineteen, who were finishing their secondary schooling at the lycée. But little by little older boys came along, people with more self-confidence and harder to know. They were scholars from the colleges of letters, science, medicine, pharmacy, law, the schools of advanced agronomy, chemistry, physics. The Movement was growing at the pace of a living cell. What is more, it had a name. We called ourselves the Volunteers of Liberty.

Every week I gave an account of my decisions before the Central Committee. So-and-so was admitted unconditionally. He joined the group from the College of Law, on an equal footing with the others. So-and-so was admitted "on probation." He would be under surveillance for the time being. A founding group existed only if it included two members, one in action, the other revealing his intentions to no one and with specific responsibility for watching over doubtful cases.

To anyone who has not lived through this period of the Occupation, these cautious measures may seem exaggerated. But they were not, and the future would prove it. As for our plans, were they on such a grand scale that we needed six hundred young men to carry them out? Actually, they were modest but also difficult to carry out. They justified the gathering of all our forces.

Our first task was to give people the news. The only papers which were coming out in France at the time were censored from the first to the last line. In spirit, sometimes even to the letter, they were copies of the Nazi press. Often they even went further, following the principle that traitors must behave even worse than brigands. The French people were completely ignorant of the war, and because of this they had only instincts to rely on.

True, there was the radio of Free France in London. But in nine cases out of ten, its broadcasts were jammed so effectively that you couldn't make out the words. Besides, listening to the British radio was forbidden. And even if the Germans exercised only sporadic control, fear ran wild and very few families listened. Our first job was to bring out a newspaper — a paper, or if that should be beyond our means at the start, a loose-leaf news bulletin, one we could circulate in secret from hand to hand.

A number of members of the Movement would be set to listen

to the British and the Swiss radios. We were going to gather the real news of the war, put it in order, distribute and appraise it.

It was urgent to guide public opinion and set it straight. Never forget that in those days in the middle of 1941, most of our compatriots, and almost the whole of Europe, had lost hope. The defeat of the Nazis seemed improbable at the least, or postponed to an indefinite future. It was our duty to declare, to cry out our faith in the victory of the Allies.

News was needed, surely, but courage even more, and clarity. We were resolved to hide nothing. For here was the monster to be fought: defeatism, and with it that other monster, apathy. Everything possible must be done to keep the French from growing accustomed to Nazism, or from seeing it just as an enemy, like enemies of other times, an enemy of the nation, an adversary who was victorious just for the moment. For our part we knew that Nazism threatened the whole of humanity, that it was an absolute evil, and we were going to publish its evilness abroad.

Our third task would take longer. We must uncover in the youth of France all that was left intact. We must sort the strong from the weak, the faithful from the cowards. The time for subtleties was past.

We were aware that the triumphant return of the Allies would not be accomplished from one day to the next. We also knew that when it did come, the country would need hosts of men ready to receive and help the invasion of the liberators.

Men in readiness, that meant men who had committed themselves months, perhaps even years ahead, who had tested themselves in patience and underground work, men who would be incapable of treachery or any kind of moral lapse. And for this task not just men but young men were needed. The evidence stared

us in the face. The men over thirty round about us were afraid:
for their wives and their children — these were real reasons; but
also for their possessions, their position, and that is what made us
angry; above all for their lives, which they clung to much more
than we did to ours. We were less frightened than they were. The
years ahead would prove the point. Four-fifths of the Resistance in
France was the work of men less than thirty years old.

There was another way we could help. Young as we were,
we could easily go all over, pretend to be playing games, or making foolish talk, wander around whistling with our hands in our
pockets, outside factories, near barracks or German convoys, hang
about kitchens and on sidewalks, climb over walls. Everything
would be on our side, even help from the girls if there happened to
be any on the spot.

The Volunteers of Liberty were going to build an information
network, not an organization of professional agents but something
better, an organization of agents dedicated and nearly invisible
because they looked like harmless youngsters. In the end, we
should have to get in touch with London, but even this difficulty
failed to alarm us.

Finally, we should be a movement with no arms in our everyday work. But the Central Committee was going to assemble those
of us — some twenty — who had been mobilized or had enlisted as
volunteers in 1939 and knew how to handle arms. We were going
to set up a few training centers in the outer suburbs of Paris, or
even on isolated farms in the countryside. We had already made
some contacts with farmers in the region between Arpajon and
Limours. According to a meticulous plan, we were going to maintain a hundred of our number ready for any eventuality. None of

us had the illusion of being important, but all of us were sure of being necessary.

BUT LET US GO BACK to my apartment, and the conferences I was holding there.

What picture could these newcomers — sometimes three or four of them the same evening — have had of the mysterious young man I was? The visitor only knew one thing about me, that I was blind. If he had carefully observed the rules about the bells, he followed me down a dark corridor — I almost always forgot to turn on the light. Two doors in succession closed behind him. At the end he was introduced into a narrow room with a window on the court, a bed, an armchair for him, a straight chair for me, a low slim chest. Through a door that always stood open to the second room he saw piles of Braille books extending all the way up the three walls of the room. Opposite him was a boy whose extreme youth was thinly concealed by the pipe he was always smoking. But the boy spoke with an intensity and an assurance the visitor had not anticipated — the assurance of an adult with the enthusiasm of a child or something very like it — in any case with a mixture of mystery and candor which encouraged confidences.

Was the newcomer suspicious of the blind man? But how in the world could a blind man be fishing in troubled waters? At any rate, if the visitor was still suspicious, he had eyes and had only to use them to observe. He might blush at his ease if emotion caught him, or make sudden movements with his head or his fingers, might twitch, draw back or smile. A blind man does not see these things.

While all this was going on, I was putting my every instinct to work. I had no system surely, and the idea of adopting one never occurred to me. I saw the only way to know my visitor was to test him out — in a vacuum to begin with. For the first ten minutes at least there must be no settled topic of conversation. After all, that in itself might well be a method.

I had scouted out a whole series of vague exchanges, vague or unexpected but without connection with my plans. Some of my visitors were irritated immediately by this hit-or-miss way of going at things. Anger being an emotion it is very hard to fake, and one which never rings true when it is simulated, I gained time with these people and came to know them right away.

But most of them were disconcerted, and rather uneasy. Then they tried, by every means possible, to get over it. They stammered out complicated explanations. And nothing is more revealing of any individual — as every psychologist knows well — than elaborate explanations. But in the end every one of these tactics amounted to very little. If I could plumb these hearts and consciences — and I felt sure I could — it was because I was blind and for no other reason.

When I was very young I had acquired the habit of guessing since I could no longer see, reading signs instead of gestures, and putting them together to build a coherent world around me. What is more, I admit I was madly happy to be doing this work, to have men in front of me, to make them speak out about themselves, to induce them to say things they were not in the habit of saying because these things were set too deep in them — suddenly to hear in their voices the note above all others, the note of confidence. This filled me with an assurance which was very like love. Around me it drew a magic circle of protection, a sign that nothing bad could happen to me. The light which shone in my head was so bright and so strong that it was like joy distilled. Somehow I became invulnerable.

Then too I became infallible, or nearly. And my comrades in the Central Committee and all the rest in the Movement knew it.

They told me so, some of them embarrassed and half ironical as they said it, the others, like François or Georges, with the conviction of faith.

As each day went by, some of us had to get used to some strange phenomena. Since we had been in the Resistance our mental powers had grown stronger. Our memories were unbelievably agile. We read between the words and the silences. Deeds which only two months before seemed impossible to us, putting walls or phantoms in our path, were now broken down into a dust of easy little tasks.

Georges was right when he called our state "the state of grace." As far as I was concerned, I was aware that my conscience was in touch with the conscience of hundreds of others, growing in rhythm with their sufferings or their hopes.

These reinforcements came with every day. I was surprised to find I knew things they had not told me, surprised when I awoke in the morning feeling a sense of purpose strong and entirely new to me — one which I found out was shared, three hours later, by two or even ten of the comrades. The spirit of the Resistance was born, and was using me as its instrument. Yet who could have said what it was, the spirit of the Resistance? Among the Volunteers of Liberty it had twenty faces.

For example, Georges was a nationalist — I mean a patriot and a jingo, to the point where if he wanted to sing the "Marseillaise," he could never get to the end of it. It made him weep like a little girl. How we teased him!

So, if he was making resistance, and he was making it like a lion, it was to save France. Germany could die the death, and England and the five continents along with her! I had undertaken to convert him to a world freed from national fanaticism, but this conversion took me more than three years, and it was never really completed.

Claude and Raymond were the philosophers. They thought France was only one among the circle of democracies, and that it was democracy itself that must be defended, deserving every expenditure of courage.

Others, like François and Jean, and before long the majority, put their reasons for fighting less clearly, but knew them better. The words mattered as little to them as to me. They were fighting for honor, liberty, the ideal, the right to live, purity, Christianity, respect.... Quite simply they could no longer stand civilians being bombed and starved, lying in public in accordance with the law, looting in the name of friendship and practicing police tyranny in the name of protection.

Above all, we did not want people to go on treating a monster — or even a man, Adolf Hitler — as if he were a god. "God is neither a German nor a Russian nor a Frenchman," I kept saying to Georges. "God is life, and everything that does violence to life is against God."

We did not want them to torture prisoners because they were prisoners, or kill Jews because they were Jews. But the Nazis were torturing and killing everywhere.

Since the morning of June 22 and the German invasion of Soviet Russia — how right our history teacher had been — they had been scorching the earth in Galicia, White Russia and the Ukraine, field by field and house after house.

On August 23 we got the news that they had shot two Frenchmen that day, Gabriel Péri, one of the Communist leaders, and D'Estienne D'Orves, a conservative Catholic officer, both of them heroes. This double death was official. London had confirmed it.

But what was less known — though known to us — was that the eighty-seven members of a Resistance network had been arrested ten days before. There were several distinguished anthropologists and ethnologists among them. They were men and women who had thrown themselves into the fighting through idealism just as we had. They had published two underground papers, *La France Continue* and *Résistance*, and we had been receiving these papers in bundles of a thousand copies. The members of the Movement had then passed them around. We learned that several of these men had already been beheaded at the Fresnes, the Santé and the Cherche-Midi, the three largest prisons in Paris, and that the others had been moved toward Germany, toward the fortresses and concentration camps and a slower death.

Everyone was becoming more frightened, we saw that too. German victories in Russia were crushing as the summer went on. London was being bombed. America did not move. Perhaps our resistance was without hope.

All this gave François a new lease on life. He would shake me and say, "What a ball! Just think! What a celebration if after all this there is not a chance! They are just ghosts, the ones who think people fight to win! They fight because they like it."

Surely we were happy to fight, even on such a modest scale. In my own efforts I was throwing sparks. I passed the second *bachot* like picking a flower, with the mark "very good." It was so much less difficult than the Resistance! And now I was about to enter the University.

It was at this point that Gérard, my friend who was held hostage because his father was in London, was set free for no reason we could see. He rushed off to my house and talked for five hours. When he left he had joined the Movement.

Yet he was one who knew the score better than anybody else.

He had seen men coming back mutilated after questioning by the Gestapo. He had heard and seen that they were killing every day. But that didn't stop him, on the contrary. Besides, none of my friends were hesitating any longer. To tell the truth, many of them were burning to die. Death at twenty is still possible, so much more so than it is later on. All of us had plunged into courage. It was our element. We were swimming in it and had no eyes left but for the shore.

11

THE BROTHERHOOD
OF RESISTANCE

THERE WAS NO LONGER ANYONE over me, and the loneliness of command was beginning to cost me dear. I had told my parents about the kind of activity I was involved in. They had courageously silenced their fears. They had given me their full support, but we were agreed that from now on I should not tell them anything. What good would it do to multiply the risks? They were putting their apartment at our disposal, and that already was dangerous enough.

Even in the Central Committee I found no one to advise me. When we were in trouble we were in it together. All of us were apprentices, but what I needed at all costs was a chief. The man who has no admiration or respect for anyone but himself is in a bad way. His soul is sick. I had to find someone I could confide in, someone who would vouch for me. And this had to be an exceptional person because what we were doing was quite out of the way. One day Jean, who felt the need as much as I did, took me to see our history teacher.

This man was superlative. He listened to what we had to say, approved, but interrupted us very soon. "Now I know quite enough," he said to us. "Keep the rest to yourselves. You have my full confidence. Come back and see me once a week. Each time you come I will give you two hours. Bring me your troubles. They concern me deeply. In return, whenever I can I will help you." That was all I needed. With this support, this confidence behind me, I was ready to meet the dangers, even the disasters if they came.

Jean, for his part, had a hard time adapting himself to our new life. Suspicion he regarded as shocking. It was not that he was short of courage. With him it was a question of decency. Like the rest of us from here on he had to suspect people, assume they were hiding their plans or lying, on occasion he even might have to lie himself to be sure they were telling him the truth. But to beat around the bush, to besmirch the heart! The idea made poor Jean tremble with disgust. He could never have believed that the pursuit of the ideal was such a jumbled business.

His greatest joy had always been in giving himself, right away, to the people he liked, and then never drawing back. The boy was as transparent as glass. And how can glass make itself cloudy? To me he used to say, "I shall never be a good soldier of the Resistance. It is only through you that I shall be able to be in it. Send me wherever you want to. If I go there in your place don't be afraid. I will go. But remember, if I were all alone, I should do nothing for I should not have the strength."

At this point, Jean began to travel all over Paris on errands which I entrusted to him. Since he had enemies and knew it, but could not think about them because he found it too painful, he went straight ahead, with the stiff gait of his long legs, and never looked around. He was not careful. "Caution disgusts me," he used to say, "it is so stupid."

François and Georges, on the other hand, were in their element. The more they had to conceal, the more intelligent they grew. François particularly had adopted the manners of the gentlemen's gentleman in a comedy. He no longer went into bourgeois apartment houses except by the back stairs, in order to avoid putting the concierge on her guard. To look less like a student he dressed like a workman. He was so much in the habit of looking around that even when we were alone in my room he kept turning his head. None of this affected his health. I should say not. He had a job to do, and he was doing it well.

He had turned himself into a secret agent, full-time. To do more for the Movement, to work for it day and night, he had stopped his studies. He lived in a garret, at the top of a dark house, in a maid's room which could be reached over the rooftops to make escape easier when it was needed. Collections taken up in the Movement assured him of the thousand francs a month which kept him from starving.

For two years he lived like this, getting thinner and thinner, more and more agile, and always happier. There was an electric quality in the tone of his voice. It seemed to say that he could have made heroes out of cowards. "All this comes from my Polish ancestors," he said; "they have been persecuting us for five centuries."

Even Jean could not blink away the fact that we had enemies. Our activities were growing fast. Twice a week we put out a bulletin for communication and for information. The object was to keep our people clearheaded and always on their guard, and also to denounce Nazi atrocities as we heard about them. They were taking place all around us in great numbers.

Ours was still only a bulletin, not yet a real newspaper. Still, we had to have paper, and since the sale of paper was entirely controlled by the Army of Occupation, we had to steal it. Georges and François had organized the raid.

Later there was the business of the ink and the machines for mimeographing. Without accomplices we could get nothing. Yet each accomplice was a potential traitor. But when and where could the duplicating be done? This question the Central Committee addressed to me. They all seemed to think I was blessed with a special gift, the gift of somehow finding the answers. And in a surprising way they were right. For the very next day I had a visit from a doctor, a young psychiatrist a comrade had sent me because "he had some useful information."

Henri, the psychiatrist, had friends in the French police. From time to time he would be in a position to let us know, an hour or two ahead of time, about police blockades set up by German order. This information would be very valuable.

But it was not long before our conversation touched on his patients, the poor crazy women he was treating at Sainte-Anne, the psychiatric hospital. The solution to the problem of mimeographing had slipped out almost without the doctor's knowing it. Sainte-Anne had padded cells reserved for violent patients. As a rule not all of them were in use at the same time. One could serve as our workshop. Henri took the arrangements in charge. When I gave the news to the Central Committee, they accepted it as a matter of course. They were a bit too quick in forming the habit of miracles.

Though our bulletins were not very well written, they were potent to say the least. They circulated throughout the Movement, and we had even made up three teams to distribute them outside. François was in charge of the first, Georges of the second and Denis, a newcomer, of the third.

Denis, what a man he was! A good-natured lad of twenty,

blond as wheat, with innocent eyes, a pink and white complexion, something timorous, even entreating in his voice, hands hot and a skin as soft as a girl's; devout (he was often telling the beads of the rosary in his pocket); ready to laugh at anything but never doing it for fear of arousing the curiosity of others; and always so polite with us, with an old-fashioned, rather clumsy politeness, almost as though he regarded himself as a small child and us as old men weighed down with honors.

The distribution of the bulletin meant trips to apartment houses in Paris, copies slipped under doors, one boy on our team watching the exits to the building while the others flew from one floor to the next with their shoes in their hands. Traitors were coming closer. Nothing was to be gained by deluding ourselves. It was not the professionals we were afraid of. We knew they were not common and almost always maladroit. But there were still the unintentional ones, and they were the devil. Just try defending yourself against people who are crazed by fear.

Disagreeable as it might be, it was necessary to swallow the bitter pill. Half of Paris was made of people of this sort. Their intentions were not criminal. They would not have hurt a fly as the saying goes. But they were protecting their families, their money, their health, their position, their reputation in the apartment house. To them we were terrorists, and they did not hesitate to say so. They talked about it among themselves, on the doorstep and over the telephone. If only we had not had them to reckon with. But they were worse than the Gestapo. Like all frightened people they were flighty. They would gossip about us without reflecting. They would denounce us without giving it a second thought.

They did denounce us. In January 1942, a member of our Movement was arrested because his neighbor on the same floor used to say at the grocer's and the baker's that he had no idea what the printed matter was that the boy across the hall was carrying around, but that if he were his father he would put a stop to it because it was dangerous.

One day Georges said to me, "I must introduce you to Nivel. This character doesn't seem to be at all reliable." Like the others Georges had the idea that, being blind, I had greater faculties — tremendous ones — for seeing through people. He was going to have me meet Nivel, who for some time had been much "too well-behaved," too zealous, too knowing. Georges thought the accusation was probably ridiculous, but he wanted to get to the bottom of it.

So one evening he took me to a spot between the Place d'Italie and the Gare d'Austerlitz, to a vacant factory warehouse where, in the midst of piles of empty crates, scaled-off walls, coils of rusty wire and many drafts, the test took place.

This Nivel was not known to me, and I was not really relying on Georges's fears. But as soon as Nivel came in, bursting out with a greeting full of gaiety, the diagnosis came without groping for it: "Let this character go! Get away from him as fast as you can!"

The warmth of his voice, the well-turned phrases made up the face I saw first. But under it was another, perceptible almost immediately, now withdrawing and hiding, but then again in evidence in spite of all he could do. It gave the impression of something swollen, for there were lumps in the man's voice.

He chatted for half an hour. He may have thought we liked him. After he was gone, I told Georges he had been quite right to be suspicious. And then Georges told me that during the whole interview I had seemed far away.

It was true that I had gone down into the depths. Inside me there was a secret chamber, and when I had a notion to go there, everything at once became simple and clear. People, above all, found themselves washed clean of appearances. I could hear a threat in a soft word and fear in boastfulness. And, strange as it may seem, this place of brightness was nothing more than the inner space which had become familiar to me when I went blind at eight years old.

I never knew exactly what mishap my intuition had spared us. But some months later Nivel, the suspect, was seen among the special police of the Rassemblement National Populaire at a meeting for collaboration with Germany. He was wearing the badge of the party, and along with the others was shouting, "Heil Hitler."

THE TIME WAS SURELY BLESSED when I was only aware of my body as something that gave me pleasure. The fifteen-mile hike I took with Jean each Sunday was enough to wipe away the small physical discomforts that came from mental strain. At night we were dead tired. The next day, when we got up at five o'clock, it was as if it were the first day of the world.

The well of my strength never dried up. The later I stayed up, the better I slept. The more I learned, the more I was able to learn. My memory only knew how to say yes. It made room for everything, for the thousand and fifty Paris telephone numbers I needed for my work in the Resistance, and which I had learned by heart in 1942 to keep from writing anything down. It made room too for the system of monads according to Leibnitz, for Turkish history in the nineteenth century, even for those fifteen pages from the letters of Cicero in Latin. Whenever a new contingent of facts presented itself, my memory, instead of tightening up at their approach, expanded. It was much simpler that way.

My mind was a world in growth, one which had not found

its limits. And if my intelligence hung back a little at the effort, I could always turn to other worlds within myself, to the worlds of the heart and of hope. They immediately sent up a relay, and I kept running continually.

I had not yet acquired the hardness of a man, and was still as resilient as a child, a fact which accounts for my accomplishments between 1941 and 1943. When I think of them now at the midpoint of life with its weariness, I find it hard to understand them.

I had entered the University of Paris in the fall of 1941. I had chosen the field of literature, which fitted in with my ability and my tastes. At the end of these studies there shone the prospect of the only professions I could care for, the ones which would put me in direct touch with other men — the professions of diplomacy and teaching.

Nevertheless, I had not turned into a run-of-the-mill student. On the advice of my teachers I had gone into a special class which, I believe, exists only in France, the Upper First. In the country as a whole there were not more than a dozen such classes. They gathered in the brightest students of literature from the graduating classes in the lycées, same forty students to a class and all of them involved in a highly competitive game. The passion which others devoted to physical sports, we devoted to the sports of the mind. But how frantic they were!

At the end of two or three years of study, depending on the circumstances, the pupils of the Upper First went into the competition which opens the way — for the ones who are accepted and that is not easy — to the highest institution in the French educational system, the school of schools, the Ecole Normale Supérieure in the Rue d'Ulm.

The work to which we were subjected was intensive — a sort

of production line of knowledge — in any case not to be compared with the regular courses at the University. Thirty hours of class work a week, in which teachers chosen for their talent and learning were supposed to teach us all of Latin, Greek and French literature, philosophy, the history of the ancient world and world history from 1715 to the present day. Don't smile at these ambitions! In the Upper First, everyone was in earnest, both teachers and students.

I had to stand this hellish pace for two years, and to my great surprise I managed it successfully. But at the same time I had to work in the Resistance. Could I succeed in combining both tasks or could I not? I had made it a point of honor to set up a balance between my two lives, the public and the secret. My days oscillated between studies and action at a frightening pace. In the morning between four o'clock and seven, I walked through books two or three steps at a time. From eight to noon I listened to the teachers, took frenzied notes and tried to absorb knowledge as fast as it was given out. In the afternoon, from two to four, I was still in class. Then at four o'clock the Resistance began.

There were trips across Paris by routes set up in advance for greater safety, meetings, surveys, judgments, discussions, orders to be given, worries, putting the doubting ones back on the road, supervision of founding groups, calls for coolness to those who thought the Resistance was like a detective story, deliberation over the articles for the bulletin, sifting of news, time lost in the kind of summons which could be made neither by letter because of the censorship nor by telephone because of lines tapped. By this time it was already eleven o'clock at night, and I believe I only stopped because of the curfew.

Alone in my room at last, I immersed myself in my studies again, and kept on learning until my fingers grew stiff on the pages of Braille. Since my interest in life and my confidence in it were boundless, everything seemed to me as significant the tenth time I encountered it as it had the first. And that gave me an enthusiasm which enabled me to go through fatigue without feeling it, through food which was already very bad, even through cold.

Those winters of the Occupation were freezing. The good people said it was always like that in wartime, most of them claiming the winter was frigid because of the war, but others, more daring, saying that there was war because it was cold. In any case, in Paris there was nothing left to heat with. French coal was all going to Germany. In the evening just one stove was lighted at our house, and since I had to shut myself off in my quarters I got hardly any of the good of it. To be able to read Braille — the sense of touch does not function adequately below ten degrees Centigrade — I had to keep the meager heat of an electric bowl only an inch away from my fingers.

I repeat that none of this bothered me. For all the ones like François, like Georges, like Denis and for me, there was eternal spring. Even in the difficulties of living we found an exhilaration that gave us strength. Somehow difficulties only sharpened the edge and made us better able to cut through the barriers. We had our miseries, but they were different, and most pressing of all was the fact that we were the exceptional ones. This none of us could disregard.

We, the exceptional! But why, when we were convinced that we were doing the simplest thing, the "only thing to do"? Without a doubt. Yet there were not many of us. We had no illusions about the six hundred active members belonging to the Volunteers of Liberty in 1942. To keep six hundred boys we had had to turn down six thousand. And yet young people represented a picked group in society, the most disinterested and the most reckless. After two years of Occupation, the Northern Zone had yielded only a few handfuls of Resistance fighters. In the nature of the case they could never be counted. The optimists, like Henri, the psychiatrist, said there were some twenty thousand.

In the two Upper Firsts at Louis-le-Grand, the elite classes as they were called by the teachers who did not mind putting a point on it, out of ninety boys we had found only six, counting Jean and me, who had agreed to enlist in the Resistance. The others never even considered it, some because of moral laziness (Jean said, "I promise you they will never be happy in life"); others because of the disease that often goes with an overdeveloped intelligence, the inability to choose; others because of bourgeois selfishness, even at nineteen; still others because they had cold feet. Finally, and most painful of all, there were the ones who had chosen the other side.

To be sure there were not many of these. But the two or three in class, who patiently noted all the signs, being careful to write them down, who spread the rumor that the six of us were involved in the Resistance, who never missed a meeting of the Association France–Allemagne, who harped on the swift coming of Fascism all over the world; the ones who spied, informed, denounced — we should find this out one day to our cost — those two or three made us more unhappy, because they were what they were, than all the rigors of a bitter winter.

They symbolized the fact that Hitler could count cowardice without a country and without boundaries among his allies (for our part, we much preferred the Germans who were going out to be killed in Russia). They proved that Nazism was not a historical disaster confined to a single time and a single place, a German disaster: "Let us kill the Boches, and the world will be happy." They proved that Nazism was a germ to be found everywhere, a sickness endemic to the human race. It was enough to cast a few handfuls of fear to windward in order to gather in the next season's harvest of treason and torture.

As for the six of us in the Resistance in the Upper First, with each day we had a better idea of our reasons for being in it, and they were not limited to patriotism. For it was not just France that was threatened, it was man himself.

When we had a teacher of French literature who was "a collabo" — there was one — all six of us had to hold ourselves under a tight rein, and consult each other ten times over to keep from spitting his shame back into his face.

I shall not try to defend our cause to anyone who may still think we were too harsh and behaving like "real young lunatics." This kind of severity was a thing to take or leave. But have you ever known anyone to choose indulgence as a weapon in a fight?

ONE DAY WHEN FRANÇOIS ASKED ME what fault I found hardest to bear in other people, my answer shot out with the speed of a bullet — "Dullness." We laughed a lot because just at the moment when I was shouting my reply, he was shouting his and they were the same. There was no doubt that we were completely in tune with each other.

Dullness, mediocrity! Whether they were Catholics, Jews, Protestants, freethinkers or not thinkers at all, all the men of the Resistance shared the same credo. For them life was not made to be lived halfway.

This conviction was second nature to us. "It has reached the point where I have to hold on to myself," as Georges put it. "If some character says yes to me to be obliging and just to be let alone, I want to hit him." Society for me was divided into two parts, the Hard and the Soft. It was not cowards one found among the soft ones, and certainly not traitors, for traitors were almost always the hard ones who had gone wrong, but the formless race of the procrastinators, all the ones who approved of what we were doing and were careful not to be involved in it. These, of all times, were not times for meaning well.

The year 1942 was very black. Seen from the vantage point of Europe it seemed several times to be a complete loss. The German advance into Russia was deeper than anyone had predicted. Toward the end of the summer its force was broken in the suburbs of Stalingrad. But Stalingrad, as we saw it, was already past the heart of the U.S.S.R.

For the first time, the Germans were making some of their killings public. The names of Auschwitz and Bergen-Belsen had appeared in the bulletins of the Volunteers of Liberty. It was true that America had come into the war. Our history teacher had been a good prophet. But America was still far away and completely absorbed in the Pacific, in battles which we knew were terrible but still an unknown quantity.

At last, on November 8, the Allies had made a landing in North Africa. This was Europe's first piece of good news in two and a half years, but immediately afterwards the Germans had occupied the Southern Zone. The last scrap of French independence was gone, and as a result it became necessary to organize the Resistance not just from Nantes to Paris and from Paris to Lille, but from Lille to Marseilles and all over the country. Those of us who hated dullness were suddenly faced with acrobatic feats. May God forgive us, but we were almost at the point of rejoicing in the misfortunes of France.

Since in those days I was being nourished at the springs of universal wisdom, I began to have scruples, saying to myself, "I am too positive." The philosophers never stopped saying it, saying that everything in this world is tempered with good and evil; there are always at least two faces to truth. What another man does which seems to us a crime is often only the result of a first mistake, a mistake so small and so hard to detect that we too may be making it from one minute to the next. This was the kind of sermon that some of my friends had been preaching to themselves for some time past.

At the end of December Georges, who didn't read the philosophers because they gave him a headache, said to me, "You are falling by the way, my boy. Throw all your brainy schemes to the winds, they are nothing but nightmares. The Movement is stagnating. For three months our number has stayed at six hundred. We are still just passing out the bulletin. Don't you see that this damnable war is moving at a faster clip than we are?"

I did see it, and it disturbed me. But what we needed was new ventures, and I didn't know how to go about them. Fortunately Georges had an idea. He said there was only one way to set me on fire — girls.

I balked, knowing this side of Georges very well, his night side. He was three years older than I was, and having enlisted in 1939 had been thrown into the life of the barracks at the age of eighteen, and had a coarse idea of love. "Have fun while there is still time," he would say. "Later, we'll be starting a family."

I had some real battles with François about Georges. In this respect as in every other, François was angelic, but that didn't keep him from understanding Georges. "Whatever road men take to their source of strength, so long as they reach it, I bless them for it." Here perhaps was another occasion for compromise. Moral purity was not necessarily bound up with the purity of the body. As Georges liked to say, "Real soldiers have always been real rakes."

So they undertook to cure me. The treatment was not what you might expect. Georges respected me too much to take me to disreputable places. It never even entered his head. But one day, since I couldn't resist the temptation to talk to him about Aliette, he made it plain, without openly making fun of me, that I was a rare kind of fool. Loving a girl who had never given you anything but smiles — and even that only in passing because it made her more beautiful — loving her without knowing if she returned it, and still loving her after two years of separation, without ever having been tempted to put another girl in her place, this kind of stubbornness seemed to Georges not just ridiculous but downright dangerous. It represented an unbelievable lack of realism, and was quite enough to account for the sluggishness of my ideas.

So, for weeks on end I was dragged from one party to the next. These gaieties far outshone the modest dances in the family circle that I had been frequenting for two years. It was hard for me to understand how Georges could have so many friends and such frivolous ones without my knowing anything about it. Because hard liquor was scarce in occupied Paris, we were drinking a brand of sparkling wine that made us tipsy, but slowly.

Most of the girls had nothing in their heads. That didn't seem to bother anybody and I got used to it too. I did my best to overcome my shyness, and most of all the notion, quite new to me, that my blindness kept me from attracting people. As a matter of fact, I was as successful at this as the others — once I put aside my seriousness which was absolutely no help. It was enough to talk nonsense, if you did it in a certain way, to pretend you were at a show and that nothing really mattered. All you had to do was drink, get worked up over unimportant feelings, and keep dancing. You got your reward right away. Girls were a strange breed. They managed to breathe life into your body and even into your mind.

It was not that they were beautiful, at least not to me. My companions would whisper, "Dance with Henriette. My boy, she is divine." But not to me. Being brittle and selfish, how could she be beautiful? She had such a way of belittling everything, and of sharpening her claws under the caresses of her smooth hands, that I wanted to run away. I turned to the girls who were not so pretty but who, at least, seemed capable of love.

Never mind if my sense of beauty was not just like the others'. One thing we had in common, the sense of intoxication. Putting your hand on a girl's hip, following the budding curve of her arm, embracing her shoulder, diving, with empty head, into the many-colored brightness that comes from a girl's body, hearing the rustle of a skirt or a handkerchief, not wanting to stop dancing, because so long as the girl is close, with her hair against yours at each step, the world can go to pieces without your caring. All these things were making me well as Georges had said they would.

It was at this point, as we were leaving a dance in the front hall of a rich house in the suburbs, that a new idea suddenly came to me — it had to do with those Allied airmen shot down every day by German fighters. I had been told a hundred times that most of them survived thanks to their parachutes. If they fell in German territory they were lost, with only one chance in a thousand. But what if they fell in France? They were lost just the same (most of them didn't know a word of French), lost unless people like us took them in charge.

By now we had our cells in Normandy, in Brittany, in the Nord and in Franche-Comté, and I was about to notify the provincial sections of our Movement to be on the lookout for fallen airmen, and to send them on to us in Paris. The rescued pilot, dressed in civilian clothes, must be accompanied by a member of the Movement. Our man was not to move an inch away from him. A fine plan, but what to do with the flyers once they were in Paris? How to send them on to the Spanish border and get them across?

When I submitted my bright, impossible idea to Georges, he burst out laughing. He knew the answer. Running a small risk would do the trick. For the last six months he had been in touch with a man named Robert — a settled person, forty years old, married, a Catholic — Robert had never said exactly what he did. But by all kinds of signs Georges was convinced that he was doing just what we had in mind. The two of us would go to see him and offer him the services of the Movement.

As a matter of fact, Robert had been repatriating Allied airmen for two years. He had set up an amazing system of camouflage in Paris and the surrounding country. His network had about fifty accomplices on the Spanish border, on the Catalonian side and in the Pays Basque. They were mountaineers and customs men. Only one thing was missing, at least in part: groups of men in the provinces, men who were brave and fast, and capable of getting information in the country without giving the show away. We were all he needed, and now we were available.

Once more ideas were in ferment. After the airmen came the turn of the false papers. In Paris, where the number of professional fighters was growing every day — besides François, we already had five others in the Movement — the business of false identity became urgent. You could no longer eat without food stamps. Everything, including bread and potatoes, was rationed, and in the town halls tickets were given out only to people whose papers were in order. Besides, what a terrible risk for the families, if one of them, the one in the Resistance, should be arrested under his own name. The Volunteers of Liberty would have to see to the making of false papers.

None of us was deluded into thinking this would be easy. My first order of this sort I sent on to the groups in Arras and Lille. In May and June, in the north of France in 1940, many villages had been bombed or totally destroyed. The papers in the town halls had disappeared, but the people had vanished along with them. We could find out their names by questioning the inhabitants carefully. Our first false cards of identity would be made out in the names of men who could not be found and were believed dead.

In January 1943, we were on the brink of great things, but we were a long way from guessing that in a short time we should be walking into history by the front door.

Jacques Lusseyran (center) at age eight in 1932. The boy to his right in white is his younger brother, Pascal.

Lusseyran at age nine, in 1933.

Lusseyran's class at Lycée Louis Grand in 1941. Lusseyran, age 17, is the fourth from the right in the front row. His dear friend Jean Besnié is the fourth from the left in the second row, with glasses and a white handkerchief.

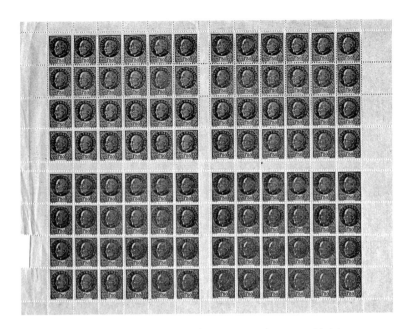

Fabricated stamps used by the Resistance for all correspondence to avoid giving money to the Vichy government.

Lusseyran (left) and a radio journalist in 1953.

Lusseyran in 1953.

Jacqueline Pardon, a fellow member of Défense de la France, in 1943. Pardon was Lusseyran's first wife. They were married from 1945 to 1954.

Author and philosopher Albert Camus (left), Lusseyran, and Jacqueline Pardon, Lusseyran's first wife, in 1953.

Lusseyran in 1963, the year And There Was Light was first published in the United States.

Lusseyran in 1968.

Lusseyran in 1971, the year he died in a car accident in France. At the time, he was a professor of French literature at the University of Hawaii, Honolulu.

[12]

OUR OWN DEFENSE OF FRANCE

L IKE EVERYTHING ELSE IN LIFE that matters, it came about
not at all as expected but much faster and more simply. It happened through a young officer in the tank corps whom I was about
to receive at Georges's request. But within five minutes the man in
front of me was no longer an officer. He was a philosopher, a con-
spirator, a big brother, and my chief, Philippe.

Let me explain. It had taken only a month to tie up the threads
of Robert's network and our Movement. Four RAF flyers had
already been brought into Paris by our people, two from the hills
around Dijon, one from near Reims, the fourth from the suburbs
of Amiens.

At the Gare du Nord, the Gare de l'Est and the Gare de Lyon,
Georges and Denis were the ones who had taken them in charge.
Quite rightly they were the only ones who knew where Robert's
hiding place was. We had never had any serious doubts about this
man, but on this occasion we revered him. Picture a face that was

always full of fun, a traveling salesman with the gift of gab, but one who also had the gift of meditation. All of a sudden Robert would stop making jokes and retreat into himself. What was he doing there? Praying I feel sure, building up his reserves of courage. And he needed plenty every minute of the time. Of all the men in France he was one of the most exposed.

He knew very well what would become of him if this Donald Simpson or John Smith, RAF pilots, turned out to be German spies. It had happened in some of the networks near us. Then it was not one man who would die, himself, Robert the chief, but thirty or fifty of them, and after what kind of interrogation!

He was even able to joke about it and without ever abandoning his humility. He was so modest he never spoke of himself in the first person. He would screw up his eyes and say, "The network wonders whether...The network has decided that..." The man was a missionary, indulgent to the faults of others, without pity for his own, fighting his way into Nazi territory as though it were the land of the heathen.

But Robert did not want us to help him too much. He believed our work should be completely divided from his. And finally he insisted that we should not continue to meet. "I smell fire," he said, "and if I am going to be blown up, I prefer to be blown up without you."

But in his final meeting with Georges he had made us a gift of a name — Philippe, an officer in the war of 1939–1940, twenty-six years old. And he had added, "I can't do better"; that was always his last word, whatever else he might have said.

On January 31 at about ten o'clock in the morning, Paris was shivering in the cold though the sun was shining — that is just how clearly details can be imprinted on the memory — Georges and I were waiting for Philippe. I must admit we had no high hopes of this event. For all Robert's blessing, we were on guard, with every hair bristling. "Please," Georges said to me, "if this individual doesn't please you, give me some kind of a sign to keep my mouth shut. For officers I have a weakness. And if he is an officer in the regular army, I am likely to lose my bearings."

It was not a professional officer who came through the door, but a great hulk of a man. Over six feet tall, broad in the chest, with strong arms and powerful hands, a quick and heavy step, the sense of brotherly protectiveness emanated from his person. Besides, he had a voice which was warm though not very resonant, a voice which came close to you immediately, which got right inside you because it was so convincing.

I am describing him badly. This was not a man I saw approaching, but a force. There was no need to tell you he was a leader. He could handle himself any way he wanted to, sprawl in every armchair in the room, pull up his trousers and scratch his leg, be unintelligible because of a sputtering pipe that got in the way of his speech, run his hands through his hair, ask tactless questions and contradict himself. In the first ten minutes of our meeting he had done all these things many times, but somehow you didn't mind them.

His coming placed a mantle of authority upon your shoulders. The well-being you felt in its enveloping folds was something you could not contain. His authority was not false and certainly not calculated. Instead, it was like the spell cast by some women as soon as they come near you. You were seduced, you were almost paralyzed, at least to begin with. For the first half hour, Georges and I would have been physically incapable of voicing the least objection.

I looked at this casual, tempestuous devil in front of me, and wondered what kind of monster we had drawn from his lair. But it was no good my calling on all the presence of mind and all the distrust I had left, I could not manage to be disturbed. They say that strength enchants. The magnetism of this man was his strength.

He seemed to have endless mines of energy. He exuded feeling, purpose and ideas. Here was a real phenomenon. Shaking his mane of hair, stretching his arms as though he were lazy, then suddenly coming to attention, he was at once great and good, gentle, talkative and secretive, precise as a watchmaker and vague as an absentminded professor. Confidences and meaningless generalizations were all mixed up in his talk.

Since he started in an hour before, we had learned that he was married and in love with his wife, that his wife was expecting a child and that he adored the child even before it was born. In the same breath he had spoken several times of Saint Augustine, Empedocles, Bergson, Pascal, Marshal Pétain, Louis XVI and Clémenceau. I can vouch for this, for I heard it with my own ears. I couldn't tell you what part they played in the conversation, but all the same they were in it. As I said, Philippe was phenomenal.

In an hour he had expressed what most people would never tell you in a lifetime. As you listened, it seemed as if nothing remained that would be hard to do, even in the Paris of January 1943. He tossed solutions at insoluble problems right on the spot. He took them by the hair of the head, shook them in front of his great face, looked them straight in the eye, and laughed out loud. When they got this kind of treatment, the insoluble problems just didn't come back.

Besides, Philippe had a good way of putting it: "In some circumstances nothing is easier than being a hero. It is even too easy, which poses a frightful moral problem." And then he began quoting Saint Augustine, Pascal and Saint Francis Xavier all over again.

As you may have guessed I was dumbfounded; in other words I was happy. This was not the happiness of love, but for all that it was happiness: mine and Georges's (though he had not opened his mouth I knew he was as captivated as I), and last of all the happiness of Philippe. Already he seemed to know us well though he had hardly heard us speak. He confided in us fully, told us how much good we were doing him, carried us along on his saddle and never stopped talking,

He said he was glad to be in the Resistance as we were and along with us. To him this last point was a mere detail, and he had already settled it. I may have given you the false impression that Philippe was flighty, or that Georges and I were, in following him at such a pace. Nothing could have been further from the truth. In those days when every meeting was a matter of life and death, relations between people were clearer than they are today. Either one was on guard or one gave oneself. There was no third choice, and one had to choose quickly. Let us say further that Philippe had laid his whole hand before us. "I am going all out," he said. "If it doesn't work, you won't be seeing me again."

He had known Robert for three years, and Robert had vouched for him. Just before the war he had been a student in the Upper First like me. We had had the same teachers and friends in common. In the end, he had decided not to ask us our secrets but to tell us his.

He had organized a Resistance movement at exactly the same time as I had organized the Volunteers of Liberty, in the spring of 1941. His was called Défense de la France. He had an underground newspaper with a circulation of ten thousand a month, not mimeographed but printed, the genuine article. Georges and I were familiar with it. Our Movement had distributed some of the issues.

Défense de la France had a print shop manned by amateurs turned professional. It had presses, paper, arms and machine guns, ten underground branches in Paris, one with cork-lined walls for the noisy work, several small trucks disguised as delivery wagons, a factory for counterfeit papers which could produce twenty-five hundred "absolutely genuine" fake cards a month, an organized editorial board for the paper, a radio transmitter which though improvised was able to function, an open channel to General de Gaulle's government in London, dependable supporters among the peasants of Seine et Oise, south and north, thirty miles from Paris — and others in Burgundy in case escape from the capital should be necessary — and fifty agents with two years' experience, "dependable," according to Philippe, as he was himself. Fifteen of them were already working full-time in the underground.

For us Volunteers of Liberty who were vegetating, not ingloriously, but without making any further progress, a new world was opening, a world of the immediate and the real. Already our usefulness was making itself felt, for Défense de la France, which had all the things we lacked, lacked what we had, a general staff, a commissariat and a corps of engineers but no troops. We were an army with generals — Georges, François, Denis and I — who had never had time to complete their training.

Without further precautions I turned to Georges, looked at him hard and heard him say under his breath, "Go ahead." Then, to Philippe, I said that plans for our working together in the Resistance had become clear.

As a founder of the Volunteers of Liberty I was going to exercise my rights. I was going to ask all my people to join Défense de la France, and within a week I should know about all the ones who might refuse to follow me out of fear or confusion. With them I would break off, whatever the cost.

The industrial resources of Défense de la France made it possible to increase the run of its newspaper and multiply its circulation ten times over in a few weeks. Georges and I gave our word to do this, and Philippe gave his. To carry it out we needed only to supply the human material to correspond with the machines. Our six hundred boys made up the material.

Perhaps we had not succeeded in making them accomplish great things in the last two years, but we had sharpened their morale to a razor edge. We had them in hand, and could answer for them as for ourselves.

Barely two hours had gone by since the officer-philosopher had taken possession. With us he exchanged a complicated system of drop-offs, mailboxes and hidden communications. He gave us the wartime names of five or six of his agents, three girls among them. I was astonished, as I had never dreamed that women could be in the Resistance. But it wouldn't be long before I found out how wrong I was.

Philippe took his leave, but we should be seeing him nearly every day for the next six months. Georges and I had hardly enough strength left to speak or comment on what had happened. We were filled with contentment and with a conviction which could not be described in words. We were moving toward the unknown, toward a fate that was sure to be victorious and as certain to be terrible.

THE NEXT SIX MONTHS were a battle, of a special kind but without interruption. Only the facts concern us here, and I will report them without comment. Less than a week after our first interview, Philippe asked me to meet him in the back room of a small restaurant. My house, with all the going and coming of the past year and a half, was too easy a mark for informers.

I had the right to run the risk but he didn't. He couldn't come there anymore. He told me that the Executive Committee of Défense de la France was inviting me to join it. Georges was taken in at the same time, as my inseparable partner, my double. I was to go to the meetings with Georges, and never with anyone else. Besides, the principle had to be established that for all the important moves from now on Georges would be the only one to accompany me. "For your security and ours we need someone with eyes in the back of his head, and the reflexes of a wild creature. Georges is our man."

At the very first meeting of the Executive Committee which I attended I understood that every dimension of the task was altered. I saw that we were acting for the country as a whole, and officially, for all we were underground. Philippe was there, two other young men between twenty-five and thirty, a young woman and a girl. They were the ones who held the reins of the Movement. They held them soberly, and each held his own, without telling the others about it.

Since each member of the Executive Committee had the right to sit on the editorial board of the paper, I took part in this work also. My new friends said our presence was justified by their hope that we could carry out our promise to set up a system for distributing the paper, and one which could be worked out in six months. The resources of Défense de la France were entirely at our disposition, but we alone were charged with the job.

The night before, at the Central Committee of the Volunteers of Liberty, I had signed the marriage contract between my old Movement and Défense de la France, or as we now called it DF. I had counted on some opposition from Claude and Raymond, my two philosophers. I knew them to be nobly entangled in arguments and hesitations, and as it turned out they did not fall in with the decision made so abruptly. It brought us a loss of some thirty members, who were their followers. But the merger of all the rest with DF was an accomplished fact.

I turned in some figures to the Executive Committee of DF which surprised everyone except Georges and me. Could they print twenty thousand instead of ten thousand copies of the next number of the paper by the middle of February? If, as we believed, the teams for distribution which we were offering to DF — and they were already organized — could absorb the first shock, we would ask that the issue of March 1 be thirty thousand, increasing after that at the pace of ten thousand per issue, until our forces were stretched to their limit. I had no way of judging this limit, but I felt sure it was far off. I knew our six hundred boys, their discipline and their impatience. The Executive Committee made me responsible for distribution of the paper all over France.

It was then, for the first time, that my blindness was mentioned. The Committee believed that its effects were only physical. Someone was needed to watch over every one of my actions in the Resistance, and warn me of all the dangers that only eyes can see. This same person would have to carry out my decisions or any move I made, from the point where they required the use of eyes. Georges said quite simply: "That will be me." A perfect pairing, for Georges could do all the things I couldn't and vice versa. From this moment — to be truthful — I should no longer say "I" but "we."

Our principal weapon was a newspaper. *Défense de la France* was a real paper, poor, covering only two pages — we had to wait four months to grow to four — but printed. Besides, our four opposite numbers in the underground press, *Résistance, Combat, Libération,*

Franc-Tireur, were not doing any better. Each was doing the same thing on its own. Their papers passed through our hands regularly, but we had no channels which allowed us to go to the source. That was the special curse of the fight in the underground. It had to be carried on in units that were hermetically sealed. The risks being what they were, no kind of overall organization was conceivable or even desirable. If one of the papers was captured, the others must, at all costs, remain unknown.

In 1943 a real paper was a precious thing. Every line of print was drawn from so much courage and so much skill. Every line of print held within it the possible death of all those who had written or composed it, put it through the press, carried it, distributed it and commented on it. There was blood at the bottom of each page, and not just in a manner of speaking.

The name *Défense de la France* bore witness to the will to patriotism, and that we certainly had. Still, our paper was far from being nationalistic. If we were defending France, that was because she was being attacked, above all because she was being threatened — we repeated this in every issue — with a fate worse than the death of the body, the death of the spirit. The paper's chief task was the awakening of conscience.

We had several ways of bringing about this awakening. The first, as always, was news. In February 1943, for instance, we said what no one in Europe was saying at the time, specifically that the Nazi army had just fallen into a trap at Stalingrad, and that the future course of the war was about to be reversed in the ruins of that city. Then too we told the French people about the terrible things of which we had proof in mounting numbers every day. If it hadn't been for us they might have suspected them, but they could not have known them. We told how the Gestapo's arrests were carried out and where, and what happened in their interrogations. We exposed the existence of political prisons and concentration camps in Germany, and the most incredible fact of all, the systematic extermination of the Jews across Europe.

We advised the population about ways of spreading passive resistance. Most of all we made it clear that there was an active Resistance at work, and one that was growing from day to day. It was invisible to our readers and must remain so. The only sign it could give at this stage was our two-page printed sheet.

To the public we suggested ways for them to help us, when and how to keep silent, what news to credit and what attitudes to maintain. Our goal was to keep France from abdicating, to see to it that she was present and intact when she was liberated.

Ours was not a political paper. Not one of us at *Défense de la France* had any commitment to a doctrine. We were too young for that, and other things were more pressing. We placed our trust in the ideal of Western democracy as embodied then, in forms that differed but were of equal merit in our eyes, by Charles de Gaulle, Winston Churchill and Franklin Roosevelt. To perfect democracy would be the task of the peace. We had no partisan cause, no material interest to defend. We were poor and full of ardor.

The only belief shared by all the members of *Défense de la France* was the survival of Christian values. Ours was frankly a Christian paper. But let us be clear on this point. We were not protecting any one church at the expense of the others. There were many Catholics among us and very devout. But there were also Protestants, equally sincere. We were not even speaking in the name of the churches, for some of our people did not belong to any. It was simply that we stood for Christian morality and its absolute demands for respect and love.

We signed all our articles with pen names of course. Philippe was "Indomitus," the unconquerable. We edited the paper from beginning to end, all ourselves. Paris at this point was not a town where you could telephone people to ask for their help. At whatever cost, we had to live in secret and sufficient to ourselves. Still, there were certain men who were known personally to some one of us. That was how, on several occasions, a Catholic bishop, Monseigneur Chevrot, and a member of the French Academy, Robert d'Harcourt, came to give us articles that they had written.

Every word was weighed by the editorial board of the paper, not for its literary value, as you may guess, but for its power to impress. Besides, in each case, we had to consider whether what we were saying was going to do good or harm, to safeguard lives or place them in jeopardy. When we had to publish our first article on the tortures administered by the Gestapo to arrested members of the Resistance, we had more than thirty concrete proofs in our hands. Still, should such horrors really be brought to light? We decided unanimously that they should. But the decision was made only after whole nights without sleep, and even at the last minute our fingers trembled.

It was the same way the first time we had a chance to publish a picture in the paper. It was a picture of a common grave, an open pit of bones on the edge of a concentration camp in Germany. It was authentic, for a prisoner heroic to the point of madness had stolen it from the archives of the Gestapo in Hamburg. But it is too soon to tell this story. Let us go back to February 1943.

THE FIRST WEEKS WERE A GAMBLE. We knew our comrades were prepared, but we had no idea they were prepared to this extent. We had to call for emergency measures at the Executive Committee, specifically for the printing of fifty thousand copies of the March 15 issue. Georges, in his turn, had become a professional operator, he was on hand at all hours. And that was not excessive, for the sections had to be reorganized from top to bottom.

For us there was no longer any question of recruiting from the ranks. This was much too risky and too fruitless. Our contact now was with the chiefs of the groups, and only a dozen of those at most. The group chiefs were people we had known for at least a year. They were entirely responsible for their sections, making all the decisions about admission or exclusion and without appeal. Of course, every group was to receive an alias and false papers to correspond.

In two months the number of people in charge of circulation grew from six hundred to about five thousand. The Paris region had to be divided into well-defined zones, five for Paris itself, seven for the suburbs. The work in the suburbs was easier, for there the police had not drawn such a tight net.

Provincial France posed a more difficult problem in communications because of the distances involved. For each region we needed a responsible person of the first quality, one who knew neither fear nor fatigue. It broke our hearts but we had to cut ourselves off from François. He alone could take care of Brittany, as the model province, the place where the percentage of Resistance fighters was highest at the earliest date. Champagne and Franche-Comté were turned over to Frédéric, the older brother of one of our first comrades. We had someone for the Nord, and someone else for the Touraine. But one of the key problems was not solved.

Since November the Southern Zone had been occupied by the Germans. Yet the myth was maintained, with the line of demarcation which cut France in two. Every mile of the border was patrolled night and day. Private cars and trains were searched, and young men were almost always arrested if they tried to cross over.

On February 16 a German order had started its ruinous work: all the young men over twenty-one were to be sent to Germany for forced labor. Only certain categories of students and heads of families would be reprieved. But this threat, put into practice promptly, gave us our wings instead of clipping them. At all costs prevent a single leader of the Movement from being taken off to Germany. All at once, nearly eighty boys became professional underground operators. Fortunately DF had the funds, and for once the extreme youth of our forces was a help, no doubt about that. Most of our members were not yet twenty-one.

At Lyon and Marseilles in the Southern Zone, DF had solid working cells. Our only problem was to open a channel of communication with them. It was imperative that the paper be distributed in the Southern Zone as it was in the North.

Unfortunately, there was no possibility of carrying twenty thousand copies of an underground paper in suitcases twice a month, with one of our band in charge. Obviously, every suitcase on the trains from Paris to Lyon or from Paris to Toulouse was not opened every day, but at least half of them were. And a Denis, a François, a Gérard, with their proud young look, would be natural suspects for the dullest Nazi. Finally, people who have never done this work can't imagine how much space is needed to carry twenty thousand newspapers.

It was at this point that we remembered the girls who were with us. They were our solution, and there was no other. Georges, whose crude ideas about women you already know, argued that we would never find a girl, still less a number of girls, who could do such heroic deeds. For them, especially if they cast themselves as ingenues or women of easy virtue, the risks would be much less than for us. But Georges thought they would still be far greater than anything we could expect of people "unless they were as mad as we were." Then Georges got a dressing down from the Chief — the only thing that could have brought him round. "You idiot," said Philippe, "you will learn something from women every day."

Catherine set out for Lyon, Simone for Bordeaux. They went just at a signal we gave them, without asking for any explanation. When they came back, we had a hard time getting them to tell us anything about it. Both of them said nothing had happened. They wanted to know when the next delivery would take place. The answer was, two weeks later of course.

The suitcases on their way to Lyon, Marseilles, Toulouse and Bordeaux were already loaded with an explosive which, as soon as it was discovered, would lead our friends straight to the firing squad. It was the simplest matter to add a few arms to the papers the next time around. The matter was hardly discussed at the Executive Committee. As for Simone and Catherine, they closed their eyes to it.

Toward the end of March there was an accident. One of the Paris shops where *DF* was being printed must have been under suspicion by the Gestapo. For three days, every time one of our comrades came out, he was followed. Of course there were techniques for shaking off such spies, and the boys in the print shops knew every trick of the game: how to enter a familiar bakery by the street door, leaving it by the service entrance on the next street; how to climb aboard a subway train and then, at the first station, just when the automatic doors were closing, hurl oneself out onto the empty platform, take one's shoes in one's hand and run away silently through the night. But this time every device had been blocked, because they followed us right from the door of the print shop, and that called for a move out in less than twelve hours.

At the very least this emergency involved three steps: finding a new shop, finding a vehicle to carry the machines away, and managing it without being seen. The last point was simpler than you might think. Since the informers were ambushed on the job and were limited in number, it was enough to find out that there were five of them, and then choose five of our comrades who would arrange to be followed at a given hour in five different directions without being caught. We had five men at the print shop, and they would do the job themselves since the informers were accustomed to them.

As soon as the spies had scattered on the false trails, five other comrades would roll the press and all the other equipment onto open lorries covered with tarpaulins which had conspicuous signs glued to them: *Fragile. Optical instruments. National Meteorological Observatory.* As for the shop, we were already holding one in reserve against bad times.

The operation succeeded, and immediately became legend in our large family. The moral Philippe drew from it was this: "Children, if we are still around to tell the tale, the day will come when we shall say that the Resistance was the easiest time in our lives. Just think of it! Not a single moral problem to cope with, only material ones!"

WE NO LONGER HAD ONE POLICE to cope with, but two. For some months now a corps of French spies and torturers had been working along with the Gestapo and its agents. Organized at Vichy, if not at the explicit order of the government, at least in the muddy waters around it, this Political Brigade had the task of covering the whole of France with its net, and killing the Resistance. The people in it were French Nazis, fanatics of the most aggressive kind, or more often just bums disguised as gentlemen, on the track of German bribes, altogether a treacherous and sadistic lot.

These bands were more dangerous to us than all the SS put together. We knew their tactics were to infiltrate the Resistance movements. My instinct for traitors was to be put to even greater tests. Still, in the Executive Committee of DF, we were not exactly elated. We knew our intuition was not infallible. "It is inevitable that we make mistakes," Philippe said, "each of us at least once. We must expect trouble."

In the first days of April, a scrawled message came to us, we could recognize Robert's signature: "Caught at the Gare du Nord with three birds. Pray for me," ran the message... "Three birds." It was all too clear — three airmen. We never expected to see Robert again in this world. A great man.... How had he managed to write the note and get it through to us? That was something else we should never know.

Less than a week later, four members of the Lyon group disappeared. They had gone together to a meeting place in the forest. They had not come back. In May the family of one of them had a telephone call from the Brigade Politique, telling them that their son, brother and husband, refusing to confess his crimes, had been killed.

As the size of DF grew from one day to the next, the risks of being caught mounted at the same pace. We used to call it a biological phenomenon. No way of escaping it, it was the law for us and all organizations like ours.

On April 15 we were delegated by the Executive Committee to set up communications with the Movement called "Résistance" — which had lost its head as you may remember in August 1941, but

had later come to life again — and with the Movement "Combat."
The government of Free France, established by now in Algiers,
was asking the Resistance organizations to coordinate their activities as much as they could.

No doubt the order was justified, but the job to be done was
almost superhuman. Each movement in itself was a pyramid in pre-
carious balance. If you pulled out one stone, the whole structure
threatened to fall in ruins.

Combat, started in the Southern Zone, published a newspaper,
like DF. So did Résistance in the Northern Zone, and also Franc
Tireur. Besides the underground press, there were activist groups
of the Secret Army, usually under the command of professional
officers, which were building stores of arms and ammunition, and
laying the cornerstone of the first Maquis. The networks of information and repatriation of flyers were in between the two.

We were all working side by side, sometimes on the same sidewalk in Paris, without knowing it. The only channel to our neighbors in the Resistance was the government of Free France. Our
meetings with the people from Combat or the Secret Army would
be arranged from London or Algiers, and from there passed on to
us in code or over the radio.

In this way I came to have several meetings with the editor-
in-chief of the newspaper *Résistance*. I was struck by the identity
of their hopes and ours, and by the similarity of our difficulties.
It strengthened our morale immensely to learn that we were not
alone. At about the same time I was in touch with the delegates
of Combat. They did not tell me that a young man named Albert
Camus was working with them.

The Communist Party was a thorn in the flesh of the Resistance. We had all kinds of proof that the Communists were hard at
work. Several hundred thousand copies of *L'Humanité* were being

distributed underground. The Communists were way ahead of us in techniques of sabotage and terrorism. Only in Résistance, Combat and DF there were no Communists. The origin of all these movements was humanist, even Christian.

Furthermore, if the French Communists were resisting, it was not in defense of their country. They had proved the point by not opposing Nazism between the Russo-German Pact of August 1939 and the invasion of the U.S.S.R. by Hitler's armies in June 1941. For them the fight was strictly ideological and partisan. Should we try working with them? A grave question, raised in the Executive Committee, where it was decided to make contact as soon as possible, despite all the evidence. We were in touch in June, but our contacts were cool. It was clear that the Communists looked upon us as outsiders.

Each day now, twenty times a day, we had to face the likelihood of imminent arrest. Georges and I had built the entire system of our work in the expectation of this event. If one of us should be captured, the other must continue, taking all the reins into his hands within a few days. In this way we were setting the example for the whole Movement. From now on, all of us would be operating in units of two, with the partners interchangeable.

A hundred thousand copies of the May 15 issue had been printed. Mad as it might be, we were determined to distribute it. The number of workers in the provinces had grown so fast that we had had to give carte blanche to the regional heads. The complexity of local operations was such that something like the administration of a flourishing factory would have been needed to direct them from Paris. Yet the rule about committing nothing to paper was more rigorously observed than ever.

Particularly in the Nord, DF was on the crest of the wave, but our agents there were swamped. What we needed was a chief on the ground, and the kind of dependable friends who had covered a good piece of the road with us were all engaged elsewhere. So this time we had to make an exception. We had to confide the work to a new man, one we hardly knew. He had come to see us only recently. He was called Elio.

He was twenty-five, a medical student in Paris, with black hair and a handshake that was too heavy. He had been sent to Georges by a group leader in the College of Medicine, in itself the best recommendation. Only at the start he had made one mistake. He had appeared on his own at my apartment without being summoned.

At once all my senses were on the alert. Then something unusual took place. This man threw my mechanism out of gear; my inner needle kept oscillating, not settling either on the "yes" or the "no." Elio spoke in a low voice, too low. His voice was like his handshake. It lacked clarity and straightforwardness.

I had a long argument with Georges, who had been present at the interview. Did we have the right to trust this man? Georges hesitated, as I did too for the first time. Something like a black bar had slipped between Elio and me. I could see it distinctly, but I didn't know how to account for it.

Elio had been in the Resistance for a year. He was well informed and definite. He had undeniable influence over his fellow students in medicine. Besides, as a native of the Nord, he knew the industrial and mining country as though it were his own village. He volunteered to give up his studies on the spot and go to Lille the next day. He was really the perfect answer to our problem in that quarter. He seemed to radiate courage and wisdom from head to foot.

Still, because of our doubts, we couldn't make the decision on our own. Philippe himself and François, as he was passing through

Paris, would have to investigate Elio in their turn. The investigation over, Philippe grumbled that we had no right to be too cautious, and François thought we should give it a try. But I could see that none of the four of us felt the familiar and heartening satisfaction of finding the right man.

Elio took off for Lille and did extraordinary work there. Within a fortnight on the ground he had mastered the network. His reports were more detailed than all the others, adroit and discreet at the same time. I tried to convince myself that in future it would be better to beware of these manifestations of vision without eyes. There too, optical illusions were to be feared.

To transport the quantity of paper Elio was demanding for Saint-Quentin, Valenciennes and Lille, we had found the ideal carrier in Daniel, a blind man who had only recently lost his sight in the explosion of a grenade in 1940, and, like me, was entirely without vision. He was twenty-three years old, very strong and determined — a real bulldozer.

In other ways he was not at all like me, not having a head overburdened with thoughts. A coach in a lycée at the time of the accident, he was the outdoor type. Thanks to him I made the discovery that all kinds of people can be blind. He was not one to make guesses, and did not seem to be aware of human beings. But he had physical powers which filled the void magnificently. He went all over Paris by himself, regardless of conditions, traveled alone on the trains, made his way through police blockades with his suitcase in his hand, groping awkwardly with the end of his white cane. He was a real hero without knowing it.

In May, June and July things happened so fast that I can't describe them, only list them. Denis, our devout and easily blushing friend, had planned and directed a new method for circulating the paper. Now it was a question of making it a public instead of a private affair. Slipping copies of the paper under doors, passing them hand-to-hand to people one could trust was not enough. It was necessary to work in the light of day.

In Paris and around it, Denis organized teams for distribution in the open. He placed picked squads of men and women on the squares in front of the big churches in Paris, after High Mass on Sundays. The member of the squad forced himself on the faithful, waved front-page headlines before their eyes, slipped the papers into their pockets or their handbags. While this was going on, a cover guard watched all the approaches to the church. Denis got bolder and bolder. Our slim romantic friend was turning into a professional soldier, the kind of knight the Middle Ages must have produced in the age of chivalry.

Raids on the factories at Renault and Gnome-et-Rhône followed the raids at the churches. Danger was growing by leaps and bounds. But it was as if Denis had taken the cross. No one could stop him. He had organized the first workers' cells of DF, among the mechanics at Renault and the men working on the Métro.

And then came July 14. This date may be nothing more than a symbol, but it is the symbol of liberty, and in days of misery symbols are the bread of life. DF was determined to have its July 14, the first anniversary of the underground press.

The special issue of the paper, and the one just preceding it, had reached the two-hundred-and-fifty-thousand mark. We had kept the promise made in February, 250 percent of it. François came back from Nantes for the occasion, Frédéric from Belfort, and Elio from Lille. Even Georges left me for forty-eight hours. The shop where type was set and all the print shops had beaten their own records. The entire Executive Committee had been writing for the paper, and had set the wheels of the operation turning with its own hands. Finally, just to show that life never ceases, the night before the fourteenth Hélène had given Philippe a son.

Operation Denis, Operation July 14, would continue from morning until night on the Paris Métro. It all came true. Forty squads of ten members each passed out seventy thousand copies of the paper between eight in the morning and five o'clock in the afternoon on the subway cars, publicly, calmly, from one passenger to the next, and smiling as though it were the most natural thing in the world. Soldiers and officers of the German army, not to mention spies in plain clothes who could not be identified, turned astonished eyes on the object that had just been handed to them.

Reports crowded in that night at the Executive Committee: not one paper left in a corner in a hurry, not one squad broken up, not a single arrest. It was a perfect performance. We had given public opinion the shock it needed so badly — the proof that the Resistance was there and could strike.

All the same, the thing that made Denis proudest was that no one had used his tear gas pens. Recently we had had to arm our squads, and London had dropped in whole cases of these pens. There was nothing about the little objects to distinguish them from the usual instrument by the same name, nothing but a safety catch which, when pressed, released enough tear gas to put an enemy out of operation for three or four minutes. Though he knew it was impossible, Denis's great dream had always been to make war without killing or wounding.

STILL, ALL THIS TIME I was a student, and perhaps you should be reminded of it. Since the passion for living cannot be divided, I devoted the same ardor to my studies as I did to the distribution of *Défense de la France*. I shifted from one kind of activity to another ten times a day, without any more circumstance than there is in flicking a switch. In the end I had acquired such flexibility in changing over that I could even dispense with the switch. The two parts of my brain were working at the same time. One recorded the latest information, supplied by François on his return from Brittany, about the crews for distribution and intelligence at Rennes, Saint Brieuc, Brest, Quimper, Lorient and Nantes. In the forest of local names and happenings it tried to uncover some unsuspected relationship which could lead to an alliance, to some consistency in the work. This part of my brain was on the scent of friend and enemy or planning a campaign. Meantime, the other part reviewed the financial disasters brought on by nine successive ministers of Louis XVI in the fifteen years before July 14, 1789 — disasters they pronounced essential to success in the competition for entrance into the Ecole Normale Supérieure.

These parallel mental processes, so hard to maintain when one is older, I could manage because I was eighteen years old. Memory was a factor — my mind then was like a photographic plate — but so was intensity. I had two equal passions at the time: to suppress Nazism and to be admitted to the Normale Supérieure.

In my studies, as well as in the Resistance, I was living under a threat. The year before — it was in July 1942 — the Vichy government had issued a decree. It was a strange document, like some others which this diseased age unfortunately produced. It listed the physical qualifications required of candidates for public employment in the magistracy, in diplomacy, in government finance and last of all in teaching.

Thus far, one must admit, the state had relied on only one criterion for the recruitment of its civil servants — common sense.

The government was satisfied not to appoint a deaf teacher of music, or a blind teacher of drawing. But aside from these clear cases, everyone suited to a profession by ability or character could enter it without difficulty.

In this way, before the war, some twenty blind people had taught in the French lycées and universities. At Louis-le-Grand there was Fournery, an English teacher who was more respected and beloved by his students than most of his colleagues — everyone was agreed on that. Or on a still higher level, there was Pierre Villey, undisputed master among the blind in the generation before mine, Pierre Villey who was appointed professor of French literature at the University of Caen, and who had published authoritative scholarly works on Montaigne. He was killed in 1935, at fifty-four, in a railway accident. But all that was in time past — in the age of reason.

Stunned by the Vichy decree, I had consulted my teachers and some of the officials in the Ministry of Public Instruction. I was one of the first to be affected. Normale Supérieure was a state school, putting students on their way to a state competition, the Agrégation, which was designed to recruit candidates for posts in the universities. Under the new law the Agrégation was closed to me. What is more, I would not have the right to take the examinations for admission to the Normale Supérieure.

If I have not said that blindness was treated by the new decree as one of the conditions most likely to exclude an applicant from public employment, that is because blindness was only one of the clauses in a long list. My history teacher, an old hand at interpreting official texts, explained this one to me: we were dealing with a racist document, fascist to the core.

The Minister at Vichy who had originated this document, Abel

Bonnard, a thoroughly neurotic man, had undertaken to imitate the Nazi laws in the most servile fashion. From active service in society he eliminated not only the blind but also the one-armed and the lame — everyone who had some physical defect. He even went further. He laid down the law that all those with any kind of serious deformity would be barred from public service. Can you imagine it? Hunchbacks were forbidden in their turn. The decree even prescribed the maximum length of nose for future civil servants!

How was I to defend myself? It would have been very hard for me. I had no union to resort to, not even any organization. In 1942 there were not more than ten of us blind in advanced studies in France. The only way out was through judgment of each case individually. That was the course I was advised to take, and I was successful. In January 1943, the Director of Higher Education, informed of the situation by some fifteen of my old teachers, had granted an exemption in my favor. He claimed that my record in school and in the University made me a special case. He authorized me to compete for the Normale Supérieure on an equal footing with my sighted classmates.

So, on May 30, I presented myself for the first test in the competition, with only the anguish of the ordinary candidates — considerable in itself — and added to it the concern of a person who at all costs must forget for a week that he belonged to the Executive Committee of a Resistance Movement.

My chances of being admitted to the school were among the best. I had finished third of forty-five in the regular examinations in my second year in the Upper First. I had completed the history composition and the composition in philosophy. I was full of courage when the blow fell.

As I was going into the room where the third examination

was to be held, an attendant handed me a letter — it was signed by the Minister, Abel Bonnard. In the style which is usual in this type of communication, it informed me that the Minister "had not confirmed the exception granted by the Administration of Higher Education on the 31st of January"; that, as a consequence, the Minister did not authorize me to present myself for the examination in literature for the Normale Supérieure, and "called upon me to break off the tests which I had just passed." I think it would be fruitless to go into the grief and anger I suffered in the hours which followed.

For me it was not an examination, not even a competition which was at stake. It was my whole future in the social system in my own country. What was I to do if the only professions I was made for — the intellectual professions — were closed to me? Even more serious, what the satrap at Vichy was placing in jeopardy was my victory over blindness, at least the part of it I had won in the world of the mind.

It was made plain to me that this order from Abel Bonnard, delayed and arbitrary as it was, was illegal, and that I should appeal through the Council of State and bring suit. But how could I have done it that June in 1943? I was not a professional operator in the underground. I was still using my own name. I was not on the blacklists of the Gestapo or the Vichy Political Brigade — not yet. But my real situation was hardly better for that. I was one of the seven people chiefly responsible for one of the five or six most important Resistance movements. The most rudimentary common sense told me not to invite official attention.

As you can imagine, the distribution of *DF* did not leave me much time for self-pity. Yet the blow had gone to the quick. For the first time in my life I was faced by an absurd situation. Up to now my blindness had always made sense. Now they were rejecting me for the first time. And it was not as a person — they hardly knew my name at Vichy — but as a category of the human race.

The contrast was too flagrant. My blindness conquered or skillfully offset — this is not the place to choose between them — had, in the last two years, won me the admiration, and far more important than admiration, the confidence of hundreds of men. It was my blindness which had turned me from the boy surrounded by friends but centered on himself, which I was at sixteen, into a new man linked on all sides with thousands of other lives, committed to the cause and effectiveness of thousands of other people. It was the very same blindness which, all of a sudden, had cut me off from society or, to put it in the most moderate terms, classified me as unfit.

Philippe and Georges had the same reaction. I must not give another thought to this accident, which after all was only a tiny episode in the war in which we were engaged. At the end of the war lay victory, and people would only laugh at Vichy's decrees.

But before we laughed, we still had to win the war, and this was not just a contest of arms, nor a clash of nations hungry for power. The whims of a French minister reminded me, in case I needed to be reminded, who was the real enemy. There was a whole world to be rejected. Where it was the maps showed only very dimly. At present, its capitals were in Berlin, Tokyo and Rome, but the centers of contagion were multiplying.

In this world the only thing that counted was brute force — and not even force but the semblance of it. To have the right to live one had to prove oneself an Aryan without physical defect. The diseased in mind and the sick of soul had their place immediately, and were pushed into the front ranks. But woe to the one-legged, the hunchbacks, the Negroes and the Jews! In the biological laboratories, the latest inventions of modern science, they were preparing a convenient end for all of them: extermination in the gas chambers, sterilization, at best elimination by slower stages.

A society was being developed in which moral and spiritual factors would finally be given their due, as the waste products of a dead civilization. With these happy times to look forward to, human stud farms had already been established all over Nazi Europe, where selected Aryan men mated, at fixed hours, with selected Aryan women to give birth to a new race.

I did not take part with hands or eyes in DF's Operation July 14. But I prepared for it in my head with a conviction and a precision that I don't need to explain here and had no need to explain then to my comrades. Their plans were definitely settled only after they had been checked with mine, hour by hour, and from one subway station to the next.

No, OF COURSE NOT, Jean has not left us. If I have let you think him absent for some time, it is only because words describe some relationships so poorly. For instance, how was I to tell you that at those parties, half decent, half indecent like life itself, where Georges used to take me and where Jean was not invited, it was Jean who kept me straight with the girls, still respectful when the girls, befuddled by dancing and by their youth and mine, seemed on the point of giving themselves?

How was I to explain that in the Executive Committee of DF, to which Jean did not belong, in six months I had never said a word or made a decision without consulting Jean? Not in words, of course, and neither Philippe nor perhaps even Georges could have guessed the consultation was taking place, but without it I should have been nothing but a poor fool.

I no longer needed to question Jean to know the answers he

would give, or talk to him to have him follow my train of thought. He was my friend, first and foremost among all the others. He was the mirror to which I returned to find the best side of myself. Absent or present, he was my witness.

For Jean, at any rate, there could be no easy women and no Executive Committee. He was not a man of the world. The world was both too complex and too ugly for him. He used his strength to keep it at a distance, but not to the point of forgetting his obligations. He had joined the Resistance, and he had asked me to give him an assignment somewhere in the middle of the ladder. Since we had gone into DF, he had been coordinating the activities of several groups of beginners from the Colleges of Literature, Science and the Law. He was incapable of attempting anything he was not sure of carrying out.

Together we went to class — he was also in the Upper First. Several times a day I found him standing in the doorway between the two rooms in my little apartment, not much more talkative than he used to be, except possibly when something important happened; getting taller and taller, steadier and steadier of voice, holding my hand without being able to let it go, in a grip which sometimes made me wonder how much of it was tenderness and how much fear. We were all frightened in those days. You mustn't think otherwise. We were full of passion, but we were not mad. From time to time Jean saw death hovering in front of him. But, unlike the others, he talked to me about it.

His tranquility at moments like these was almost unbelievable to me. He was serious in his explanations, but barely, just a little more attentive than usual, like a person leaning over something which is hard to see, and who only tells you what he perceives a little at a time.

Jean saw his own death but not mine, and this theme kept

repeating itself. He did not understand why, but he recognized that this period of history was on too vast a scale for him, too vast and moving too quickly. Something seemed to be crushing him. Might it not have been life itself, the life for which he was not made? It was not that the activities we were engaged in did not suit him. Nothing really suited him. If he had not been involved, it would still have been the same.

On the last two occasions his premonitions became more pressing. "When I am gone," he said, "you must not think about me anymore. That would be harmful. Besides, I will be with you even more than before. In you, though I can't say how."

When they hear this, many people will think I should have forced Jean to be reasonable right then and there, made him drive out those evil dreams, have spoken harshly to him, as one can among close friends. But that would only be because these people were not there as I was, and had not heard him speak with such conviction.

The very last time, it must have been in June 1943, Jean told me I was made to live, even to the point where anything could happen to me, I would still stay alive; but that he was not made for life. I knew at the moment that we were not talking at cross-purposes. There wasn't time for that. The essential things had to be said. I replied to Jean that we were on the edge of an abyss. But I couldn't go on, because the reality of the things he had just said was growing too fast inside me. It is true that Jean in those days was more and more intelligent, but he was also less and less adroit.

It was at this point that he made a noble attempt at living. I was happy, believing him saved when he got engaged. Not to Aliette, for Aliette belonged to the past, but to a brave working companion, a lively little woman, someone I must admit I had not thought of for him, but whom he had chosen with determination, the way he did everything else; someone he loved and who loved him in return. Wasn't it strange that Jean should be plunging headfirst into life ahead of me? When things like this happen, none of the signals count.

Remarkable that that year I almost never said, "I myself think, I want, I believe." There was always someone else there to believe with me, to think in my place. Usually it was Jean, but sometimes it was François, Denis, Simone, Philippe, Catherine, Frédéric. And for them it was the same thing. There was not one of them who didn't recognize it, not only with pleasure, but with the sense that his whole being was in process of growth. This fraternity was the greatest virtue of the Resistance. But fraternity is a poor way of expressing it. It was really a sharing of the heart.

There were about twenty of us, living intertwined with our hearts open to each other, one protecting the next man, the next man protecting him, in a traffic of common hopes so close and so continuous that in the end it made an opening in our skins and fused us all into a single person. Such a thing can no longer surprise or shock you. During the night before July 14, when Hélène, Philippe's wife, gave birth to a son, the child was for all of us, our son also, born in a sacred spot.

To know François, Georges or Denis, I didn't need to keep on saying to myself, as people commonly do: "But where are they now?" Or, "What would they think in this case?" I carried them with me, complete in every part, even when I was reading a book or taking examinations for the Normale. And it was easier and easier, because they were growing lighter and lighter.

Aside from Philippe, who had a family — what a load and how proudly he carried it — I had not a single friend who had anything left to lose. They had given up literally everything except life. As a result there was not a trace of frivolity left in them, none of those little sidelines which usually make people so insipid.

Georges had not become a saint. He was still frantically running after skirts, the little beast. But he had grown sharp as a knife. His body was like a blade because he was so thin. His voice, naturally nasal, hewed out the sentences, you could see its tracks. He never wandered idly from one place to another. He followed his course straight to the target, and went through every obstacle along the way.

Hadn't he recently been faced with a German patrol after curfew without a reason for being out? He was an easy mark for arrest. Besides, that night he was armed with an authentic 7.65, "a big fat risk" as he described it. But as a knife he had done his job! He had gone through the patrol without looking to right or left or behind him, without slowing down or hurrying up, without reaching for his gun, without thinking about what he was doing — he swore to this next day — and the Germans, mystified, had let him through. Georges said in conclusion: "If only you go all out, you are untouchable. That's as true as the existence of the good Lord."

As for Denis, it was hard to remember that July that he had ever been timid. He was in his hour of command, and among the five hundred workers of the Open Distribution — fifty of them were real toughs — there was not one who opposed his orders or his right to give them. I think I was the only one to know that Denis was not as strong as the others thought, at least not strong in that way.

Denis made short visits to my house, just to unwind he said. And then the artless boy in him reappeared. He was full of superstition. He still believed that all men were good in spite of the evidence. He would tremble and sometimes even weep silently.

François? He was the one who had changed the least. He was born flame, and flame he remained. Only he burned more brightly than before, that is all. Unlike Jean, he loved the realities of life, and had an all-embracing tolerance for them. He, who had never touched anything more than a girl's wrist, was completely understanding of the party boys, the dissipated ones, the prostitutes and even the pimps, he insisted on that.

On my word of honor, the air was different where my friends were. There you could smell joy. How can I say more? Even when they were sad and talking about their own death, the smell of their talk was good and gave you a lift.

However it is waged, war is a dirty business. But oh, if only in peacetime men could find a way of being more like the friends I made in time of war.

[13]

BETRAYAL AND ARREST

THAT NIGHT — IT WAS JULY 19 — Philippe and Georges had held a long conference at my house. The matters we discussed included the steps to be taken to increase the circulation of *DF*, how to arrange for the feat of the fourteenth to be only the first of a series, and how to go about turning me into an underground agent, full-time.

The risks that my work at the Boulevard Port-Royal brought on my family, not to mention myself, had reached the proportions of an alert. On the other hand, *DF* could not do without my services. I was to continue to supervise its distribution but in a more carefully protected anonymity. I would go to live in one of the P.C. of the Movement in Paris.

When he left, Georges took with him the twenty tear gas pens I had been holding in reserve for the last five days. He had also taken a stock of counterfeit identity cards to turn over to Frédéric, who was going off to Besançon at seven o'clock the next morning.

That night was one of the happiest of my life. A storm was rumbling over Paris and I couldn't get to sleep till nearly four o'clock. But the sleep I lost was not because of the storm, it was because of the friendship of Philippe and Georges. I had known it intimately for months, but I had never known it to reach such a point. Friendship was salvation, in this fragile world the only thing left that was not fragile. I promise you one can be drunk on friendship as well as on love.

From the depths of my happy sleep about five in the morning I heard my father's voice: "Jacques, the German police is calling for you." Arrest! Here it was.

"Just a minute, please," while I jumped out of bed and dressed with trembling hands.

Around the world for the last twenty years, there have been so many men and women arrested by so many police agents for so many reasons, and so few of them have survived, that I feel I should not make much of my personal experience. So let me give only the plain facts.

My father's voice sounded pretty much as it used to when he was talking to his small son. He wanted so much to protect me, but of course he could do nothing. Strangely enough, it was more my job to protect him, at least to keep them from arresting him or my mother or my little brother. That was the first thing to be done, but how to go about it?

There were six Germans, two officers and four soldiers, and these imbeciles were armed. Perhaps no one had told them that I was blind. They were not brutal. They gave me time to get ready. They let me take a package of cigarettes and my lighter. They searched my two small rooms methodically, if you can call it that, since their system consisted in scattering five or six thousand sheets of Braille which they obviously could make nothing of. In any case what they were looking for wasn't there. It was in my head, and at the time my head was in a confusion from which the most diabolical policeman could not have extracted anything at all.

The question I asked myself was monstrous. Who had denounced me? First, see to it that Mother and Father were not arrested, then find out who the betrayer was. Already there was a plan. Granted, a plan, but there was not a single idea in its place in my head, not one lucid fiber in my whole body. When you are caught in a trap you cut a poor figure in your own eyes. Not liking yourself, you would willingly injure yourself.

Fortunately one of the officers who was questioning me didn't know how to go about it. He had a paper with names on it in his hand. His French was bad and he got all the names jumbled. To gain time I was trying to play the terrified little boy and mixed everything up. The SS officer got nowhere but it didn't seem to bother him. He ended by taking me by the arm in a fatherly way and leading me down the stairs. Thank God, they were taking only me. They had let me say good-bye to my parents.

Now on the pavement in the car which was already moving, as I leaned against those heavy immovable German bodies, it was much less difficult. Things were getting interesting again. So there was a future after all. If only one could arrive later, later still.

The car stopped in the middle of a large courtyard. And from that time on for hours on end, without any explanation, I was taken from office to office and floor to floor by ten surly but silent Germans, who handled me as though I were breakable. The only thing they asked me, all of them and often twice over, was whether I was really the Blind One. I answered, "Yes, I am the Blind One," and that seemed to make things easier for them.

For that matter on that day it was appallingly true. I was stone blind. Because of my creeping anguish about what was going to happen, I hardly saw anything at all. For hours, nothing had been going on while they were walking me around and showing me off. How could I tell? They sat me down in a parlor on a soft bench, and told me to eat a thick pea soup I didn't want. Finally, a man fell on me like a rock, waving his fist in front of my eyes and cursing, and pushed me into a room where I could hear the sound of a typewriter.

So far it was nothing, nothing but the questionnaire about identity. They asked stupid things, whether my father's parents were Jewish, or his grandparents. They seemed delighted to learn that it wasn't so. I asked why I was arrested. Everyone laughed, from the orderly to the typist. But all the same I was right to ask the question, because the man who spoke French was giving the underground names of Frédéric, Denis, Catherine, Simone, Gérard and ten others just as real. He wanted to know if I knew why they had all been arrested. He wound up with these words, "Where are Georges and Philippe? They are the only ones we are still looking for."

I felt as though I were breathing in gas. My nerve centers stopped functioning. And then all of a sudden I was set free. Literally, I was no longer afraid. Electric lightbulbs went on in every corner of my head. I saw the man from the Gestapo and the secretary. I had to clench my teeth to keep from bursting out laughing. If I stayed like this, they could keep on forever and never find out anything.

At random I made up three or four names out of whole cloth. I asked if they had been arrested, if they had really caught all the people who were at that surprise party at Saint-Germain-en-Laye two weeks before. There never was such a party, but to my amazement I saw that my questions got them all mixed up.

But this was only a bright interval. They took me back to the soft parlor where I had not eaten the soup. They left me there a long time. In succession about ten people were let into the room. Every time one of them came in, I said, "Who are you?" But none of them answered. They must have known that we were being watched. There must have been a jailer somewhere. My eyes, I would have given so much to have my eyes. If only they could be loaned to me just for a week!

At night — it was night for I had just heard nine o'clock strike — they left me in a washroom. There were a basin, a chair and a transom high under the ceiling. I could hear them sliding the bolts. I was by myself for twelve hours.

The most distressing thing in such circumstances is that one keeps on thinking in spite of oneself, and not thinking straight. I have been over the subject with hundreds of men, of every character, from every social class and of every age. On this point they all agree.

Thought runs away from you, like a car abandoned by its brakes in the middle of a hill. It no longer bothers about you. You can stay in it or jump out. It is a machine and doesn't care at all. Thinking is always a machine, especially in people of intelligence. And I put this question to those who still doubt it: "Have you ever spent a night all alone before being interrogated by political police?"

Your thoughts slip through your fingers; you reflect in a vacuum. Meanwhile your body goes off in another direction by itself. It is nothing but a miserable shell with slackened muscles. And when the muscles stiffen it is no better, for then they quiver. Something hurts all the time, either dryness in your throat, buzzing in your ears, rumbling in your stomach or tightening of the lungs. And at all costs, don't try saying to yourself, "I am a man of character, it can't happen to me!" It happens to everybody. And as for character, that is something else again.

Obviously, I had learned the truth about the arrest of fourteen of the chiefs of DF. Philippe and Georges had not been taken. But these arrests in themselves were very likely to mean fifteen deaths in the coming days or weeks. My own death among them I couldn't bring myself to think about. It was one of the few things which the machine had cast out when it got away from me on the slope.

But what about Denis, Gérard and Catherine? It was surely not by accident that they had made such a catch. It was mass betrayal and so fantastic that it didn't seem real.

I said a prayer, two prayers, and surely more. Words flowed. Then, by chance, I hit my elbow hard on the wall. It hurt a little, and then did me a lot of good. I cried aloud, "I am alive, I am alive."

One small piece of advice. In a spot like this don't go too far afield for help. Either it is right near you, in your heart, or it is nowhere. It is not a question of character, it is a question of reality. If you try to be strong, you will be weak. If you try to understand, you will go crazy.

No, reality is not your character which, for its part, is only a by-product — I can't define it, a collection of elements. Reality is Here and Now. It is the life you are living in the moment. Don't be afraid to lose your soul there, for God is in it.

Make all the gestures you like. Wash your hands if there is a place to wash them, stretch out on the ground, jump up and down, make a face, even shed tears if they help, or laugh, sing, curse. If you are a scholar — there is a gimmick for every category — do what I did that night. Reconstruct, out loud, Kant's arguments in the first chapters of his *Critique of Pure Reason*. It is hard work and absorbing. But don't believe any of it. Don't even believe in yourself. Only God exists.

This truth, and it holds good always, becomes a miraculous healing remedy at such a time. Besides, I ask you, who else is there that you can count on? Not men, surely. What men? The SS? Sadists or madmen, or at best enemies patriotically persuaded that it is their duty to dispose of you. If God's pity does not exist, then there is nothing left.

But to experience this pity you do not need an act of faith. You don't even need to have been brought up in an organized church. From the moment when you start looking for this pity, you lay hold of it. It lives in the fact that you breathe and have blood pulsing in your temples. If you pay strict attention, the divine pity grows and enfolds you. You are no longer the same person, believe me. And you can say to the Lord: "Thy will be done." This you can say, and saying it can do you nothing but good.

There is forgiveness for every misery. And as misery grows, forgiveness grows along with it. I had learned many vital things during the night of July 20, 1943.

AND WHAT ABOUT JEAN? Why hadn't he been arrested? They hadn't mentioned his name just now, but if they knew me, they knew him. It seemed inevitable, and yet perhaps it wasn't.

And François? The day before yesterday, François had started back to Brittany. Surely he had escaped them, but not so surely. Among the fourteen names they had named in my presence were those of four chiefs of our groups in the Nord. They must have made arrests at Lille, in the provinces, as they had in Paris. In that case why not Elio?

When you are a prisoner you know nothing, are sure of nothing. That's just what prison is. You are shorn of confidence, they cut you off from it at one blow. Then you are born into a hideous world in which nothing holds together, where the only remaining law is human. And all of a sudden you realize that man is the greatest of all the dangers in the universe.

The next day about nine o'clock they brought me coffee, but they didn't give me time to drink it. They pushed me by the shoulders down the corridor to an office. There was an SS Major there — everyone called him that — and a secretary.

Immediately the major made a long speech to the secretary in German. Obviously he was convinced that I didn't understand it, but I did, word for word. But how right I had been the day before to tell them I didn't know German. In a minute, while the secretary was translating, I should have time to collect my thoughts. The major told me I had been condemned to death for subversive acts against the occupying authorities. I had heard perfectly, but I didn't believe it.

And now the secretary was repeating it in French. I believed her even less than I did him. Had I lost my mind in the night? Had they made me drink a drug which wipes out imagination? "They tell you they are going to shoot you. Believe them! They are telling you why." Their reason for killing me, they said, was that they could prove that for six months I had been responsible for distributing *DF* all over the country. What could be truer?

But there was nothing to be done about it, I still didn't believe them. It was the first thing I said to the secretary in French when she had finished translating. I said it in a voice that surprised me for it was very calm. "You have not condemned me to death."

The Major must have expected every reaction except this one because, instead of shouting or laughing, he seemed to be thinking it over. At last he ordered the secretary to take the record and read it to me from one end to the other.

That is how the impossible came about. But even today I can't say what miraculous intervention accounted for it. The bottomless stupidity of an SS major? Really? At all events heaven was taking my affairs into its own hands. The Gestapo was laying down its arms one after another in front of me. But see for yourselves.

For five hours by the clock the secretary read aloud, hesitating over the words but never stopping. There were about fifty pages, obviously written in French and admirably drafted. A faultless document of denunciation.

From the first of May on, my activities in the Resistance were recorded day by day, on occasion hour by hour, even to my own words — at least every act and every decision connected with the distribution of *DF*. For strange as it may seem, my membership in the Executive Committee was not even mentioned.

I had been betrayed so meticulously, and this was revealed to me so fast, detail after detail, that I didn't even have time to get angry, nor time to understand or suffer. The only thing that counted was to fix in my memory all that they knew.

But mine was not the only record in the dossier. Unfortunately Georges, Frédéric, Denis, Gérard, Catherine, François, Elio, and twenty others were there too....I could no longer count them. And Jean whose name kept coming up, Jean whose relations with me were described more precisely than I had ever heard anyone describe them.

Still not a sign of the Executive Committee. Philippe's name was mentioned twice, with a description of his appearance which was very like him. Nothing more. I had no time to suffer, I was hunting for the betrayer, the author of the dossier. I had to find him. I focused my attention almost to the bursting point. Nevertheless the reading was drawing to a close. The evidence they had against us condemned us without any possibility of reprieve. Still, even more than before the document was read, I knew I was winning. In dropping the document on the trail they had made me master of the game, at least one game. And they could count on me to play it. For five hours my brain had been manufacturing lies, twenty to the minute.

Then it was the officer's turn to speak. Where did the man get his patience? He asked in German whether I wanted to add anything. In German I answered that I did. The odd thing was that I had thought of everything else. I had not consciously decided on revealing my knowledge of their language. But that still was nothing. Here I was in their language saying things so dangerous that they frightened me almost as soon as I had uttered them.

I explained that I was knocked out. Since I knew they knew everything, I could no longer lie and was about to tell the whole truth. There was nothing their informer had not seen. But several times, I pointed out, he had been wrong in his interpretation of the facts. I would confine myself to correcting his mistakes. As to proof that I was telling the truth, they had it. I knew German. Even that I could no longer hide.

They were cowardly words I spoke. I made them come out as though I were faltering. I increased the trembling of my hands as much as I could. But my heart was full of courage. On my honor, on my life, I had resolved to deceive them. Blind as I was, I couldn't escape, couldn't even see to it that I was killed in flight. But even if I had no eyes, I had a head. I would use it, even if it should burst. I would fight with it till I lost it.

Believe it or not, now it was I who was questioning the major. My voice asked, "Why don't you tell me who betrayed us?" The major got up, furiously angry. But I got up too, shouting, "It is Elio, isn't it? I know he is the one."

The Major sat down again. But I was no longer interested in his reply. Besides, he did not reply. It was Elio and I knew it. I had remembered the black bar, the kind of omen I had not wanted to rely on that first time Elio had come to see me. And the first time was on May 1, the opening date of the record.

In my head I was going over the whole record of denunciation in reverse. The evidence fascinated me. What there was in it was what Elio had seen and heard. All the things the record did not contain were the ones Elio had not known. His final ruse had been to include himself in the denunciation, to record his own activities in the Resistance as fully as ours. Even more fully. How had I missed this the first time? When it revolved around Elio the record included even notations of his expenses.

The major was grinning. He seemed to think the last episode was pure farce. The fact that I managed to guess who was the traitor, and the sight of my frightened face, made it up to him for several hours of boredom.

He squeezed my neck into his great fist, and led me slowly down five flights into the courtyard. He made me sit next to another German in the front seat of a car. It was all over for the day. An hour later I was in the suburbs south of Paris at the admitting office of the Fresnes prison.

The rest of the story is hardly worth telling. It moves too slowly and is too commonplace. From July 22 to September 8 I was taken thirty-eight times from Fresnes to the Paris headquarters of the Gestapo in the Rue des Saussaies. They came for me about seven o'clock in the morning in my cell, and brought me back there at seven in the evening. The rest of the time I was being questioned or waiting to be questioned by five SS men who worked in relays.

One day one of the five took it into his head to beat me up. With all his strength he threw me against one of the walls of the room, picked me up and threw me again. I lost my temper and shouted, "You are a coward. Even if I wanted to I couldn't defend myself." Then the brute laughed. They didn't touch me again.

Was there anything those people respected? It certainly wasn't intelligence or courage. Was it something more indispensable, more at the core of things? It was a fact that when I managed to forget their presence, when I forgot everything except what I found in the depths of my being, in the innermost sanctum of my inner world, in the place which, thanks to blindness, I had learned to frequent, and where there is absolutely nothing but pure light — when this happened the SS did not wait for my answers; they changed the subject. Then, naturally, they didn't know what they were doing, and I knew it hardly any better. No, they did not respect courage. Courage is a human attribute, and therefore made to be broken.

One morning at the end of July, as they were about to take me from Fresnes to the Rue des Saussaies, they had locked me up in one of the compartments of the prison van as usual. But the van didn't start up. They seemed to be waiting for someone. At last the door of my compartment opened again, and the body of a man fell in a heap against mine. For two men to be crowded into that small space, only one posture was possible, two men embracing each other, face to face.

"Holy Virgin, Mother of God," the man muttered, "it can't be you, little one." The man who was rubbing his prickly beard against my face and who never stopped praying was Robert. The Robert we thought had already died; the Robert to whom we owed Philippe and Défense de la France. The two of us had an hour on the way to Paris, to tell each other everything. They were torturing him systematically at the Gestapo. One of his ears was torn.

His voice whistled through the few teeth he had left. Sweat poured down his arms and off his hands, as if he had just come out of the water.

He told me that but for his steady concentration on Christ, he would willingly have allowed himself to be killed. He told me that since his arrest the Boches had not caught a soul in his organization because he had not given them a single name. They were going to shoot him but he couldn't say when. All he had to hope for was that it wouldn't be too late. "One might speak without even knowing it. That's the worst of it," he said. Robert too had faith. He had it a thousand times more than I. Then tell me, why was he not protected?

THE PERIOD OF INVESTIGATION OVER, it was prison for six months, a space four feet long and three feet wide, with walls like a medieval fortress, door three fingers thick with a peephole through which the jailers watched day and night, and a sealed window.

Still, you shouldn't think of Fresnes as nothing but a prison in the summer of 1943. It was a church underground. There were seven thousand prisoners there and nearly all of them from the Resistance movements. There were no guilty men and there was no remorse.

On the walls of the cells inscriptions had been cut into the plaster with the point of a nail: *March 17, 1937, three o'clock in the morning, the last hour of Dede the Black. Pray for his soul.* Or this one: *Forgive me, God, forgive me, Mother,* with a cross after it. So in this same place there had been men without hope. But that was long ago, in another world. Blood was pulsing in our hearts, call it courage or liberty. It sang with a voice that was louder than fear.

When night came, it was not fear tapping against the wall

of our cells with those precise little blows, to transmit messages from one prisoner to the next. It was not fear either which made us slowly loosen a windowpane and shout the watchword through the opening from one level to the next. Nothing could stop us, not threat of the dungeon, nor threat of the blows received there. At the end of a few hours I had learned that it was not so hard to be brave when so many brave men were so near that all you needed was one more small leap of the heart and the turning of the imagination in the right direction.

To know yourself one of seven thousand men striving to sustain patience and hope, yearning for liberty and life and their homes once more, creates for you a second soul and a second body: your own has only to dwell therein.

We had felt this before at the Gestapo. In the final weeks of the interrogations they were swamped with the flow of prisoners, and had thrown us pell-mell into prison vans, up and down stairways and into waiting rooms. Finding Gérard once more like this, and Frédéric, Denis, Catherine, Simone and twenty others, coming in contact with their voices and their hands, and hearing my own name on their lips, I had gained much more than solace. I had gained an exaltation which neither the Germans nor I myself could hold in check. You hardly suffer when you are not suffering alone. I was beginning to find that out.

They had not passed final sentence on us. They had closed the file of the DF case, one might almost say out of exhaustion. It is true that many people were still being executed, but no one was ever condemned. There was no time for it. I was just like my seven thousand comrades behind the walls. I didn't know where I was going to be, nor for how long.

In the meantime, I was alive. Even that was hard, because this kind of living was not at all like what you used to call life outside.

You had to give up your individuality. It would have been in your way, like clothes when you are swimming. Never forget that the enemy has every right over you: the right to kill or not to kill you, to dress or undress you, to befoul you. The only thing to do is to think about it as little as possible; to think of your comrades who are enduring the same thing. I had to remember that I, for one, had finished for the time being with my beautiful new identity as a blind young intellectual. Now I was the prisoner in cell 49, in the second division. I was in solitary confinement, and on the door outside there was a comical inscription: "Watch out! Dangerous prisoner." Me, dangerous!

The hardest thing was not remembering I was in prison, but remembering why. Twenty times a day I lost track of the connection. Everything was happening as if my actions of the past two years — not just my acts, but even my thoughts and my dreams — had turned to stone and were burying me alive. My fate was no longer that great indescribable substance in the future or in the stars, but walls, chipped mess tins, shouting, keys endlessly knocking against the steel of guns. My fate had become an object. I could hear it and touch it.

Solitary confinement I hated and it made me flabby. How have men managed to stay in solitary, sometimes for years on end, away from the voices of others, from the flesh and blood of their own kind? Humanity is a precious thing. Just to have one of my fellow creatures near me I would willingly have associated with the worst rogue.

I had only one way of finding peace once more in this solitude: by closing my eyes. That surprises you because of course you think my eyes are closed. Unfortunately, that isn't so. I saw walls and only walls. I longed to bore a hole in them, to go down into myself all the way to bedrock, to the solid place inside where time and space no longer exist, where prison slips away and vanishes into thin air, as they say mirages do. As a matter of fact prison is still there, but then it is I who contain it.

Finally, one morning, two jailers came to get me. They made me climb four flights of stairs. They shoved me into another cell. There I found three other men. The desire to cry filled my mouth with the taste of brine.

This longing to cry was still with me hours later but for a different reason. The three men didn't want to have anything to do with me, at least two of them didn't: the furniture salesman from Toulon and the road inspector from Normandy. As for the third, he said nothing to anyone. He just lay back on his pallet, collapsed like a bundle of clothes.

I had told them right away who I was and all about it. I thought that was the natural thing to do since we were going to be together day and night. I must have done it too fast and the wrong way around. They didn't return the compliment.

The road inspector, a man thirty years old, the bossy type, with a loud voice, told me immediately he was "a big wheel in the Resistance," and pledged to silence. That was a stupid thing to say. I had no intention of telling him my secrets or asking him about his. The furniture salesman was a little old grayish man who laughed easily and was more approachable with his Provençal way of talking. But he hardly dared speak without the permission of the road inspector.

My coming had upset them and they made me feel it. Having been together in that cell for two months they had made it into a cozy confinement, a comfortable spot to be in. I was not welcome with my free and easy way, my hot youthfulness which overflowed and which I did not know how to hold down. For whole days I was wretched. "What should I say to them? There are certainly things not to be discussed, but which ones?" The Provençal and the Norman were having private conversations which lasted a long time but were almost incomprehensible, with all kinds of allusions to events and people only they knew about, the kind of things married couples say to each other.

I was slow to catch on. It seemed really unbelievable. These two men had a grudge against me because I was only nineteen, because I was doing advanced studies and because I was blind. The road inspector ended by saying to me in an aggressive and confused tone of voice: "The Resistance is no place for a blind man." I answered that it was the place for honest men, like him or me, blind or not blind, young or old. But he didn't want to talk about it.

So I had only the third one left, the big flabby one lying on his mattress. All day long he only left it for half an hour to take care of his bodily needs. Then he fell back, flat on his back with his arms outstretched, and quiet as a down quilt — except once in a while when a small whistling noise came out of his lips, and seemed to convey something full of irony.

At last, on the second day, he spoke up to ask me some simple and affectionate questions about myself and to give me a warning: "Pay no attention to those two fellows. They are no account" — just this in a bright clipped voice in the presence of the two others who didn't even notice.

So the four of us had to live there in a space of twelve square yards, without heat, without friendliness, almost without speaking, in full view of the bucket standing wide open in the corner. My ears were pressed against the inner rumblings of these strange bodies, so close to them I sometimes didn't know whether I existed as a separate being. So near and yet so far. I had expected everything but this kind of misery.

I would not be content with this defeat. These were men, no more, no less than I. They didn't even seem particularly spiteful. Perhaps they were just unhappy. They pierced my ears with the sound of their woes. But if I tried to help them — that would have made me forget my own unhappiness — they sent me packing. God, how clumsy man can be!

It became a trial for me to see those two so close. Literally I could think of nothing else. When, by chance, they talked about their wives in short sentences badly turned, they did it in such a way that I felt as if it were I and not they who was caressing them or sleeping with them. Oddly enough, to free myself of the muck, I had to think of the third one, the big lazy one on his mattress. He took nothing from me; it was more as if he were giving me something. In short, the two who were talking I didn't understand, while the one who said nothing I understood right away.

Two weeks later, going on from a guess to a certainty, I realized that the Norman and the Provençal were petty bourgeois patriots and the other one refuse, as the two of them liked to say again and again: half tramp, half housebreaker, a great man for chasing girls, with a foul mouth and thoroughly disreputable. My ideas of society were in for a rough correction.

The habit grew on me. By the end of September I was an old hand at turning phrases without thinking about them, at never asking questions, even indirect ones, at stringing together endless idiotic jokes as one strings a set of pearls; even an expert at complaining, an art that was well received. If the Norman was crying over his lot, you had to cry over your own longer and louder if you possibly could. That made you a member of the family.

For sure, that was not what they had taught me about men at the University. They had even taught me just the opposite. But why? All that learning in my head was doing me no good. I was an empty wineskin, empty but transparent, no doubt because of my age. Everything went through me, and I saw it clearly, too clearly.

From a point so close at hand you can imagine how easy it was to resort to my inner vision, to depend upon the sound of voices. I spent hours at it. In time it became my only occupation.

By the way, when you are in prison, you must think of anything but the world outside. That is forbidden, materially, because of the walls, but above all spiritually. What is outside wounds you. It is dreadful to think that other people are going on living while you are no longer alive. Already you begin to tell yourself that they are growing old away from you, and that you will never see them again as they were. The idea is foolish, especially when you have not spent two months in prison, but it is inescapable and destroys you. You must not let it in.

In prison, more than ever before, it is within yourself that you must live. If there is a person you cannot do without, not possibly — for instance a girl somewhere outside the walls — do as I did then. Look at her several times a day for a long time. But don't try to picture her wherever she is at the moment, out there where there is free air everywhere and open doors. You won't manage it and it will hurt you. Instead, look at her inside yourself. Cut her off from everything that is space. Focus on her all the light you hold within yourself. Don't be afraid of using it up. Love, thought and life hold so much of this light you don't even know what to do with it. In this way you will see your mother, your sweetheart or your children perfectly. And for a long time you will not even realize you are in prison. Believe me, that is what the inner life can do.

[14]

THE ROAD TO BUCHENWALD

WHERE WERE MY FRIENDS? All at Fresnes like me. I couldn't shake off the foolish notion that I would have suffered less if I had known exactly where they were. In the cell above me, the cell under me? Was I going to see them again someday? Did Denis, Frédéric and Gérard have cellmates as ordinary as mine? And if so, how were they behaving, hot-blooded and demanding as they were? Were we moving toward the same fate? The Gestapo had said nothing. Oh, if only we could share the same sentence! Live together or, if not, die together. But not apart! All of them were thinking as I was at that very moment, I was convinced of it.

Early in November I was called for medical inspection in a cell on the ground floor. When a sad cry of joy greeted me, I stammered, "Is it you, François?" What? François there too? François, whom I had thought was one of the few to have escaped the raid of July 20, because that day he was in Brittany, and no one, dear God, no one, could pick up his trail.

I listened to his story. He had returned to Paris from Brittany July 27, coming into the Gare Montparnasse. On the platform Elio was waiting for him, not quite normal that, because of the strict rules of the Movement, but still possible. Then Elio led him to a small bistro nearby. He described the huge catch of the week before. He told him that the Executive Committee had charged him, Elio, with the task of rounding up all the forces that remained of the decimated Movement. At that point he handed over a 6.35 caliber pistol, passing it to François under the table, and François, distracted by the tragic news, had not had the presence of mind to refuse it.

Two minutes later, Elio snapped his fingers as if he were calling the waiter. Immediately, two men in plain clothes threw themselves on François, and jamming his arms behind his back, put on handcuffs. François had come very close to dying, for the Gestapo had tortured him, he said, because of the gun. They certainly had tortured him. He had a dislocated shoulder. His voice had grown horribly nasal. But what strength he had! He was like a burning bush.

The medical examination took place, apparently to no purpose. François thought they would send him to Germany for forced labor. "But you," he said, "they are going to release you." He had no way of knowing that, and I for one didn't believe it. I didn't want it. I wanted my freedom of course. But if I was the only one to receive it, it was a rotten fruit. It was unthinkable that François or Jean should go on to suffering and I, at the same time, to happiness.

One evening after the guard had been changed, a jailer, a stocky old man, and one we had spotted for his timidity and gentleness, no doubt a peasant from the Territorials, came into our cell. He shut the door behind him, a thing that had never happened before. Then he handed me a scrap of paper which Jean had signed. One of my cellmates read it to me: "I am in the third section. They have done me no harm. I have high hopes for you. I love you more than myself. Jean." I dictated a word of reply which the jailer took. It was over. I had had my news. And it was the last.

"I have high hopes for you." Did Jean, like François, mean they were going to set me free? The three characters in my cell thought it was a sure thing. Again the road inspector said: "What in hell can they do with a blind man?"

It was no good my saying to myself that all three of them were talking like that to please me, or because they were ignorant, or because, like everybody else, they couldn't keep from talking even when they had nothing to say — it was incredible how talkative we had grown as time passed — still the idea of my liberation obsessed me and the idea of my blindness along with it. Blindness again, but this time in a strange dress, since perhaps my blindness was going to protect me. At the Gestapo they had had such a hard time believing in my guilt. A cripple must be harmless in spite of all appearances. Or else he must be another man's tool. They had looked for the other man, but they hadn't found him.

Weeks passed, and a delicious sense of relief came with them, the relief that habit brings, I suppose. I was no longer bothered by the presence of the other three. It is true that the road inspector had left us, set free suddenly one day at noon after a single interrogation. Then it was the turn of the furniture salesman from Toulon. But in his case we didn't know where he was going. Others had taken their place: an old peasant from the Auvergne, with heavy speech and the smell of the soil, like a fish out of water in that prison; then the proprietor of a small restaurant in Burgundy; then a young officer of the regular army.

Here at last was a man, lively, gay, open, warm. He reconciled me to the human race. Only I had changed a great deal even before he came. I was no longer the spoiled, precocious boy. I no longer expected everybody to be like me. I had found a refuge for my hopes inside myself, to keep them from being blown out by the breath of other men.

Keeping up one's illusions is always harder than one thinks. On January 15 in the evening, in a great lyrical outburst, I had pointed out to my officer pal how and why it was inevitable for the Germans to set me free. He, as a rule so cautious and so suspicious, seemed convinced. I had not felt such fever in my head or heart since the night before I was arrested.

The next morning, very early, an SS lieutenant opened the door to our cell. He consulted a list. He was in a hurry. He called my name. I had ten minutes to get ready. Either it was freedom or its opposite. But suddenly, while I was picking up my small package of clothes, the outcome became unimportant. I was already dreaming, but I couldn't tell you what I was dreaming about, perhaps about the return of the SS man in three minutes, even in one. I was breathing in my destiny greedily.

We went downstairs. I asked the lieutenant, "Where are you taking me?" In passable French he explained that I was lucky, because they were taking me to Germany, and Germany was a great big generous country. The mechanism of hope in our hearts must have a thousand springs, almost all of them unknown to us, because when I heard this news about Germany, the most dramatic they could have given me except for the announcement of my own death, I felt a kind of passionate pleasure. It was bitter and sudden, cutting as a wound, but pleasure for all that. That's the only way I can describe it.

The danger which had been hanging over me for three years, since the day when I joined the Resistance, suddenly stopped being a danger to become the minute ahead of me, my tomorrow. At least this time I knew where I was to go. They had assigned me my place. The transformation was instantaneous. The hope of being free, which an hour earlier had raised my temperature, had become the courage not to be free, not yet and, if need be, never.

I had just spent a hundred and eighty days in a cell. My body was anemic. My legs didn't hold me up straight. The outside air scratched the membranes of my nose. My shrunken lungs blocked the entrance of air. Everything smelled to me like flint or raw steel, had the smell of the knife. My breathing intoxicated me as if it were wine. Being free could not possibly have made me more drunk.

God be praised! The others were there and they too were going to Germany. Denis, Gérard, Frédéric, all of them except the girls, who had stayed in the women's quarters, and François, whose name was not called, and Jean. Jean, the one they clearly did not want us to see. I said a prayer, with all the strength I had, begging that his absence should have no special meaning.

The hours, the days that followed, I still see them today as though they were a bacchanal. The Germans made a careful census. They counted and recounted us ten times over. The first night they made us spend in one cell, all eight of us. We didn't have a minute's sleep. We had found each other again. We overflowed with confidences exchanged. Our anguish and our joy cried aloud without knowing how. Every subject was somehow religious, with the taste of another world. During the night in the cell our hands reached out to each other. We kept saying, "You are there and I am too. They are going to take us away together." Nothing seemed hard anymore. Once more we were men.

Drunk on friendship and the cold light of a January morning, we climbed into a bus. We drove across Paris. At the Gare du Nord a train was waiting for us to take us fifty miles north of the capital, to Compiègne on the edge of the forest, to a camp which served as a clearing house.

Our bodies unfolded, then sank back again because the air was too harsh as we came in contact with it all of a sudden. The camp at Compiègne-Royallieu was not unfriendly, only unfamiliar. It had been a ground for maneuvers in the French army, a place where quarters had been put up and where some ten thousand men ran from one spot to another as fast as they could, all day long without any visible goal.

Being blind I didn't know what to do in this whirlpool of men. I went from one to the other. I don't know why, but they showed me everything and introduced me to everybody. My friends made a chain and never let me go for a minute. I seemed to be a lucky piece for them, a kind of fetish. Perhaps it was because I couldn't possibly do anybody any harm.

There were lawyers there, peasants, doctors, radio operators, people in trade, teachers, hawkers, former ministers, fishermen, railroad engineers, conspirators, football champions, professors at the Collège de France, newsboys. All of Resistance France, big and little, all mixed up together.

I was taken from one dormitory to the next. I was hardly allowed to wash myself alone. There was always someone to scrub me. But why should they all be so giving? The rumor was going around that we were going to stay there a few days, and then there would be "the great summons." It always began, they said, with a search, a great big search, with two thousand men having their hiding places and their bodily openings examined to be sure they set off without arms.

The search took place in hoarfrost and sunlight. All of us who were friends pressed against each other to shut out any possibility of being sent off apart from the rest. Every ten days or so about two thousand men took off. That was how it was at Compiègne, a cage to be loaded. Every ten days the scales tipped, and two thousand men slipped down toward Germany.

Only no one knew anything beyond that. Names were going the rounds without our knowing where they came from and without their telling us anything: Neuen Gammen, Mauthausen, Buchenwald, Dora, Oranienburg, Nachsweiler. They were German names which sent a chill all through us for no particular reason.

Before the end of the week it was our turn. They told us it was our last night before the big trip. Of course we stayed up. How can you sleep, when hymns keep resounding in your head, and anguish belabors your body, when revolving searchlights make the shadows flicker like a merry-go-round, and when the darkness they puncture is also your future!

Denis, Frédéric, Gérard and I spent the night standing up. We had decided to look at each other as long as we could. We had decided to know each other as if it were for the last time, or for the very first. We were persuaded we must store up warmth as fast as we could, the warmth which might well be taken from us.

The silent column of two thousand Frenchmen walked through the town of Compiègne under the snowy sky at dawn. Hundreds of eyes stared at us from the windows. Nothing could be heard but the calls of the jailers in the convoy.

The column crossed the bridge over the Oise, and on the platform outside the station a train was waiting. About twenty cattle cars, the familiar French cars, "forty men, eight horses." We were shoved inside. In our car there were ninety-five of us, standing of course. There wouldn't have been room to sit down. The doors slid shut and were sealed. The train of cars was shaken by the locomotive.

Then there was the usual ceremony of leave-taking. Two thousand men sang the "Marseillaise" just to be sure of being French, and for auld lang syne. There has to be a song of universal friendship when fear shuts down.

We had been traveling for three days and two nights. The last time we had had anything to drink was on the empty platform at Trier. Then it was a burning salty soup slopped around in an earthenware pot. We were facing the muzzles of machine guns and were ordered to run along the tracks. The soup splashed over the edge of the pot, and what was left of it we swallowed on the run.

We had crossed the Rhine at Coblenz as it was getting dark on the second day. We knew it because there were still men in our car who could pull themselves up by the wall to the height of the metal ventilator and read the names of the stations we were passing through. It had snowed in the night, and the men in the corners of the carriage had been licking the cold moisture which seeped through the cracks between the metal plates.

No one could sit down except on someone else's knees, but this was not a position one could hold for long. Right in the middle of the car the wrestling champion was lying stretched out flat on his back all by himself. At first he used his fists to keep his place, but for hours he had been groaning like a beaten child, from thirst. His fists had gone mad and were making the whole carriage bloody. Two men who had fainted had fallen across his body.

On the second day some of the men suddenly remembered that I was blind. They were lost in the tangle of bodies in the middle of the night and called out to me to help them. Then I began groping my way through the mass of flesh, moving as delicately as I knew how after twelve years of practice. I put one foot down in the space between two heads, the other between two thighs, and managed to reach the corner the cries were coming from without hurting anybody. An old doctor from Bourges who was shaking with fever, the one I had led to the latrine, mumbled: "I could swear you were made for emergencies like this."

For forty-eight hours I had been crawling around without stopping, and it helped to relieve my pain. What was really bad was the thirst, and then our legs because of the swelling that climbed up to our knees. When I stuck my finger into the calf of my leg, it sank in the length of the whole finger.

Denis was supporting me with his prayers. He had a special prayer for every case. He prayed for me, saying I did not need to work at prayers, but only for the boys with pains in their stomachs.

We had no idea where we were. The last name deciphered was Marburg-an-der-Lahn. But now there was no one left with strength to climb up to the ventilators. We were traveling east, that was all, toward Poland. Somehow we were convinced of it.

In the car next to us they were worse off than we were, because the first night — it was still in France while the train was puffing up the long grade toward Bar-le-Duc — five men had managed to cut through the metal plates with a knife, and stretching out full length on their sides had thrown themselves out of the car in the direction of the embankment. The SS guards who were on watch everywhere had stopped the train. Machine guns fired, dogs howled, and we heard cries of pain. Then the SS guards opened the carriage from which the prisoners had escaped, shot three men at random, and took away the clothes of all the rest. These men were naked. We were not, not yet.

My body had finally turned into a soft feverish pulp, but all the time my head was growing clearer. I understood life and I understood Germany.

The train must have stopped some time back. We couldn't be sure, there was too much wailing in the car. Four men had gone berserk, the wrestling champion and three others. They had upset the bucket and were yelling and biting the people next to them. I don't know just when it was that we heard a voice through the wall of the car asking us in French if we were Frenchmen. It must have been someone outside, perhaps in a station, a prisoner who was working there. The voice droned on, saying we had reached our destination that morning in the station at Weimar, and that soon they were going to take us ten miles farther, that it was only there that everything would begin. But what? Something to drink?

In my head words floated around like small balloons: Weimar, Goethe, the Elector Charles Augustus, Frau Von Stein, Bettina Brentano. I said fatuously to Denis that we were lucky to have the chance to see Weimar. Denis was not listening — he was praying.

The train started up again but not for long. There was a steep grade. Then the doors slid open. We had arrived. Some of us called out, *"Trinken! Bitte, trinken!"* The answer was a hail of blows raining down on flesh and blood in the car, blows of clubs and rifle butts. The men standing too near the door fell out.

We had to form a line and walk fast. All around us there were dogs biting the ones who hung back. It was almost impossible to move because of our swollen legs. We felt as if we were walking on knives. I was angry with myself for not being stronger, but I was not really miserable. My body was, but not I myself.

The SS guards were charging into our lines by fits and starts. Lamouche (he was a youngster eighteen years old, from Nantes, who loved me and wanted to protect me) had his wrist broken from the blow of a rifle butt. If it hadn't been for him I would have gotten it full in the forehead. A few minutes later we suddenly heard a military band drawn up on either side of a monumental entrance.

The music it made sounded like dance tunes. The inscription over the gate read, *Konzentrationslager Buchenwald*.

I passed through this gateway going in the opposite direction fifteen months later, on April 18, 1945. But here I come to a halt. I can't say how, but it is no longer I who am conducting my life. It is God, and I haven't always understood how he went about it.

I think it would he more honest to warn you that I am not going to take you through Buchenwald, not all the way. No one has ever been able to do it. A Frenchman like me, who got there at the same time, David Rousset, has written two books about Buchenwald. An anti-Nazi German, Eugen Kogon, has written his own version. I can testify that these books come very close to reality. Still, I can't say that they are "true."

There is no truth about the inhuman, any more than there is truth about death; at any rate not on our side, among us as mortal men. Such truth could only exist for our Lord Jesus Christ, absorbed and preserved by him in the name of his Father and ours.

Of the 2,000 Frenchmen who went into Buchenwald with me at the end of January 1944, about thirty survived. According to the count made after the war, during the fifteen months of my stay, in the camp itself and in the commandos which were its direct dependencies, 380,000 men died: Russians, Poles, Germans, Frenchmen, Czechs, Belgians, Dutchmen, Danes, Norwegians, Hungarians, Yugoslavs, Romanians. There were even Americans, thirty-four of them, all officers, brothers-in-arms who had been parachuted into the Resistance in Western Europe. There were very few Jews, for Jews only went to Buchenwald through administrative error. They were sent to Lublin, to Auschwitz-Birkenau, Theresienstadt, for quick extermination by scientific methods. Our extermination was only to take place after we had been exploited. The process was much slower.

The survivors of deportation have never told all they saw except to a few friends — each of them can count them on his fingers — and to a few women, their wives above all. But there is one record you are entitled to, the record of one handicapped man, a blind man, and how he managed to live through it. About this I shall try to be as precise and detailed as I can.

A few hours after we arrived at the camp, we were shunted through the offices. A Nazi concentration camp is highly organized, full of red tape, aimed at persecution and death, but extremely complex, hierarchical and artful to the nth degree. The ultimate artfulness consisted in leaving the SS, who were the real masters, out of the everyday routines. There were 17,000 of them to supervise our camp but we prisoners hardly ever saw them. When they came in, it was in groups, heavily armed, for mass hangings or shootings.

In January 1944, there were 60,000 prisoners at Buchenwald. Six months later we were 100,000. Like all the rest I went through the different offices. For the last time I had to identify myself. Immediately after that you were given a number. Mine was 41978. Of course the offices were manned by prisoners, our comrades. One of them, a Pole, learning that I was blind, did not falter for a minute; he merely recorded the fact. But when he found out I was a student at the University of Paris, he slipped in this piece of advice in a muted voice in German: "Never say that again. Once they know you are an intellectual they will kill you. Name a trade, never mind what it is." My answer came out — I don't know who dictated it: "Profession: interpreter of French, German and Russian." Then my fellow prisoner in the office muttered, "Good luck," and seemed relieved.

That's how I acquired an official profession, entered on the books the first day and recognized as of general use. Without that protection I would not have lasted a week. It was true I knew German, but at the time I didn't know a word of Russian. My notion to mention that language could have been expensive. Luckily I wasn't put to the test for two months, and by then I could make a pretense of understanding Russian, as long as they kept to simple things.

All through February they kept us in quarantine in crowded barracks removed from the active center of the camp. It was hard to bear because of the cold. In the dead center of Germany, near the edge of Saxony, and on the top of that high hill, fifteen hundred feet above the plain, the thermometer fluctuated between five and twenty degrees below zero.

They had dressed us in rags. My shirt had only one button, my jacket had holes in ten places. I had open wooden clogs on my feet, and no socks. The cold literally winnowed out my comrades. Nearly two hundred of the two thousand died of it before the end of February, particularly the boys between twenty and twenty-five who looked strong. Eating so little, being so cold and so frightened killed them off.

I was much less bothered by my body, which was of medium height, on the small side, and which since childhood I had trained to live on the defensive. Like everyone else, the cold hurt me very much. But Denis, Gérard, Frédéric, all friends from DF, were with me. I didn't have a single failure of courage. Together we made an island of human warmth. From one day to the next we managed to put off the hour of despair, though it had already fallen upon many of the others. When it did they died right away, sometimes in less than twelve hours.

I must be frank. The hardest thing was not the cold, not even that. It was the men themselves, our comrades and other prisoners, all the ones sharing our miseries. Suffering had turned some into beasts. But they at least were not malicious. They could be calmed with a sign or a word, in the toughest cases with a blow. Worse than the beasts were the possessed. For years the SS had so calculated the terror that either it killed or it bewitched. Hundreds of men at Buchenwald were bewitched. The harm done them was so great that it had entered into them body and soul. And now it possessed them. They were no longer victims. They were doing injury in their turn, and doing it methodically.

The man in charge of our quarantine barracks was a German, an anti-Nazi who had been there for six years. Rumor had it that once he had been a hero. Now, every day, he killed two or three of us with his own hands, barehanded or with a knife. He struck out in the crowd at random. It was a satisfaction he could no longer live without. One morning when it was snowing hard, we discovered that he had disappeared. When the snow was swept off the steps of the barracks, they found his body with a large knife wound in the back.

At the end of February I thought I was lost. Frédéric, Denis and Gérard had been called for commando service outside. That meant they were going to other secondary camps, and that I was to stay at Buchenwald alone. They left. I stayed. That day the cold was so bitter I thought I wasn't going to be able to stand it.

[15]

THE LIVING AND THE DEAD

I CAME VERY CLOSE TO DYING. But how can I make you believe it alive as I am today? I shall tell it badly, but since I have
promised, I am going to tell my story.

In March I had lost all my friends. They had all gone away. A
small child was reborn in me, looking everywhere for his mother
and not finding her. I was very much afraid of the others and even
of myself since I didn't know how to defend myself. One day out
of two, people were stealing my bread and my soup. I got so weak
that when I touched cold water my fingers burned as if they were
on fire. All month long a blizzard which had no beginning and no
end had been buffeting the Buchenwald hill.

Being blind, I still avoided one of the greatest miseries, the
labor commandos. Every morning at six o'clock all the men who
were fit left the camp to the blare of the orchestra, an efficient
orchestra and functional, the liturgy of forced labor in caricature.
The whole day these men moved rocks and sand in the quarries,

dug into the frozen ground to put down pipes, carried rails for the tracks, always in range of submachine guns and SS *Kapos* who were blind with rage. The prisoners came in at five o'clock at night, but never all of them. The yards were littered with the day's dead.

They were dying whatever they might be doing: pulled down by the weight of a rock on the slippery paths in the quarries; felled by blows or bullets in the night; executed with ceremony before the eyes of 100,000 fellow prisoners, under floodlights clouded by a snow-storm, to the strains of a funeral march, to set an example on the square where the roll was called; or hanged more obscurely in the barn they called the movie house. Others were dying of bronchial pneumonia, of dysentery or typhus. Every day some were electro-cuted on the charged wires that surrounded the enclosure. But many were dying, quite simply, of fear. Fear is the real name of despair.

I was spared the labor commandos because I couldn't see. But for the unfit like me, they had another system, the Invalids' Block. Since they were no longer sure of winning the war, mercy had become official with the Nazis. A year earlier being unfit for physi-cal work in the service of the Greater German Reich would have condemned you to death in three days.

The Invalids' Block was a barracks like the others. The only difference was that they had crowded in 1,500 men instead of 300 — 300 was the average for the other blocks — and they had cut the food ration in half. At the Invalids' you had the one-legged, the one-armed, the trepanned, the deaf, the deaf-mute, the blind, the legless — even they were there, I knew three of them — the apha-sia, the ataxic, the epileptic, the gangrenous, the scrofulous, the tubercular, the cancerous, the syphilitic, the old men over seventy, the boys under sixteen, the kleptomaniacs, the tramps, the perverts, and last of all the flock of madmen. They were the only ones who didn't seem unhappy.

No one at the Invalids' was whole, since that was the condition of entrance. As a result people were dying there at a pace which made it impossible to make any count of the block. It was a greater surprise to fall over the living than the dead. And it was from the living that danger came.

The stench was so terrible that only the smell of the crematory, which sent up smoke around the clock, managed to cover it up on days when the wind drove the smoke our way. For days and nights on end, I didn't walk around, I crawled. I made an opening for myself in the mass of flesh. My hands traveled from the stump of a leg to a dead body, from a body to a wound. I could no longer hear anything for the groaning all around me.

Toward the end of the month all of a sudden it became too much for me and I grew sick, very sick. I think it was pleurisy. They said several doctors, prisoners like me and friends of mine, came to listen to my chest. It seems they gave me up. What else could they do? There was no medicine at all at Buchenwald, not even aspirin.

Very soon dysentery was added to pleurisy, then an infection in both ears which made me completely deaf for two weeks, then erysipelas, turning my face into a swollen pulp, with complications which threatened to bring on blood poisoning. More than fifty fellow prisoners told me all this later. I don't remember any of it myself. I had taken advantage of the first days of sickness to leave Buchenwald.

Two young boys I was very fond of, a Frenchman with one leg, and a Russian with one arm, told me that one morning in April they carried me to the hospital on a stretcher. The hospital was not a place where they took care of people, but simply a place to lay them down until they died or got well. My friends, Pavel and Louis, didn't understand what happened. Later they kept telling me that I was a "case." A year afterwards Louis was still amazed: "The day we carried you, you had a fever of 104 or more, but you were not delirious. You looked quite serene, and every now and then you would tell us not to put ourselves out on your account." I would gladly have explained it to Louis and Pavel, but the whole affair was beyond words and still is.

Sickness had rescued me from fear, it had even rescued me from death. Let me say to you simply that without it I never would have survived. From the first moments of sickness I had gone off into another world, quite consciously. I was not delirious. Louis was right, I still had the look of tranquility, more so than ever. That was the miracle.

I watched the stages of my own illness quite clearly. I saw the organs of my body blocked up or losing control one after the other, first my lungs, then my intestines, then my ears, all my muscles, and last of all my heart, which was functioning badly and filled me with a vast, unusual sound. I knew exactly what it was, this thing I was watching: my body in the act of leaving this world, not wanting to leave it right away, not even wanting to leave it at all. I could tell by the pain my body was causing me, twisting and turning in every direction like snakes that have been cut in pieces.

Have I said that death was already there? If I have I was wrong. Sickness and pain, yes, but not death. Quite the opposite, life, and that was the unbelievable thing that had taken possession of me. I had never lived so fully before.

Life had become a substance within me. It broke into my cage, pushed by a force a thousand times stronger than I. It was certainly not made of flesh and blood, not even of ideas. It came toward me like a shimmering wave, like the caress of light. I could see it beyond my eyes and my forehead and above my head. It touched me and filled me to overflowing. I let myself float upon it.

There were names which I mumbled from the depths of my astonishment. No doubt my lips did not speak them, but they had their own song: "Providence, the Guardian Angel, Jesus Christ, God." I didn't try to turn it over in my mind. It was not just the time for metaphysics. I drew my strength from the spring. I kept on drinking and drinking still more. I was not going to leave that celestial stream. For that matter it was not strange to me, having come to me right after my old accident when I found I was blind. Here was the same thing all over again, the Life which sustained the life in me.

The Lord took pity on the poor mortal who was so helpless before him. It is true I was quite unable to help myself. All of us are incapable of helping ourselves. Now I knew it, and knew that it was true of the SS among the first. That was something to make one smile.

But there was one thing left which I could do: not refuse God's help, the breath he was blowing upon me. That was the one battle I had to fight, hard and wonderful all at once: not to let my body be taken by the fear. For fear kills, and joy maintains life.

Slowly I came back from the dead, and when, one morning, one of my neighbors — I found out later he was an atheist and thought he was doing the right thing — shouted in my ear that I didn't have a chance in the world of getting through it, so I had better prepare myself, he got my answer full in the face, a burst of laughter. He didn't understand that laugh, but he never forgot it.

On May 8, I left the hospital on my two feet. I was nothing but skin and bones, but I had recovered. The fact was I was so happy that now Buchenwald seemed to me a place which if not welcome was at least possible. If they didn't give me any bread to eat, I would feed on hope.

It was the truth. I still had eleven months ahead of me in the camp. But today I have not a single evil memory of those three hundred and thirty days of extreme wretchedness. I was carried by a hand. I was covered by a wing. One doesn't call such living emotions by their names. I hardly needed to look out for myself, and such concern would have seemed to me ridiculous. I knew it was dangerous and it was forbidden. I was free now to help the others; not always, not much, but in my own way I could help.

I could try to show other people how to go about holding on to life. I could turn toward them the flow of light and joy which had grown so abundant in me. From that time on they stopped stealing my bread or my soup. It never happened again. Often my comrades would wake me up in the night and take me to comfort someone, sometimes a long way off in another block.

Almost everyone forgot I was a student. I became "the blind Frenchman." For many, I was just "the man who didn't die." Hundreds of people confided in me. The men were determined to talk to me. They spoke to me in French, in Russian, in German, in Polish. I did the best I could to understand them all. That is how I lived, how I survived. The rest I cannot describe.

THE IMAGE OF JEAN NEVER LEFT ME. Through all my illness it stayed with me constantly, watching over me. When, too weak to face the world outside, I was living entirely inside myself, his image was still there, my one remaining picture of the world without. For whole days and nights I had held Jean's hand in my thoughts, but in my mind it had shielded me more than his hand could have done in the flesh. How can I explain this strange phenomenon? All the longing for the life which Jean had not lived had flowed over into me, for, though I have put off saying the words, Jean was dead.

There was no question about it. They had told me the night

before I became sick, in March. Jean had died at the gates of Buchenwald. The circumstances have been almost entirely blotted out of my memory. All I remember is that I was exhausted, wandering around the camp, when a sort of large thin bird fell on my neck. Suddenly his arms were around me, his bones like thin sticks of wood about to pierce the skin. It was François. I didn't know François was at Buchenwald. He had not come there with the rest of us. He wept and so did I. We had no other way of expressing our affection. And, as always in that place, our tears were for joy and grief at the same time.

Right after that he told me a story so shocking that I made him repeat it. The first time I hadn't heard it. That day back in January when we were taken to Compiègne, they had also been called — François, Jean and three others from Défense de la France. At first the Germans treated them well. They put them in cars built for regular passengers. They had traveled all night but that was all. Politely, they were told to get out. They were then near Sarrebruck at Neue Bremm.

But Neue Bremm was an invention of the devil. The administration of the SS called it a *Straflager*, a camp specializing in punishment, a waiting room for the concentration camps on the big scale, a place where they broke men in a week or two, rapidly and methodically, until the will to live left them just as smoke leaves burning wood. They only let them sleep two hours a night. They only gave them something to drink once in twenty-four hours. They showered them five times a day with torrents of icy water. They made them crouch down and stay in that position under threat of being fired on. Still crouching, they had to hop around a pond filled with water, some days for six hours, other days for eight hours on end. The ones who fell into the pond were pulled out and beaten. It was the same kind of horror as at Buchenwald, but all concentrated in the space of a few days. Buchenwald in an abridged version. And François and Jean had stayed at Neue Bremm for three weeks.

At last one February night, when they were all on the point of dying of injuries and exhaustion, the Germans had once more sat them down in a railway carriage, without telling them anything, of course. They didn't know where they were going. The carriage was comfortable and heated, and they fed them. But they were kept going for twenty-three days. For no reason, as far as they could see, they had gone from Sarrebruck to Munich, from Munich to Vienna, from Vienna to Prague, from Prague to Nuremberg, from Nuremberg to Leipzig, from yards to stations and back to yards. At the junction of Zwickau they stayed five days and nights, still with no reason given.

François and Jean stuck together, and the Germans didn't separate them. François said it made the whole thing possible. But Jean's breathing was very bad and he couldn't sit up. He just lay stretched out on one of the benches. Two or three times a day he spoke a few affectionate words, about François, about me or his fiancée. He was without hope, but didn't seem to be suffering much.

On the twenty-third night, about six o'clock, he died in the railway carriage, as François said, "Gently, like a child going off to sleep." Two hours later the train came to a stop in the Buchenwald station. Jean had not made it all the way. François had found me in camp the very next day. Jean's death he had seen with his own eyes the night before.

Right after that I took Jean with me in my illness, to a place where, for weeks, I didn't know exactly where death or life were. When I came out of the hospital and saw François again, he did not have the strength to talk to me again about Jean's dying, nor did I to him. You see, just keeping alive what was left to us of life was a task which took all we had.

François's future worried me, certainly more than my own, for I knew he was going off on a labor commando. He was called two weeks later. But, most of all, François was much too brave, and when you are deported, that kind of bravery never spares you for long. You die of it. He had gone through Neue Bremm, I can't think how, but with everything he had. And then this Franco-Pole, this Pole from France, whose ancestors had grown hardened to suffering over centuries, had planted anguish in the middle of his heart, like an arrow in the center of its target. It quivered there.

He suffered, of course, like the others, but instead of complaining, he sang the praises of suffering. Never in his exalted life had I heard his voice more intense or seen his movements more rapid. On his way to work he carried his shovel or his stones, but always, too, those of another who couldn't carry them himself. Back from work at night he took care of the wounded, ministered to the dying, and for two hours sang all the songs he knew. François did not have an ounce of grief in his heart, not an inch of softness in his body. His skin had turned dry and rough like leather.

It made no sense to tell him to save his strength. He kept saying: "What if I die? But the boys don't know how to manage by themselves." Then François went off and Georges arrived. It was in the middle of May. That made all of us without exception. It would never come to an end.

Georges had escaped the raid of July 20. We had found that out at the Gestapo. The SS had been furious. May 13 as I was coming out of the block, suddenly I heard a cry and felt the body of a man embracing mine. I knew right away it was Georges, I can't tell you how.

I had not heard his voice yet, but it was he. Unlike François two months earlier he did not weep, he laughed like a madman. For several minutes I had the hardest time understanding what he had to say. He laughed too much, he choked over his words, he was confused.

It was a fact, he said, they had not caught him on July 20. No indeed. Georges had worked double time until January 31: "For you and for me, you understand?" On that day there was another piece of treachery and Georges had been taken. I was learning remarkable things. DF was not dead, it had even grown. How right we had been, Georges and I, to work as a team in the Resistance. Everything I knew he knew. He had put together the fragments of the newspaper's circulation, and had even increased it. In January the issue was 250,000, but it was not like the heroic feat of July 14, for now it was a regular affair twice a month, a machine in good running order. And DF had an underground fighting force north of Paris between L'Isle-Adam and Compiègne, with two thousand men under arms, waiting for the landing of the Allies.

Georges's own story, horrifying and by now so commonplace, was the story of torture. The day he was arrested he was carrying the keys of eleven underground branches in the region. They had tortured him eleven times. How had he managed to tell them nothing, how had he lived through it? I didn't understand, and I saw that he didn't know the answer. There are boys born to courage, perhaps just as others are born to weakness. But unfortunately my Georges was a damaged man. Strange, it was not so with François, but it was with Georges. There was defiance in everything he did and said, and terror as well.

To cap the climax, as soon as the period of interrogation was over, they sent him to Compiègne. And from there through an administrative error his convoy had been taken to Auschwitz. When they arrived, someone on the staff who was more conscientious than the others noticed that the two thousand Frenchmen they had brought there that day were not Jews. So for the time being they put them in a barracks, and a week later shipped them off to Buchenwald. But Georges had had time to see several thousand Jewish men, women and children lined up in a column as they were about to go into gas chambers masquerading as shower rooms. He could still see that sight, and in him it had killed both love and hope.

We had a few great days together. Compared to Georges I had suffered very little. I was almost intact. I tried a kind of artificial respiration on him. At all costs he had to have joy breathed back into him. Otherwise he was bound to go under. Strange to say, it was not physical strength he lacked, but strength of a different kind, the kind I had by the grace of God. The point was for him to make use of my strength right away. I said to Georges: "Help yourself, take all you can." And he did. He had grown terribly irritable. Sometimes he even hit people for no reason. But from me there was nothing he would not take, because I was his "brother."

One morning about eight o'clock — it was June 6, 1944 — Georges and I were together when a Dutchman whom we knew only by sight blocked our way and shouted in German: "The Allies have landed in Normandy." How this news, only four hours old and accurate, managed to reach Buchenwald so fast is still one of the countless mysteries of the deportation. So perhaps, after all, one day we were going to be set free. That was the last happiness Georges and I shared.

A week later they called Georges for the commando. I am sure of it because I was there when the column was being formed. It was only ten yards away from me, and between us was the barbed wire. I remember his voice when they whistled for them to go off. From a distance he cried out to me: "Good-bye, Jacques, I won't be seeing you again." That was something no one had said yet, not Denis, or Gérard or Frédéric or François. And right away I had the answer in my mind: "If he said it, it must be true."

Jean, François, Georges, all of them, one after the other, while I could do nothing and was nothing. Only the chief, Philippe, was free, back there in France.

To FORGET WAS THE LAW. We had to forget all the missing, the comrades in danger, our families, the living and the dead. Even Jean must be forgotten, and not just to keep off suffering — in any case suffering had settled in with us as if we were a country under occupation — but rather to hold on to the strength to live. Memories are too tender, too close to fear. They consume energy. We had to live in the present; each moment had to be absorbed for all that was in it, to satisfy the hunger for life.

To bring this about, when you get your bread ration, don't hoard it. Eat it right away, greedily, mouthful after mouthful as if each crumb were all the food in the world. When a ray of sunshine comes, open out, absorb it to the depths of your being. Never think that an hour earlier you were cold and that an hour later you will be cold again. Just enjoy.

Latch on to the passing minute. Shut off the workings of memory and hope. The amazing thing is that no anguish held out against this treatment for very long. Take away from suffering its double drumbeat of resonance, memory and fear. Suffering may persist, but already it is relieved by half. Throw yourself into each moment as if it were the only one that really existed. Work and work hard.

About the end of May, I had found my job. During all the eighteen hours in the day when the camp was not asleep, I set myself to fighting panic, the panic of my fellows and my own, for they were inseparable.

I was going to sort out the war news, and that was important. If Germany was victorious, we were done for, all of us. If Germany was beaten, but beaten too late, later than the coming spring, only a handful of survivors would still be alive, and which of us could flatter himself that he would be among them? It was important for another reason, because at Buchenwald everyone lied. False rumors flooded the camp. Since the Allies had landed in Normandy, Paris had fallen once a day; Berlin had been destroyed; Hitler was dead; the Russians were at the gates of Leipzig or Nuremberg; airborne troops had taken over from Southern Germany to Denmark. You could never find the source of such news. You could never find the guilty person who had started it. All were guilty, all were peddling rumors. Shunted from false hopes to denials, from illusions to gossip, all of our hearts were like ships capsized. Doubt and agony were taking root.

We had to make war on the disease. My comrades put me in charge of the news in the "little camp," in other words a division of about 30,000 prisoners. There was a loudspeaker in each block. Over it the SS command gave its orders from outside the camp. The rest of the time, the loudspeakers were tuned to the German radio, for official broadcasts and bulletins of the German army. Every day I took down the bulletins, all of them, from morning to night. My job was to decipher them. The fact was the army bulletins were not straightforward and not clear. They didn't describe operations as they were. They spoke by omission. They sketched the war in a void. My work, and it was hard and painstaking, was to redress the balance.

When we came to the middle of August 1944 the name of Paris
never appeared in the bulletins. No defeat, no lost city was ever
mentioned, you had to fill in the gaps without making mistakes.
Still, I announced the fall of Paris on August 26, and that was neither ahead of time nor behind it.

Once the news was picked up and deciphered, it had to be distributed. I went from one block to the next, climbed up on a table
or on benches piled on each other, and then made my statement.
You must be thinking it would have been easier to write down what
I had heard on a slip of paper, then have it translated into five or
six different languages and circulated. Unfortunately, I had learned
this would not work. Even a crowd that is happy and confident does
not welcome the news brought before it. But a crowd enslaved by
fear and despair sets itself against news as though it were an attack.

It was not facts, names or figures that all these men wanted. It
was certainties, the kind of realities that went straight to the heart.
Only a man standing before them could give them that. They needed
his calm and his voice, and it was I who had become the voice.

I started by saying I had heard the news myself, and I told
them when and where. For one thing I repeated the bulletins of
the German High Command word for word. Then I explained
what they meant, what I understood them to mean. In German and
French I did the talking myself. When it came to Russian, Polish,
Czech, Hungarian and Dutch, I had found people to help me. I
took my band of interpreters with me everywhere I went.

Since we had no maps, every day before speaking I had to find
a man who knew the zone of operations at first hand, whether it
was in Galicia or in the Ardennes. At all costs, names, positions,
distances must be exact, especially the distances, since the war
depended on them.

That was only the beginning. I have said that everyone lied at Buchenwald, some from discouragement, some from fear, others from ignorance, and some viciously. I have watched men inventing the bombing of cities, just for the pleasure of torturing a neighbor who had all his dear ones in that place.

Once the news was given out, it had to be kept straight, and that called for unending vigilance. I had put two or three people in charge in each block. Their task was to repeat accurately what I had said, and correct publicly all the crazy and vicious distortions; but, above all, to find and denounce the people who were peddling false rumors.

Some of these people were very hard to hold in check, for they believed in their own inventions. Truth slides over a man, but falsehood fastens on to him like a leech. Often the only way out was a fight. Somebody had to hit one of these characters to make him stop lying. There he was, persuaded of his garbled story, and begging you to let him tell it; like the Pole who, one night, screamed out that there was not one stone left on another in Poznan, that he had found it out, knew it for a certainty, and must tell everyone about it. But that was just the point. Such things were not to be told, absolutely not. For otherwise there would have been murders and suicides among the men of Poznan who could not bear the news.

But how were we to hold on to the remnants of reason in the swirling madness of deportation? How were we to keep some order in the utter confusion of the brain? If we really couldn't find out what was going on, at least let us not conjure it up!

So much for the official news, now for the inside story. It is hard to believe but true nonetheless. News was coming in to us from France, England and Russia. In one of the blocks set aside for medical experiments, down in the cellars, some prisoners had set up a radio receiving station made with stolen parts, and also a sender as we found out later on. If it had been discovered, this receiving station would surely have cost the lives of several thousand men. But what was to be done with news received through these channels?

Should it be passed on to all the prisoners? After all, wasn't it theirs by right? Of course it would be done without naming the source, but the risk was too great. The place was swarming with spies. Under the SS system, no one can be trusted. No, we had to keep the news to ourselves, to a little group of us in the know. It was absurd, it was cruel, but it was indispensable.

So each day I knew a little more than I had the right to tell. I was forced to measure my words, to hold everything in control, even a smile. All day long I was busy. I hardly had time to think of myself. I could say to myself that I was a kind of doctor. When I went into a block, I took its pulse. With experience I learned to recognize right away the state of block 55 or block 61 on that day. A barracks was a spirit shared, a collective body. In there men were so packed together they could hardly tell each other apart. When panic started at one end of the block, it reached the other within a few minutes.

I could sense the condition of a block by the noise it made as a body, by its mixture of smells. You can't imagine how despair smells, or for that matter confidence. They are worlds apart in their odor. So then, according to the state of things, I gave out more news of one kind, or less of another. Morale is so fragile that a word, even an intonation can throw it out of balance.

The remarkable thing was that listening to the fears of others had ended by freeing me almost completely from anxiety. I had become cheerful, and was cheerful almost all the time, without willing it, without even thinking about it. That helped me, naturally, but it also helped the others. They had made such a habit of watching the coming of the little blind Frenchman with his happy face, his reassuring words delivered in a loud voice, and with the news he gave out, that on days when there was no news, they had him visit them just the same.

How well I remember that September night when 1,500 Ukrainians set me down in the middle of their block, made a ring around me, sang, danced, played the accordion, wept, sang again — all this gravely and affectionately without ever shouting — that night I promise you I no longer needed to defend myself against the past or the future. The present was as round and full as a sphere and it warmed me many times over.

And finally, as for those men who were laughing and putting their arms around each other — for they were laughing within an hour — if anyone had told them then that they were unhappy, that they were in a concentration camp, they would not have believed him. They would have chased him away.

WE HAD OUR POOR AND OUR RICH at Buchenwald as they have everywhere. Only you couldn't recognize them by their clothes or their decorations. For decorations every one of us had a triangle of material sewed onto his jacket, red for the politicals, yellow for the Jews, black for the saboteurs, green for ordinary criminals, pink for the pederasts with records, purple for the enemies of Nazism on religious grounds. And underneath the triangle there was a square of the same stuff with our registration number and the letter indicating our nationality. Last of all, if the records said we were mad, we had the right to wear an armband with three black dots. The clothes we wore were all alike, all rags.

The only distinguishing mark was on the head. Before you had been in camp three days, they shaved your head clean, and since your beard kept on growing, it gave you a fearsome look. During the second three months of your stay, the two sides of your head were shaved, but a mane of hair was left growing in the middle. For the next six months, the two sides were not touched. They grew wild, while the mane was shaved, leaving a large stripe we used to call the expressway. By the end of a year you could do as you liked with your hair. That was your privilege.

All of us were naked, if not literally, to all effects. We had no rank, no dignity, no fortune left...and no face to save. Every man was cut down to himself, to what he really was. And, believe me, that created a real proletariat. Still, there had to be a way of recognizing people in the crowd, of knowing who to speak to. The camp was the witches' well. They had thrown them all in there together, the Benedictine monk, the Kirghiz shepherd who prayed to Allah three times a day with his face to the ground, the professor from the Sorbonne, the mayor of Warsaw, the Spanish smuggler, the men who had killed their mothers or raped their daughters, the ones who had let themselves be arrested to save twenty others; the wise ones and the fools, the heroes and the cowards, the good and the evil. The only thing was — and you had to get used to it — all these categories were dead and gone, for we had passed over into a different world.

I was lucky enough to be twenty years old and to have no habits except the few that had to do with the mind. I needed no honor except the honor of being alive. So it wasn't surprising if I was more contented than most of my neighbors.

The religious searched everywhere for their faith. They did not find it again, or else they found it so reduced in force that they couldn't make use of it. It is a terrifying thing to have called yourself Christian for forty years and then discover that you are not a real one, that your God no longer solves your problems. The people who had been generally respected ran after their lost respect, but there wasn't anything left of it. And the intellectuals, the cultivated men, the great brains, had great sorrows. They didn't know what to do with their learning for it didn't protect them against misfortune. They were submerged in that vast broth of humanity. How many doctors and sociologists, archaeologists and barristers needed comforting. And it wasn't easy to console them. They could understand anything more readily than the fact that their intelligence was out of season.

Our rich at Buchenwald were the devil and all to find in the crowd, for they had no label. They were neither religious men nor atheists, neither liberals nor communists, neither well nor badly brought up. They were just there, that was all, mixed up with the rest. My one idea was to find them.

Their wealth was not made of courage, for courage is always suspect or a consequence of something else. The rich were the ones who did not think of themselves, or only rarely, for a minute or two in an emergency. They were the ones who had given up the ridiculous notion that the concentration camp was the end of everything, a piece of hell, an unjust punishment, a wrong done them which they had not deserved. They were the ones who were hungry and cold and frightened like all the rest, who didn't hesitate to say so on occasion — why conceal the real state of things? — but who in the end didn't care. The rich were the ones who were not really there.

Sometimes they had removed themselves entirely by going crazy. In the Invalids' Block I had known two or three hundred such, and intimately. We ate, slept, washed together and talked to each other. Most of them were not harmful if you left them alone. They didn't need to be destructive. For as a rule they were content. But still their contentment was terrifying, a sort of frozen happiness and not communicable. I watched these madmen across the barrier of my reason. There was always something changeless about them which fascinated me. Take Franz, the little Silesian, whose hands never stopped trembling, who talked day and night under his breath, saying over and over that all in all Buchenwald was not a bad spot, and that the misfortunes of the others were only their own hallucinations. Franz looked as though he had the anguish of the world on his shoulders. You couldn't say just how, but still he was taking it upon himself. Some people said his face had begun to look like the face of Christ.

The feeble-minded, the ones who were short on memory and imagination, also did not suffer. They lived from minute to minute, each day for itself, I suppose as beggars do. The odd thing was that it was comforting to be with them. The tramps, the hoboes, the ones who had never had a place to live, stupid and lazy as they were, had gathered up all kinds of secrets about living. They did not complain. They passed their secrets along. With them I spent many hours.

And then, I mustn't forget, there were also the Russians; not all the Russians, of course, for among them too there were the dark ones, the burdened, especially the ones who clung to Marx, Lenin or Stalin as though they were life preservers. The ones I mean were the Russian workers and the peasants. They did not act like other Europeans. It was as if there were no intimacies for them, and no individual concerns except for the basic affections for their women and children; and even these were not nearly as strong as with us.

It was as if they were all combined in a single person. If ever you happened to strike a Russian — and it wasn't easy to avoid, there were so many occasions — in a minute fifty Russians sprang up all over, to right and left, and made you repent it. On the other hand, if you had done a Russian a good turn, and it didn't take much, just a smile or silence well timed, then all of a sudden too many Russians to count became your "'brothers." They would willingly have let themselves be killed for you, and sometimes they did just that.

I was fortunate enough to be taken into their affections right away. I tried to speak their language. I didn't talk politics and they didn't talk about it either. I relied on the strength of their people, a people not composed of individualists like ours, but charged with a current of energy which was directed passionately toward life.

Last of all there were the old men, the old Russians and all the rest, the French, the Poles, the Germans. From them too I always learned something. Because, you see, the bad old men, all those who hadn't found out how to grow old, had died. At Buchenwald many died between fifty and sixty-five. That was the age for the great slaughter, and almost all the survivors were good men.

As for them, they were no longer there. They were looking at the world, with Buchenwald in the middle of it, from further away. They absorbed Buchenwald as part of the great outpouring of the universe, but already they seemed to belong to a better world. I found nothing but gladness in the men over seventy.

That is what you had to do to live in the camp: be engaged, not live for yourself alone. The self-centered life has no place in the world of the deported. You must go beyond it, lay hold on something outside yourself. Never mind how: by prayer if you know how to pray; through another man's warmth which communicates with yours, or through yours which you pass on to him; or simply by no longer being greedy. Those happy old men were like the hoboes. They asked nothing more for themselves, and that put everything within their reach. Be engaged, no matter how, but be engaged. It was certainly hard, and most men didn't achieve it.

Of myself I can't say why I was never entirely bereft of joy. But it was a fact and my solid support. Joy I found even in strange byways, in the midst of fear itself. And fear departed from me, as infection leaves an abscess when it bursts. By the end of a year in Buchenwald I was convinced that life was not at all as I had been taught to believe it, neither life nor society. For example, how could I explain that in block 56, my block, the only man who had volunteered day and night, for months, to watch over the most violent mad, to calm them down and feed them, to care for the ones with cancer, dysentery, typhus, to bathe them and comfort them, was a person of whom everyone said that in ordinary life he was effeminate, a parlor pederast, a man one would hesitate to associate with? But here he was the good angel, frankly the saint, the only saint in Invalids' Block. How account for the fact that Dietrich, the German criminal, arrested seven years before for strangling his mother and his wife, had turned brave and generous? Why was he sharing his bread with others at the risk of dying sooner? And why, at the same time, did that honest bourgeois from our country, that small tradesman from the Vendée, father of a family, get up in the night to steal the bread of other men?

These shocking things were not what I had read in books. They were there in front of me. I had no way of not seeing them, and they raised all kinds of questions in my mind. And last of all, was it Buchenwald, or was it the everyday world, what we call the normal life, which was topsy-turvy?

An old peasant from Anjou whom I had just met — how strange that he was born only six miles from Juvardeil — insisted that it was the everyday world which was askew. He was convinced of it.

[16]

My New World

Progressively, from day to day, the Eastern front and the Western front were closing Germany in a vise between them. The liberation of Europe was approaching, but the more the Allies' chances of victory grew, the more our chances of survival shrank. We were not ordinary prisoners. There were no codes of international law for us, no humane conventions. We were the hostages of Nazism, the living witnesses of its crimes. If Nazism was going to blow up, it had to blow us up at the same time.

In September 1944, a rumor was spreading. The SS corps had been ordered not to leave a man alive in the concentration camps in case of defeat. The charges of dynamite were ready, and whatever explosions and fires might not accomplish, machine guns would finish off. Soon it was not just a rumor, it was a directive which even the SS were not trying to hide.

At Buchenwald, as in all the rest of the camps, we were caught in a trap. Seven concentric circles of electrified barbed wire cut us off from the world. Nothing less than a divine accident could save us. No fragment of the future belonged to us. We didn't even have the right to look ahead. Besides, we didn't have the strength.

During the winter of 1944–1945 the food ration had been cut down to less than a quarter of a pound of bread, and less than a half pound of thin soup a day. Whatever we had in the way of energy we consumed on the spot, for it was the only thing we had left. Our nervous vitality was so reduced that it could no longer nourish our dreams. Hope is a luxury — a thing one doesn't ordinarily realize — because as a rule there is a superabundance of the life force.

In March 1945, when the Allies crossed the Rhine, a strange indifference blanketed Buchenwald. The news was impressive, but to us not sufficient to diminish or increase our courage. Leaden bodies and muted hearts were the only things to be found those days, and the ones like me who hadn't given up life held it pressed close to them. It was not a thing they were expending or talking about.

From this time on, every night long flights of planes we couldn't see passed over the Buchenwald hill. The whole sky resounded like a metallic shell. Giant firebrands rose from the surrounding plains — factories blown up, cities destroyed. One night the fire was in the distance toward the east — this time the flames burned for twenty-four hours — they said it was the synthetic gas factories at Merseburg.

SS control over the camp had been somewhat relaxed, but when it came back it came back in furious force. March was the time for the most ghastly public hangings. At last, on April 9, there was no longer any doubt about it, those concentrated bombardments over Weimar and near the camp, that cannonade to the west in the suburbs of Erfurt, some fourteen miles from us, could only mean that our forces had arrived.

The news fell on us as though it had been dropped into a well that was too deep. We could see it falling and then lost sight of it. Our bodies were terribly weak, and then on the same day the food ration stopped altogether. On the tenth an order was suddenly passed along. We were given a choice, but just what did that mean?

The SS command offered an alternative to the Buchenwald prisoners. They could either stay in camp at their own risk and in great danger, or they could leave within two hours on the roads to the east, escorted by SS guards. That was the hardest blow of all. How could we choose? No one was capable of it. There was no reasoning power, no human reckoning to go by. Which way lay safety? Which way life? What was the SS offering?

I saw panic all around me. The ultimate absurdity, the false freedom to choose their destiny, held men by the throats more tightly than any threat. Some said, "They will exterminate the ones who stay. They are giving a chance to the ones who leave." But the opposite was just as likely.

At this point I made my decision to stay. More than that, I dragged myself across my block and across the ones next to it. I called to everyone to stay, cried out that stay they must. I remember hitting a comrade brutally to keep him from taking off. Why? I didn't know any more than the others. Nothing had been revealed to me. Still, I was determined not to go, I knew I must not go. Instead of arguing, I spoke the words without any plan: "You don't run away. You stick to the ship." What ship? God save us. In the course of the afternoon, of the one hundred thousand men at Buchenwald, eighty thousand left. We, the twenty thousand who stayed, had nothing to say. We didn't have the courage. On the morning of the eleventh hunger was such agony that we were chewing the grass in the paths to fool our famished stomachs. The fight was raging six miles off, at the foot of our hill. We could barely hear it.

Toward noon I couldn't take it any longer. I had to have news. I suddenly recalled the existence of the loudspeakers. There was one in each block connected to the General Headquarters of the SS, and it was through this channel that they always gave their orders.

I dragged myself toward the private room reserved for the prisoner who was in charge of our barracks. That was where the loudspeaker was located. Nobody else was around. All the men were outside, trying to follow the sounds of the battle.

I knew that out of this loudspeaker would come life or death — one or the other. The instrument was obstinately silent. At one-thirty, I heard the familiar SS voice, very deliberate, ordering the SS troops to proceed with the plan for exterminating all surviving prisoners within the half hour.

What hand was holding my senses in check at that moment, what voice was addressing me? I have no idea. But I do remember not being frightened. I don't remember believing the SS, and I decided not to inform my companions.

Twenty minutes later, a fourteen-year-old Russian boy, supple as a monkey, who had climbed up on the roof of the block, fell into the middle of the crowd from a height of twelve feet. He was shouting, "The Americans. Here come the Americans."

They picked him up. He had hurt himself badly when he fell. Some people were running, others were crying out. A French comrade took me by the arm and dragged me outside. He was looking and kept looking toward the entrance of the camp. He cursed and blessed between his teeth. He looked again and it was there, quite real — an American flag, an English flag, a French flag were flying from the control tower.

The days after that were days of stupefaction. We were drunk but with an evil drunkenness. We still had thirty-six hours to go without food, for the SS had spread poison over the stores in the camp, and so we had to wait. One doesn't pass over all at once from the idea of death to the idea of life. We listened to what they were saying to us, but we asked for a little time to believe in it.

There was a very strong American army, the Third Army, under a bold, supremely bold general, Patton. Patton knew what Buchenwald was and what dangers it held. He knew that a three-hour wait meant 20,000 dead. Against every rule of caution in strategy, he had mounted an armored attack, an enveloping attack on the hill. At the last minute, the SS troops were cut off from the camp, forced to flee or surrender. The underground receiving set, in the hands of the prisoners in the cellars of the medical block, told the Americans what to do.

But where was the joy of freedom, or the joy of living? The camp was under an anesthetic, and it would take hours and hours to lay hold on life. Finally, all of a sudden, it burst upon you, blinding your eyes, stronger than your senses, stronger than reason. It came in great waves, every wave hurting as it came in. Then the tension relaxed, and everyone fell into a stupor as small boys would if you gave them a strong drink. It wasn't always a pretty sight, for in happiness men reveal themselves as much as in misfortune, Besides, in the first week people were dying in great numbers. Some died of starvation. Others died from eating too much too fast. Some were thunderstruck by the mere idea of being saved. It was like an attack which carried them off in a few hours.

ON APRIL 13, THE CAMP RADIO — its free radio — announced the death of Franklin Delano Roosevelt. His was the first name of a real man that we had heard — Roosevelt, one of our liberators — and it was he who had died and not we. When the news came I was carrying my pail in a water detail with about fifty other men.

Most of the pipes had burst. I remember it well. The whole team put the pails down on the ground, and everyone knelt, French and Russians together. For the first time in a year, the death of a man had meaning.

Life came back to most of us, mixed up, incoherent, tempestuous, ironical, difficult, like life itself. I was proud of the comrades who had survived. It may have been foolish, but I was proud of them.

Seventeen hundred officers and soldiers of the SS, taken prisoner by the American army, had been placed in a block of the camp at our disposition. It is certainly worth reporting that there was not a single act of vengeance, not one SS man killed by a prisoner, not a blow struck, not an insult. Nobody even went to look at them.

On April 16 we learned through official channels that the 80,000 prisoners who had gone off on the roads on the tenth had been machine-gunned en masse by the SS, at a place sixty miles southeast of Buchenwald. They said first there was not a single survivor. We learned later that this was wrong; ten were still alive.

On April 18, just a week after the liberation, as I was coming in from a water detail, a voice suddenly burst out fifteen feet away from me, warm as sunlight, impossible to believe, but crying, "Jacques." It was Philippe's voice. It was Philippe himself. He was holding me against him. He was there, Philippe the chief, Défense de la France, France personified. I was not dreaming. Philippe, that daredevil, a captain now in the army of the liberation, had crossed France and Germany in three days and three nights, throwing caution to the winds, without a military pass, a real Resistance fighter, a real man of the Maquis, to call for his own men, at least those who were in Buchenwald, those of them who were still alive.

Philippe was life itself. It was the triumphant equation. He was the last man I had seen before I went to prison. He was the first man I saw when I came out. I was alive, and two others from Défense de la France were also living. Philippe gathered the three of us together. A French car was waiting for us, a car belonging to *DF*, for *DF* was no longer underground; it had become *France-Soir*, the most important daily newspaper in Paris. When we got to Paris, the chauffeur, a boy who had never been in prison, drove us around the Place d'Appel in his car, to pay tribute.

Epilogue

THERE ARE STILL SOME FACTS TO REPORT. François died on March 31, twelve days before the liberation of Buchenwald, somewhere near Leipzig, in circumstances unknown. Georges died in the first days of April, it seems of exhaustion, aboard an armored car, near Halle an der Saale. Denis died in Czechoslovakia on April 9, killed by an SS bullet on the roadside. Twenty-four other members of DF, arrested along with me on July 20, 1943, did not return. You certainly have the right to know about them.

HERE MY STORY ENDS, as it must, for the man I am now, husband, father, university professor, writer, has no intention of telling you about himself. He wouldn't know how, and he would only burden you. If he has recorded the first twenty years of his life at such length, it is because he believes they no longer belong to him as an individual but are an open book, for anyone to read who cares to. His dearest wish was to show, if only in part, what these years held of life, light and joy by the grace of God.

And now, in conclusion, why has this Frenchman from France written his book in the United States to present to his American friends today? Because today he is America's guest. Loving the country and wanting to show his gratitude, he could find no better way of expressing it than in these two truths, intimately known to him and reaching beyond all boundaries.

The first of these is that joy does not come from outside, for whatever happens to us it is within. The second truth is that light does not come to us from without. Light is in us, even if we have no eyes.

ABOUT THE AUTHOR

J ACQUES LUSSEYRAN (September 19, 1924, to July 27, 1971) was a blind author, professor, and French Resistance leader. Born in Paris, he was blinded in a school accident at the age of seven. At age seventeen, less than a year after the German invasion of France, Lusseyran formed a Resistance group called the Volunteers of Liberty with fifty-two other boys. Because of his ability to read people as a blind person, he was put in charge of recruitment, and the group grew to over six hundred young men. The group later merged with another Resistance group called Défense de la France, which published an underground newspaper that eventually achieved a circulation of 250,000. After the war, it became one of France's most respected daily newspapers, *France Soir*.

In July 1943, Lusseyran was arrested, along with twenty-five other leaders of Défense de la France, and spent nearly fifteen months in the Nazis' Buchenwald concentration camp. When the U.S. Third Army arrived at Buchenwald in April 1945, Lusseyran was one of roughly thirty survivors of a transport of two thousand French citizens.

After the war, despite his service as part of the underground and his brilliant schoolwork, Lusseyran was denied admission to the École Normale Supérieure, an elite university for training French academics, because of a decree passed by the Vichy government barring "invalids" from public employment. Although for years he was prevented from becoming a professor, he repeatedly presented his case and was eventually able to teach in France. Later he moved to the United States, where he first lectured at Hollins College and then became a professor at Case Western Reserve University in Cleveland. He was a professor at the University of Hawaii in 1971 when, at age forty-seven, he was killed in a car accident with his wife, Marie, not far from Juvardeil in France, where he had been happy as a boy.